THE STORY OF
LOTUS
1947–1960 Birth of
a Legend

THE STORY OF LOTUS

1947-1960: Birth of a Legend

by

Ian H Smith

MOTOR RACING PUBLICATIONS LTD
28 & 32 Devonshire Road, Chiswick
London W4 2HD

ISBN 0 900549 10 6
First Published 1970
Reprinted 1978
Reprinted 1982

Copyright © 1972 Ian H Smith and
Motor Racing Publications Ltd
All rights reserved

Printed in Great Britain by
Page Bros (Norwich) Ltd, Norwich

Chapters

1	Bangers and mash	7
2	Wings over wheels	12
3	Colin plays his port trick	19
4	Trials and triumphs	26
5	Six sets the scene	29
6	A matter of aerodynamics	42
7	Town and country planning	53
8	A pair of Nines	58
9	Reverse at Le Mans	68
10	The first Eleven	73
11	Return journey	89
12	Room for one only	94
13	Improving a winner	104
14	Celebration in the Sarthe	114
15	Better late than never	122
16	Joining the Elite	127
17	The championship trail	136
18	A matter of handling	147
19	Simplicity breeds success	155
20	And one for Junior	169
21	Rapid therapy for Moss	174
22	One man's Mille Miglia	176
	Lotus cutaway drawings	184
	Lotus catalogue of models	189
	Index	191

Preface

TODAY LOTUS ranks alongside Ferrari and Porsche as one of the great names in the world of motor racing and high-performance cars. Lotus cars have taken drivers to the sport's highest honour – the World Championship, they have caused a technical revolution by breaking the American domination of Indianapolis, and they have won major international successes from Europe to Australia and New Zealand. The Lotus Story, in fact, is one of the great success stories of the automotive industry in the second half of the twentieth century. It is also a fascinating story, and never more so than during those formative years when the Lotus legend was born.

It is a story which begins in a tiny lock-up garage in North London when Colin Chapman was a student at London University and in his spare time indulging in the popular post-war hobby of buying and selling "Old Bangers". This was the birthplace of the marque Lotus, the development of which Ian Smith – a close associate of Chapman in the fifties – traces in fascinating detail, from Chapman's first tentative steps as a kit car manufacturer to his ultimate emergence as a successful manufacturer and entrant of Grand Prix cars.

The Story of Lotus, 1947–1960, is based on Ian Smith's earlier work, Lotus – The Story of the Marque, but it contains many revisions and includes important additional material relevent to this period of Lotus history.

The late Gregor Grant contributed an additional chapter, based on his experiences with a Lotus 11 in the 1957 Mille Miglia, shortly before his tragic death in 1969. At the time he was busily engaged in updating The Story of Lotus, and much of his manuscript is to be used in a companion to Ian Smith's book, covering the years 1961 to 1970.

The author and publisher are most grateful for the generous assistance they have received in illustrating this history of a make of car which was not always as prolifically photographed or drawn as it is today. In particular they wish to thank Iliffe Transport Publications Limited for their permission to reproduce the excellent cutaway drawings and sketches previously published in *Autocar*, Geoffrey Goddard for so painstakingly and successfully delving through his earlier photographic files, and Simon Taylor, Editor of *Autosport*, for offering access to several rare pictures which appeared in past issues of the Haymarket Press magazine. Sincere thanks are also due to all the photographers whose work has been reproduced on the following pages, and by no means least to artists David James, whose sketches illustrate the jacket, and David Murray, who was responsible for overall design and layout.

1.

Bangers and mash

IN OCTOBER, 1945, at the age of seventeen, Colin Chapman entered University College of London University to study engineering. Already he travelled on wheels—a Panther 350cc motorcycle which was doomed to a short life. He arrived at the "Freshers" dance in November swathed in plasters, having written off the bike by driving it through the door of a taxi—much to the surprise of the fare! Luckily for Colin, Christmas was not far off, and to his joy his parents presented him with a maroon 1937 Morris 8 Tourer. No doubt they considered his accident with the Panther decreed the extra protection provided by a car.

Colin lavished much care and attention on the Morris and became most fussy about its appearance. He used the car a great deal as transport from his home in East Finchley to the University and as passengers would often have Hazel Williams, who lived in Muswell Hill, and fellow student Colin Dare, who came from Friern Barnet. Colin met Hazel, who worked as a secretary in Wigmore Street, at a dance during the summer of 1945 and consequently their routes to work tallied conveniently.

Even in those days Colin drove with a style of his own, which might best be described as hectic. He never liked to hang about whilst motoring and was always interested in setting a new record for the run from his home at 44, Beech Drive, via Alexandra Park Road—to collect Hazel and Colin Dare—and on via Wigmore Street to the University.

At College, Colin was definitely a personality. Already, however, he was becoming very interested in motor cars and this interest did not leave him much time for joining in the various activities of the University. He was always a bright spark, and when Woolwich Polytechnic stole "Phineas", the London University mascot, Colin was in the forefront of a mob of engineering students who went *en masse* by Underground to regain it. In class, Colin was always an attentive student but out of class he was definitely no "swot". He could absorb technical articles easily, with the result that he could "cram" just before an exam with very satisfactory results. An early example of the logical and clear-cut way he had of thinking is shown by his answer to his tutor on being asked to solve a geometry problem—he was chosen because obviously he was not paying attention! A question of circles and tangents was involved and after surveying the situation Colin gave his solution step by step. It was not according to the book, but gave the right answer—even the tutor had to admit that! Perhaps if his interest had not been so keenly taken up with the practical side of engineering Colin would have become a very successful teacher himself. He has a great gift for explaining the most technical subjects in a way which anyone, following his reasoning, will be able to comprehend.

Soon after entering University, Colin, in the company of his namesake Colin Dare, became interested in second-hand cars. One thing led to another and before very long quite a business had developed. Lectures would be skipped in order that "deals" could be followed up and Wednesday afternoons were always spent on the pavement in London's Warren Street. At this time, in early 1946, cars were very scarce, and such tricks as obtaining copies of the local paper immediately on publication had to be resorted to in order to beat the rush for a bargain "banger". Before very long the two Colins were buying and selling cars at the rate of one per week. A stock of three cars resided in the garage at 44, Beech Drive, forcing Mr. Chapman Senior to leave his own car out at night! The stock grew and one or two cars found their way into the lock-ups behind Hazel's home. Some of the deals proved very lucrative, whilst others were definitely difficult. There was the open MG 4-seater tourer which smoked so badly that all Colin's driving skill was necessary to hide this fact from the potential customer who asked for a demonstration. There was the Austin Big 7 which Colin decided to use himself for a few days until the rear wheel fell off and rolled serenely past him up the road.

Straightforward deals became rather tame and Colin began to modify and improve the vehicles he had in stock. This meant a lot of hard work but brought larger profits. His best deal involved considerable ingenuity when, with the aid of spares from Fiat England, he and Colin Dare converted a Simca 500 to right-hand drive.

But there was trouble ahead for Chapman, who handled all the finance of these deals. His second-hand car business crashed in October, 1947, when he was holding his largest stock of nearly £900-worth of cars—the basic petrol ration was cancelled! Nobody wanted to buy cars and the stock finally realised £400. To that date very nearly £500 profit had been made—so the nett result of all this chasing, chivvying, improvement and selling was exactly nil!

This experience would have made most mortals leave motor cars severely alone, but with the fierce determination which was to mark Colin's progress in later years, he decided to build himself a special car. He had become very interested in trials and would often be reading reports and results of these events when he should have been at a study class. One car of his depreciated stock was not sold—principally because it was the most depreciated—and this was to form the basis of his trials car. The car was a 1930 Austin 7 fabric saloon which had been found on bricks in someone's front garden. A fast deal had been effected between Colin and a rather unsure old lady which resulted in PK 3493 being towed behind the Morris Tourer to the lock-ups by Hazel's house. The tow was rather a memorable one as it took place at night and the Austin had no lights or brakes. Colin of course had no time for "On Tow" notices and worked on the basis that the quicker everything was done the less time the police would have to find out about it! As usual Colin's persuasive way won through and Colin Dare steered PK 3493 to Muswell Hill behind the Morris on the strict orders that "if you're going to hit me—hit me fair and square on the bumpers".

They say that fate plays a great part in the fortunes of one's life. Colin had been lucky indeed when he met Hazel at that summer dance, for the lock-ups behind her house were an ideal place in which to reconstruct a car. To add to the ideal nature of the set-up, these lock-ups were situated at the top of a steep unmade road—just right for a batteryless take-off when a test was demanded.

There followed a short breathing space, during which time Colin sorted out his wrecked finances. Then, having decided on the components for his "special", work began in earnest. PK 3493 was stripped completely. Very methodically the chassis was scraped and painted and Colin checked everything right down to the chassis rivets. No actual additions were made to the bare Austin frame but the main members were "boxed" by welding a fourth side to the "U" section. As the work progressed, the people concerned assumed their respective roles, Colin doing the lion's share of the work, with spasmodic assistance from Colin Dare. Hazel carried out all the painting most meticulously and brought innumerable cups of tea from her house. At all odd hours Mr. and Mrs. Williams had at least one extra mouth to feed. Equipment was far from lavish and tools consisted of a normal set of car spanners, both ring and open-ended. Colin relieved his father of the burden of owning an electric drill, which he modified to drive a grindstone, wire brush, or anything else which had to revolve quickly. There was no jack and when the car had to be lifted, people were enrolled to heave as bricks were pushed into the

Left: The Lotus competitions career began on the muddy slopes of British trials country. Here are Colin and Hazel in the Mark 2. Below: The car that started it all, the Mark 1, still bearing its Austin 7 ancestry.

required position. Colin did have a ten-and-sixpenny Vernier gauge with enabled him to get down to "two thou". There was no lathe or any other machinery, so when any welding or brazing had to be done, he co-opted a local welder. He would assemble the pieces to be fitted together and dash down to the other chap's workshop, where he would hold them for the expert.

It was not long before the neighbours began to voice their opinion of the banging that went on far into the night. Mrs. Williams, however, managed to placate them with promises of an early finish to the project. But one next door neighbour did not complain, in fact he helped on the construction of the car on occasions. He was Rodney Nuckey, who later accompanied Colin as passenger on several of his trials outings. Rodney became a firm friend, and later took part in motor racing, driving a Cooper 500 and then Cooper-Bristol racing and sports cars.

Progress on the construction of the car was slow as Colin was learning as he went—applying theories which he had read of and filling in the gaps by trial and error. The Austin 7 had the undesirable vice of oversteering which might have been acceptable at moderate speeds but was hardly to be tolerated in a more sporting car. The reason for the oversteer was obvious. The back springs sloped downwards when in a static position but as soon as the car was cornered the outside spring flattened and moved that end of the rear axle back. At the same time the other end of the axle moved in the opposite direction. Together this slewing of the axle helped steer the car into a corner. Colin was building a trials car so he could not sacrifice ground clearance by fitting the "sports model" straight springs—instead he turned the axle upside down so bringing the suspension links to the top and flattened the springs at the same time. The cure worked perfectly and the

The Mark 1 as originally completed, still with its original registration number and with full road equipment. At this point in its career the car was still officially an Austin 7.

oversteer was eradicated, without any loss of ground clearance.

A great deal of thought and design went into the building of the body of the car. Plans were drawn up at the University—no doubt during Colin's "mechanical drawing" lectures! Being interested in all forms of motion, Colin was in the University Air Squadron and naturally he read a great deal about aircraft construction principles. These principles he applied to his first car. It is interesting to note that this application of aircraft practice has continued throughout the life of Lotus.

A stressed framework with three bulkheads was built up of alloy-bonded-plywood. The construction was based on the basic principle of simplicity giving rigidity. The body, being hand-made, was rather angular but meticulously executed. No sharp edges—where a panel finished, half an inch of wood would be scooped out, and the two skins of alloy folded together, so giving a smooth rounded finish.

Trials cars at this time often suffered damage to their wings. Colin had no desire to indulge in this expensive pastime so fixed the wings of his car with wood-screws and Rawlplugs. On making solid contact the wings could leave the body instead of crumpling and then by renewing the Rawlplugs and a little attention from the screwdriver the vehicle was as good as new. The back of the body was extended so that two passengers could be carried, or alternatively ballast for trials hill-climbing. Provision was made for two spare wheels. For a finishing touch a radiator cowling, rather resembling that of the Rolls-Royce, was hand fashioned out of copper sheet.

The brakes received special attention. The Austin linkage was modified and special actuating cams were fitted. The engine required the expenditure of much labour and after a thorough overhaul the compression ratio was increased and double valve springs were fitted. Colin decided that the Austin carburettor was not satisfactory—in fact, as he put it in the jargon that develops during the long hours of tinkering, it functioned on the principle of "suck and hope". A special inlet manifold was made and a Ford downdraught carburettor fitted.

The first trial run of the car was entirely unplanned and most hair-raising. One Saturday, Colin was at work in the lock-up with an estimate in his mind of a fortnight's work before completion date when suddenly a friend, Derek Wooton, arrived, took one look at the car and declared "we'll have it going today". He proved to be right, for working as a team, Derek sat on the bonnet and worked the throttle control by hand—there was no pedal—and Colin steered. Unfortunately the "accelerator" chose to sit facing the driver with the result that his bursts of speed did not suit Colin who, at the best, was only getting a very restricted view of the road. Although rather hazardous this preliminary dash down the hill from the lock-ups proved promising and so PK 3493 was registered in its new guise and became OX 9292. As Colin did not want to own another "Austin Special" his new creation was declared as a Lotus—and so Mark 1 was born.

Two trials were entered in the spring of 1948 with the gratifying reward of two class awards. Hazel was now just old enough to drive the car legally but had to be content with the role of passenger and "bumper" on the tricky sections.

1948 was a busy one at College for Colin, and as exams were looming up there was not much time for competition work in the Lotus. The few appearances, however, brought out certain weaknesses in the basic design, as a result of which two important alterations were made to the car. Firstly, the rear wheels were changed to Ford disc units so that larger section tyres could be fitted. Also in search of extra traction, the front axle beam was split and pivoted in the centre, so providing independent front suspension. The curtailment of his hobby paid off, and towards the end of the year the name Colin Chapman could be followed officially by "B.Sc.(Eng.)".

The celebration which followed the announcement of this degree very nearly ended in a visit to jail for the driver of a certain Lotus which flashed past a police car at over 50 mph. On being overhauled by the law, the very happy lawbreaker was informed of his speed to which he replied, a little over-enthusiastically, "Was I really—I didn't know it would go that fast!".

2.
Wings over wheels

ON LEAVING University Colin realised that his interest in cars was taking on the nature of an obsession. He now knew that his first car could be improved in many ways and the method which most appealed to him was to build another Lotus—the Mark 2.

He worked on the basis of his University training; a car is but a structure, as amenable to stress calculations as any building of bricks and mortar. However, the difficulty was to learn what stresses a car must sustain and what safety factors were required. Colin spent hours trying to obtain information on this subject—he had long sessions in the library of the Institute of Mechanical Engineers and browsed through everything from the most learned papers to the non-technical articles in the motoring Press. Then he joined the 750 Motor Club and there met many people who were interested in the same problems as were facing him. By his reading and by discussion he began to formulate his ideas. Inspiration seemed to come the most readily when in the bath, accompanied by some rather tuneless humming or singing—sometimes the bathroom was occupied for very long periods!

Basically the Mark 2 was to be a trials car, but Colin also wanted a vehicle which was equally at home on the road and even perhaps on the track—there was now the prospect of circuit racing. The larger-engined trials cars were losing popularity and light, manoeuvrable Ford 10-powered cars were favoured. Regrettably, however, some of these smaller cars were becoming rather freakish. Basing his ideas on the popular Austin 7 chassis, Colin set out to build a compromise, a car which would have a sufficiently "live" chassis to be at home on trials terrain and yet retain enough stiffness to handle well on the open road. As on the Mark 1, the main chassis members were boxed-in but the cross members were removed and tubular braces welded into position. This gave a light and satisfactorily stiff basic frame.

Work had only just begun on the new car when Colin joined the Royal Air Force, and in October he found himself at Padgate for "kitting-out". As he had already reached Elementary Flying Training Standard in the University Air Squadron, with 35 hours' solo flying behind him, he was sent straight to Tern Hill, which is near Market Drayton in Shropshire, on a Short Term Engagement. It is interesting to note that Colin had done his earlier solo flying in Tiger Moths from Fairoaks Aerodrome, where Jack Brabham later kept his private plane.

At Tern Hill flying training continued on Tiger Moths and Harvards. It was not long before all of his 11 fellow pupils on the flying course knew of the car which Colin was building and very soon five more Austin "specials" were under construction at the camp.

The Royal Air Force rather interrupted work in the lock-up behind Hazel's house where the Mark 2 was being built in the wheel tracks of its predecessor. All Colin's leaves and "48's" were devoted to the car. At times Hazel began to resent the intrusion of the new Lotus as her boy friend had very little time for dates in the generally accepted sense of the word. Instead, before rushing back to camp, he would present her with a

Left: The versatile Mark 2 which, though conceived as a trials car, was soon taking part in sprints and circuit races. Below: Eric Beaumont driving the same car in the Irish Experts' Trial, still going strong after five years of active competition life.

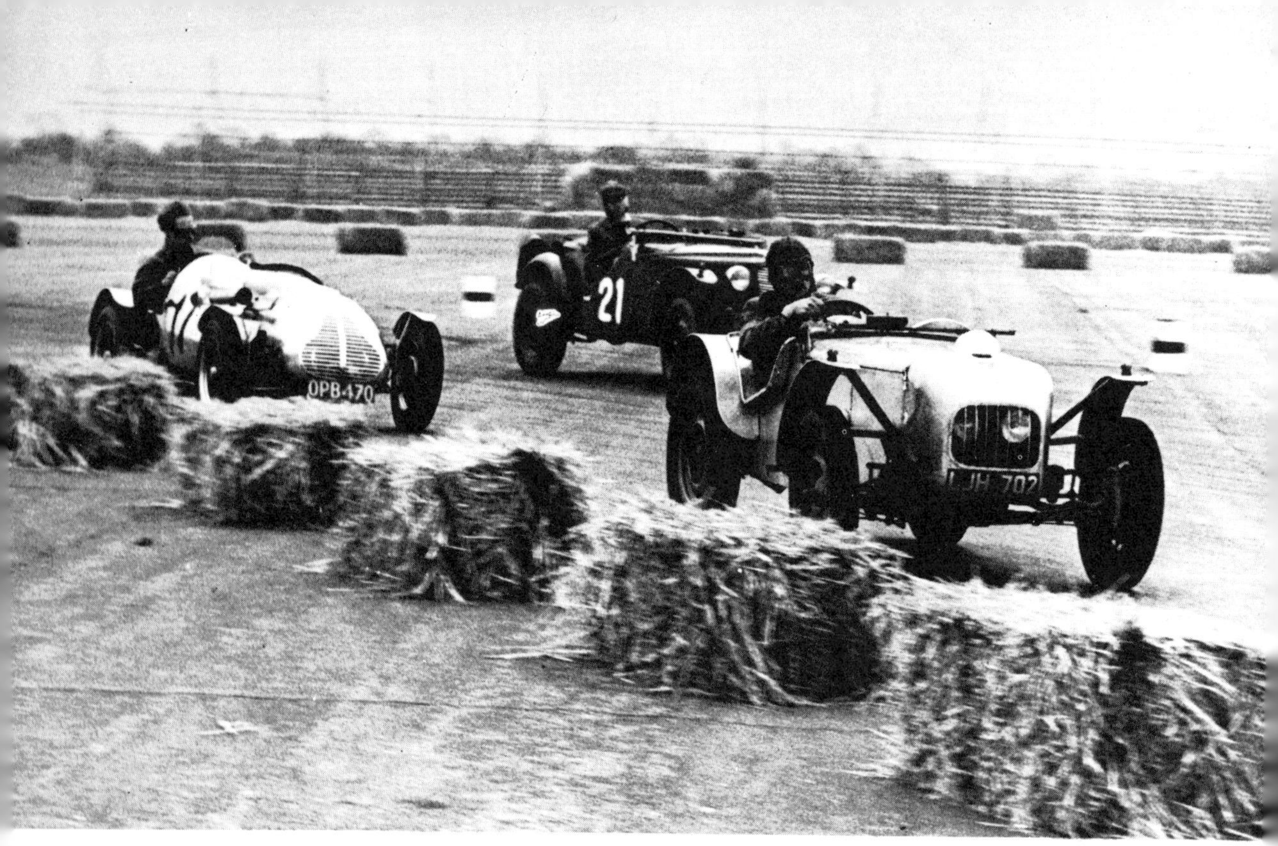
OPB 470
21
LJH 702

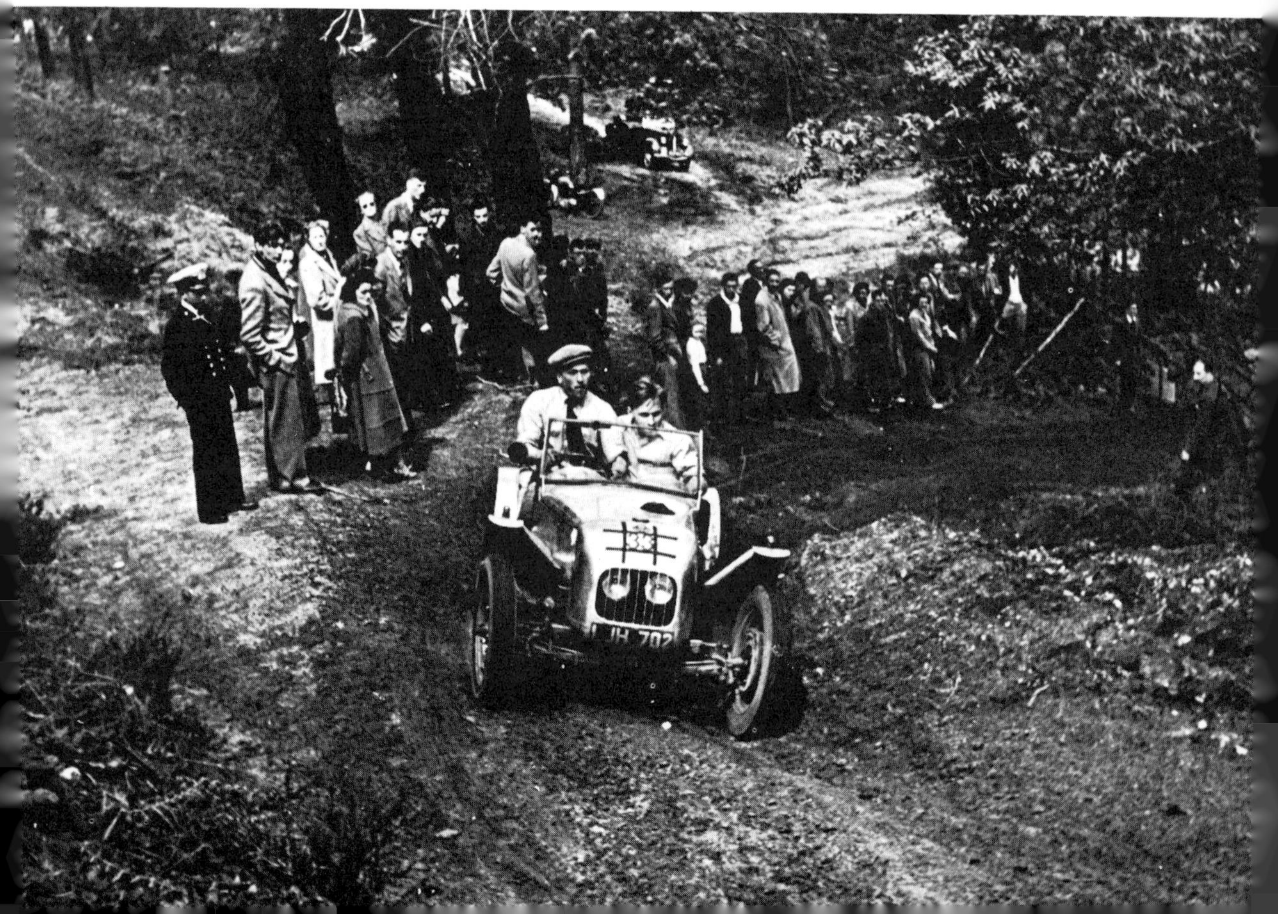

Left: Chapman's Mark 2, leading Wilks' Cooper-Rover, lapping a slower car at Silverstone. Below left: A thoughtful Chapman searching for grip on a picturesque British trials hill. Below: Silverstone again, this time leading Dudley Gahagan's Bugatti. Bottom: Michael Lawson in Mark 2, a car which was to give him many trials successes.

job list which included painting tasks, filing and drilling pursuits, polishing, and the procuring of bits and pieces, all of which had to be completed by the time the next "48" came round!

So through 1949 the car progressed slowly. The front axle was of Ford origin, but the Austin rear axle was retained. An interesting item is the way in which Colin provided the axle with a 4.55 to 1 ratio. There were two types of crown wheel and pinion available for the Austin 7—a 42-tooth crown wheel and 8-tooth pinion which gave a 5.125 to 1 ratio and a 44-tooth crown wheel and 9-tooth pinion which gave a 4.9 to 1 ratio. Colin built up the axle of his car with the 9-tooth pinion and the 42-crown wheel and then, instead of oil, filled the differential housing with neat Bluebell metal polish. The car was run in this condition for about 50 miles and then the back axle was inspected—the bearings were ruined but the crown wheel and pinion now meshed perfectly. New bearings were popped in and the 4.55 to 1 unit filled with its correct lubricant. Bodywork followed the principles of the Mark 1 but general dimensions were smaller. Ford wheels were fitted all round with large section tyres.

Funds were low by mid-1949 so a very ancient and wheezy Ford 8 engine was purchased for £5. Colin was anxious to use the 4-speed Austin gearbox so he had a cast aluminium adaptor ring made. Again, so that expense should be kept to a minimum, he made the pattern for the casting himself.

As is always the case with a project of this nature the constructor was itching to try his device, so at 2 a.m. one Monday the Mark 2 set off from the lock-up on its maiden voyage. Colin was accompanied by fellow airman John Hall, who had helped greatly in the construction of the car. At Brickhill the aged engine ran a big-end and the car had to be abandoned. As luck would have it the next car along that way happened to be going right past the Tern Hill R.A.F. Station, so a rather tired and dishevelled Chapman reported at the guard room before his pass expired at 6 a.m.

The engine was repaired and soon LJH 702 had made the complete journey to be inspected by Colin's fellow R.A.F. "specials" builders. One or two minor trials were attempted and it was immediately obvious that the old Ford 8 engine was not up to the task. A Ford 10 engine must be fitted—the question was how to obtain one, for Colin was flat broke!

Most of Colin's spare time at Tern Hill was taken in browsing round garages, peering over hedges and looking in breakers' yards in the Market Drayton area. On one of these trips he found a burnt-out Ford 10 saloon in a garage. The car was virtually a "write-off" and enquiries established that the insurance company involved were planning to sell it by auction. A brief inspection showed the engine to be unharmed by the conflagration. Hiding his real interest, Colin managed to locate the owner and casually ask him a few questions. Imagine his surprise when he learned that the engine was a brand new unit, only fitted about 1,000 miles before the fire! The snag now was how to raise the £30 which the insurance company hoped to get at the auction.

At this time a certain dealer in the Midlands was buying up second-hand Ford 8 and 10 parts—particularly if the parts included a log book! Colin therefore offered them "his" car for £35 with log book but less engine and gearbox. They jumped at the opportunity and were eager to collect the bargain. Now the tricky part of the deal was arranged—Colin found a "breaker" who was keen to make an easy fiver. The middle-man bought the wreck for £30, Colin removed the engine and gearbox, then the remains were collected and the £35 handed over. Colin returned to his camp with a free, as new, Ford 10 engine complete with gearbox. The old engine was removed at once and this, together with the unwanted Ford gearbox, was sold to his friends the breakers for £5—clear profit!

The new lease of life which this 1172cc engine gave to the Mark 2 even further enthused Colin towards motoring sport and precipitated his leaving the Royal Air Force. By September he was trained up to "wings" standard but was required to sign on for five years in order to get a Permanent Commission. A future in the R.A.F. did not appeal to any of the class of twelve at Tern Hill so they all returned to civvy street. December saw Colin working in London for a firm of constructional engineers.

Christmas of that year brought the necessary finance to give the Lotus a shapely radiator cowl. At the same time an ingenious system was arranged for the twin headlamps, which were mounted in front of the radiator block and made to turn with the steering.

For the 1950 season ahead it was decided in the interests of financial prudence to leave the engine in perfectly standard form, although as the year passed Colin could not resist raising the compression ratio, fitting stronger valve springs and incorporating a different carburettor. The car was light and the roadholding was good—on these points it was hoped the opposition could be tackled. And so it proved, as can be seen from the diary of Colin's first full competition season. 1950.

Sunday, January 15th—750 M.C. Mudlark—Hazel drives. Win nothing but get write-up in Club Bulletin.

Sunday, February 5th—Herts County Trial—1st Class award. 2nd best performance in class.

Sunday, February 12th—Tyrwhitt-Drake Trophy Trial—Hazel drives. Does quite well but damages nose cowl by trying to climb a vertical bank.

Sunday, February 19th—President's Trophy Trial. S.M.C.—Wins 1100–1500cc class against all other Ford 10 specials including Onslow-Bartlett's.

Sunday, February 26th—North London Enthusiasts C.C. Jacobean Trophy Trial—2nd Class award.

Sunday, March 5th—Hants and Berks Blackwater Trial—Hazel drives. 4th best performance of the day.

Sunday, March 12th—Lancia M.C. Bramley Driving Tests—64 starters—Win event outright and get Hamilton Trophy, 750 Club award and Team award.

Sunday, March 26th—Horsham and District Spring Trial—1st Class award. Clean sheet on hills but fluffed on reverse between trees in the special test.

Sunday, April 2nd—Hants and Berks Aldershot Trial—Failed 2 hills with insufficient power. 1/5 sec. below F.T.D. in "snake-in-the-grass".

Easter Monday, April 10th—Berkhamsted M.C.—Speed Trial—Fastest "unblown" car and 2nd fastest in class.

Monday, April 17th—Start work with British Aluminium Company as construction engineer.

Sunday, May 7th—Maidstone and Mid-Kent Speed Trial on Gravesend Aerodrome—2nd fastest in class.

Saturday, May 13th—British Grand Prix at Silverstone—Cannot go—no money!

Sunday, May 28th—North West London M.C. Lawrence Cup Trial. Rodney Nuckey passenger. Qualify for award but forgot to sign off.

Saturday, June 3rd—Eight Clubs race meeting. Qualified in one-hour trial. Win 16-car scratch race after terrific scrap with Gahagan's Type 37 Bugatti. 3rd in 16-car handicap race.

Sunday, June 4th—Miss the Lancia M.C. trial because have to attend cousin's wedding.

Saturday, June 10th—Maidstone and Mid-Kent race meeting at Silverstone—No success largely due to suspension trouble.

Sunday, June 18th—Falcon M.C. Tewinwater speed trials—Hazel 2nd in trials class. Self 3rd in sports class. Ignition too retarded.

Sunday, June 25th—750 M.C. Bisley Rally—Win event outright by a big fluke!

Saturday, July 8th—North London Enthusiasts Redcap Rally—Win event outright with George Beresford as passenger.

Saturday, July 16th—Go sailing in father's yacht. Take my boss and nearly lose him overboard in a hard blow when he gets hit by the boom!

Sunday, July 23rd—Hants and Berks M.C. Speed Trial at Great Auclum—Nasty moment when I get both near-side wheels over lip of the banking.

There was not much activity in August and so Colin was able to save for his forthcoming holiday in September. Throughout his season events had to be very carefully planned because he was supposed to work every other Saturday. This meant concentrating on Sunday events with all-night preparation before the outing.

First time out for the Mark 2, still without nose cowl and headlamps, was in the Lockhart-Bassingham Trial at the end of 1949.

Colin and Hazel had their holiday in Jersey and flew back to London at the end of September to find lashing rain awaiting them. It was a rather dampening return as they climbed into the Mark 2 which had been left at the airport during their absence. As they drove into London, Colin realised that it would be far more comfortable if he had a saloon for general use now that the winter was approaching, and idly he began to ponder the type of saloon required.

He decided it would have to be a light, responsive car—small and compact and, if possible, one having an engine with which he was conversant. There was only one vehicle that filled these requirements and that was the rather rare Austin 7 Aluminium Saloon. At the very moment he decided this they were passing through Potters Bar, and there, lo and behold, stood a perfect specimen of this breed standing in the forecourt of a public house! The Mark 2 was turned about and parked beside the little Austin. Preliminary investigation showed the car to be in beautiful condition and Colin soon decided that he must own it.

Leaving Hazel sitting in the Lotus he tried each bar in turn until he spied a peak-capped gentleman downing a pint in the public category. Colin, for the first and last time in his life, ordered himself a pint and soon was in conversation with the Austin owner. By generalisation he learned all about the little car and slowly he began to cast aspersions on one thing and another—rattling rear main bearings, high oil consumption, weak back axle, etc., etc. Soon the gentleman with the peak-cap was not so sure about his car. Colin then began to turn gloomy about the war in Korea, impending petrol rationing, compulsory inspection of old cars and the doubtful second-hand value of an Austin 7 Aluminium Saloon. By now the owner was beginning to wonder if being a car owner was such fun after all. Then as a passing shot Colin asked him if he had a hobby.

Apparently the Austin took up all the owner's time so he was surprised to hear from his new acquaintance that the hobby of breeding budgerigars was both interesting and remunerative. (Colin had happened on an article on this subject in a magazine during the flight home from Jersey.) Finally, the Austin owner could not wait to rid himself of the car and started this fascinating pastime. £45, Colin's last penny, changed hands and they walked into the forecourt to "shake" on the deal. The peaked-cap set off in the direction of the nearest pet shop and imagine Hazel's surprise, after a wait of an hour and a half, to be told to take over the Lotus as Colin hopped into the Austin.

The Austin became the Chapman "comfort carriage" for four years in which time about 75,000 miles were covered. The car was then passed on to Mike Costin, who was then working with Colin, and he brought the total mileage to over 100,000 before his brother Frank took over. Frank Costin soon had the mileometer buzzing through its "second time round" and found that there was still plenty of life left in the little car.

With alternative transport available Colin was able to plan for 1951 with an easier mind. He decided that his interest in construction and driving had out-grown trials for, whilst these were great fun, the nature of the competition allowed luck to play such a big part. Also trials cars were becoming very specialised and his real interest was to build a car that would beat all others under normal road conditions. Sports car racing appeared to be the field for this type of development—the new 750cc Formula racing in particular.

The die was cast when Mike Lawson offered to buy the Mark 2 as he was anxious to enter the forthcoming Wrotham Cup Trial. A sale was effected and then Colin and Hazel decided to compete against their old car in Mark 1.

Feverish preparation enabled the earlier Lotus to be roadworthy by October 8th and the results of the outings were very pleasing when Mike Lawson won the Cup, in his new acquisition, and Colin won the Walsingham Cup for best performance in the opposite class. As Mike Lawson successfully climbed the "Horror" Colin was heard to shout "and he was going to buy a Dellow!" However, Dellows did have their share of 1st and 2nd Class awards when the results were published. Following this successful start, the Mark 2 had a most distinguished trials career in the hands of its new owner. In the following 12 months the combination had 17 Firsts and five Seconds.

After the Wrotham Cup Trial, Colin was already thinking along the lines of better roadholding and brakes for a new car. There was no point in retaining the Mark 1, particularly as it had a good money value and he was going to need quite a bit of that. So OX 9292 was sold and took up residence in the North of England.

During the early part of 1957 the Mark 2 was seen by many thousands of cinema-goers as it appeared in the Boulting Brothers film comedy "Brothers in Law". Throughout the picture it made brief appearances—usually combined with loud engine noises! Finally, when its doting owner had emerged the winner of the hand of actress Jill Adams the car was used for the honeymoon departure, complete with large luggage grid and resplendent in a shining coat of paint.

3.

Colin plays his port trick

A CAR TO COMPETE successfully in the 750 Formula was the broad requirement of the Mark 3, and as a start Colin purchased a 1930 Austin 7 saloon for £15. This was stripped completely, the chassis side-members were boxed-in and two 14-gauge tubular cross-members were put in place of the originals.

When this stage had been reached in the construction of the new car Colin heard of two brothers who lived locally and being 750 Motor Club members were considering building Formula cars for themselves. He lost no time in introducing himself and soon became a firm friend of Michael and Nigel Allen.

The Allen brothers went in for "messing about with cars" in a big way—their garden, in Vallance Road, Wood Green, was littered with various automobiles. They also had wonderful workshop facilities, plenty of space and all the tools and equipment necessary for carrying out any work on a motor car. They appeared to amuse themselves by buying and selling second-hand cars. Sometimes they would do a considerable amount of work on their purchases but never really obtained just reward when they sold the car. The intervention of Colin Chapman decided them definitely on the 750 Formula and lacking the necessary experience they decided to build two identical cars to the Mark 3 Lotus. By now 1950 was at its close, so, in the very tidy way in which Lotus always fixed their dates for the start of a new project, work began on the three Mark 3s on January 1st, 1951.

It was not long before Colin realised that he was spending far more time at Vallance Road than in his own lock-up, giving advice to the brothers on the next move in the construction schedule. So the inevitable happened—perhaps Colin had secretly hoped for this—and he moved his chassis into the Allens' workshop so that the three cars could be built together. This simplified matters immensely, for now such luxuries as a compressor, crank and valve grinders, a lathe and a power drill were readily to hand.

To say that much midnight oil was burnt on the Mark 3s would be an understatement—even the girl friends were found their jobs. One of these was the fabrication of a beautiful sprung steering wheel which could be adjusted for "spring". It soon became apparent, however, that in spite of all the nocturnal work, the cars would not be anything like ready for the start of the season. One of the main factors in this disappointment was the long delays when a special part was required. So, in order that one car would be able to reach the starting line for the first event in the 750 Formula Championship, it was decided to concentrate all forces on the completion of Colin's car as it was the furthest advanced.

The plan was for Colin to drive in the championship events and for Michael and Nigel to take turns in the other races at the various meetings. In the meantime the other two cars would be completed so that towards the end of the season the Allens would have their own cars. How little the three knew about an amateur racing season! What happened was that by the end of the 1951 season the Allens' cars had been reduced to bare chassis frames in order to keep the one Mark 3 in racing condition!

At this point it is interesting to look at the

specification of the Mark 3 as it began to take shape, for this was the first Lotus to be designed purely for circuit racing.

The altered Austin chassis had a wheelbase of 6ft 9in. An extension was built out at the rear in 20-gauge steel to serve as a mounting for the Newton shock absorber struts and a 1930 Austin 7 petrol tank. It was found necessary to cut a portion of the tank away in order to clear the back axle casting. The rear springs were set flat and given a much softer rate than was standard. A 4.9 to 1 ratio back axle was employed with drive supplied through a late-type "Ruby" propeller shaft. A "Nippy" gearbox, with remote control, was used and the drive came through a standard clutch fitted with slightly heavier springs. Moving further forward, the flywheel was lightened to reduce torsional loading on the engine crankshaft. For front suspension a Ford 8 axle beam was used, divided in the middle to provide i.f.s. and with the spring mounted above it. Silentbloc bushes were used at the pivot points of the axle beams. Damping was provided by a pair of Newton struts and the Ford radius arms were anchored on another pair of Silentblocs. The Ford axle gave a 4-ft track and although heavier than the Austin unit was preferred because of the more durable king-pins. An Austin 7 steering box was laid on its side ahead of the axle and the drop arm actuated separate track rods via a transverse drag link. Lockheed hydraulic brakes were fitted all round with two leading shoes at the front and using the stiffer Girling drums. A Morris Minor handbrake was fitted with a cable linkage to the rear brakes.

In order to obtain a very stiff chassis a 15-gauge tubular hoop was put round the scuttle and the two-bearing Austin engine was rigidly mounted in the chassis. After the car's first race it was found that the crankcase studs of the engine were pulling out, so the rigid attachment was changed and the engine was mounted on three-shilling Ford rubbers. This resulted in chassis flexing, so a triangular brace was bolted in above the engine. This way the chassis regained its stiffness but now the engine removal necessitated the unbolting of this chassis member.

Throughout construction meticulous care was taken with weight economy. A 25-lb spring-balance was the final judge and any component that gave a high reading was treated with great disfavour. This resulted in a beautiful little aluminium body weighing only 65 lb complete with hoops. A 22-gauge undershield was made to run the whole length of the car and comfort was supplied by two well-upholstered seats and a lightweight hood. Another item receiving special attention from the weight angle was the wheels. These were specially made up by the West London Repair Company and featured special light centres which did not shroud the brake drums and granted a weight saving per wheel of nearly 4 lb.

There is no doubt that much of the astonishing performance of the Mark 3 could be credited to its engine, so let us see what was so remarkable about this little 750cc unit. Originally a two-bearing Austin 7 unit was used, but when this, at times, was taken up to 6,500 rpm the standard connecting rods were apt to bend. "Ulster" rods were not the answer, for using them with the $1\frac{5}{16}$-in crankshaft caused the big-ends to run. So early in its life the Mark 3 received a three-bearing engine. Immediately a Hoffmann-type "O" rear-main race was fitted and a Fram filter incorporated in the lubrication system in order to reduce oil deterioration due to inadequate crankcase breathing. In Colin's opinion three-bearing cranks broke only because of corrosion, caused by bad breathing, wearing away the rear-main bearing.

The cylinder block of the three-bearing engine was over-bored 0.050 in; the inlet valves were slightly enlarged and the size of the exhaust valves reduced in consequence. A "Nippy" camshaft was used with "Ulster" springs and the valves were set at a very fine clearance. Covmo pistons were fitted with two $\frac{1}{16}$-in compression rings and one $\frac{1}{16}$-in scraper ring.

Cooling was very thoroughly thought out and a modified Austin 7 radiator received water, via a three-branch take-off from the cylinder head, from a Stuart Turner pump driven from the front of the crankshaft.

A Scintilla Vertex magneto, driven from the dynamo, provided ignition and also a headache when it came to panelling the car. Finally it had to be inclined rearwards to prevent fouling the bonnet. A manual ignition control was fitted and the engine given a new set of 14-mm sparking plugs.

Michael Allen was responsible for much of the engine work—guided and spurred on by Colin. Whilst Michael had attended to the bottom end Colin had been working on an idea which had suddenly come to him after a rather hectic Christmas party a few months earlier. This brainwave had motivated his efforts to build a 750 Formula car, because on the face of it he seemed to have the answer to the major problem of tuning a side-valve engine.

After that Christmas party Colin had been thinking about the carburation intake and exhaust outlet of the car that he was about to build. He was well aware that in order to keep down production costs most motor cars had siamesed inlet ports to their cylinders. This meant that on the Austin engine he would be using, the first two cylinders would be fed from a single port as would the rear two cylinders. Now, for racing this would be most inefficient because with a 1,3,4,2 firing order the ingoing charge of fuel and air to the centre cylinders of each pair would be robbed by its neighbour as each induction stroke took place.

It was imperative to obtain good filling of the cylinders, for with the side-valve engine you are basically restricted by the closeness of the cylinder head to the edge of the cylinder bore. Increasing the compression ratio of such an engine may give you power "low-down" but it is no good for increasing your speed as the alteration has still further reduced the breathing capacity of the cylinders. It was obvious to Colin that in order to extract more power from a 2-port block he must try and get as near as possible to a 4-port head. No other 750 Motor Club constructors seemed to have given this problem a great deal of thought, but it seemed the logical way to obtain power. Suddenly, Colin saw a way to "de-siamese" the inlet ports—a way that still enabled you to comply with the 750 Formula regulation which stated that Austin 7 cylinder blocks must be used.

This was how the scheme was to work. First, open up the inlet port areas by grinding away the cast-iron on each side of the passages. Then build up a special manifold from welded sheet steel with

Nigel Allen, running a wingless Mark 3 as a racing car, chasing Metcalfe's Fiat at Silverstone.

Studies in camber as J.B. Davidson takes the Mark 3 through Becketts Corner at Silverstone and, below, Adam Currie tackles the same corner in the Mark 3B.

a vertical steel strip in the centre of the manifold. This dividing strip was to extend into the enlarged siamesed ports and, with asbestos tape fixed on each protruding end, would seal each port in two halves when the manifold was bolted on to the cylinder head. On top of the manifold a flange would be fixed for a twin-choke carburettor.

In practice a twin-choke downdraught Stromberg carburettor from a Ford V8 was used with each choke mated with its corresponding port in the top flange of the manifold. This system endowed the Austin cylinder head with the effect of a twin-carburettor induction system and permitted a clean alternate "pull" on each induction stroke. That the system was a success was shown by the fantastic performance of the Mark 3 and the subsequent incorporation of the following clause in the 750 Formula: "Inlet and exhaust ports must not be reversed in function, nor must the siamesed inlet ports be divided".

In conjunction with this special inlet manifold the external exhaust system was carefully planned. Square-section take-offs were used for numbers 2 and 3 ports with ordinary small-bore pipes from numbers 1 and 4 leading down into a double-pipe Servais silencer. This layout of exhaust ducting provided an extractor effect.

The cylinder head was assembled with a 6.1 to 1 compression ratio but during a season's racing the ratio was gradually increased to 7.2 to 1.

Trials of the completed car were very brief but they afforded the three constructors, together with helpers Derek Wootton, George Beresford and Ken Hawes, a chance, at last, to sample their handiwork. Encouraged by these test runs the car was entered for the Bristol MC and LCC's race meeting at Castle Combe on May 12th. In practice on the Wiltshire circuit Colin found that drops of fuel were being swept back into his face at high speeds so making it difficult to see. The reason for this was that the large Stromberg carburettor was mounted outside the bonnet and the accelerator pump fitted to it was causing an excess of fuel under large throttle openings—it was this surplus which was blowing back. The rate of the pump could not be cut down so a dash was made to nearby Chippenham where a garage produced a piece of right-angle radiator hose. This formed an ideal air-intake, facing forwards like a *schnorkel*. The remedy was very satisfactory and Colin was able to walk home in first place in the ten-lap race for "750 Club" cars, lapping everyone but second man L. West. His race average was 60.01 mph and he set the fastest lap at 61.33 mph. The star of this meeting was one J.M. Hawthorn, driving his two vintage Rileys.

After Castle Combe, 750cc specials constructors all began copying the Lotus *schnorkel*, believing it to be some very hush-hush device for magically producing more horsepower!

The next meeting entered was the Maidstone and Mid Kent MC's event at Silverstone, and here the Mark 3 began to show its tremendous potential. Firstly, Nigel Allen drove it in the sports car race for cars up to 1300cc and finished a very creditable fourth behind Metcalfe's Fiat Balilla, Lister's Cooper-MG and Fuller's supercharged MG PB. He was very pleased with his performance because he beat an MG TC and Buckler's chief mechanic, Drew, in one of the firm's cars. Colin then took the car out in a mixed race and in spite of stalling on the line and losing about half a mile, he managed to beat all the other 750s in a 3-lap event! For the last handicap of the day Hazel took the wheel but unfortunately received a handicap based on Colin's earlier lap times. Even though she was unplaced in the results she was hand-timed to be lapping the old Club circuit at 2 min 7 sec—some going for the fairer sex!

June 2nd had been eagerly awaited by the Lotus *equipe* for on that day the Eight Clubs were to stage their annual meeting at Silverstone, and included in the programme was a 5-lap race for Formula cars. Alas, during practice a big-end bearing broke up. However, this did not daunt Colin and his team—they removed the offending piston and connecting rod and the car went to the starting line on three cylinders. In four laps Colin built up a huge lead, lapping at 58 mph, then when in sight of the finish the crankshaft broke—and that was that.

The Austin engine appeared to like performing on less cylinders than was intended as was demonstrated again on the only occasion during the season when the car non-started. This was at Gamston, where on the way to the meeting the

Left: A triangulated tubular structure augmented the Austin 7 chassis members to make a rigid frame for the Mark 3. Note the return pipe from the cylinder head to the header tank. Below: The modified induction system which caused 750 Formula regulations to be amended. Bottom: Finding a slot between an HRG and a Morgan in an Aston Martin Owners' Club race at Silverstone.

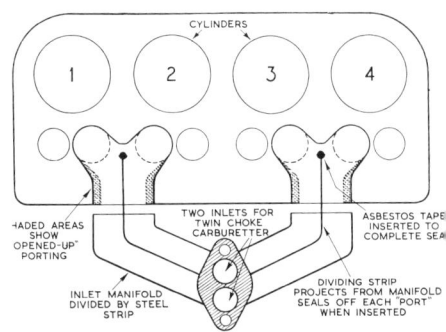

valve guides on numbers 2 and 3 cylinders worked loose and broke up. Thanks to the "de-siamesed" ports it was possible to blank off the carburettor choke nearer the cylinder head and continue on 1 and 4 cylinders only. The car did not complete at the meeting, but the performance on the road on two cylinders was amazing. On the way home Colin worked it up to 65 mph—not bad for a 373cc side-valve "twin".

Michael Allen was at the wheel of the Lotus for the Midland Motoring Enthusiasts Club meeting at Silverstone on June 30th and he took a second place in a 5-lap race behind Len Gibbs' 1089cc Riley and in front of J.M. Sparrowe's 1098cc Morgan—the Mark 3 was now really motoring! Brother Nigel notched up another second place in a 5-lap handicap race at the A.M.O.C. Silverstone meeting three weeks later, and at this same meeting we saw Miss Hazel Williams beating all the ladies in their handicap race.

Colin had a very easy win at Ibsley on August 4th when he toured round to win the 7-lap 750 Formula race. Nigel Allen, however, had to work very hard for his second place behind Ken Downing's Connaught in his race.

A hat-trick followed at the Tewin Water Speed Trials on the Bank Holiday Monday. The course lived up to its name and was soaking wet all day. Hazel won the 750cc class, Colin the 1100cc and Nigel the 1300cc class. At this meeting, Michael Allen also drove but was not placed and a similar fate befell the Lotus' fifth driver of the day—Pamela Slade. Pamela, an Australian, was the girl friend of Derek Jolly who had himself built a very fast Austin special "down under".

In September, Colin decided to try his hand at the famous Prescott hill climb with the outstanding result that after two very spirited climbs he had put up the remarkable time of 52.29 sec., which stood as a 750cc unblown sports car record for a very long time.

Directly after Prescott, Colin and Hazel crammed all their luggage into the tail of the Lotus and set off for a holiday in Scotland. That this holiday was a great success proves that the Mark 3 was a true sports car. There was no surplus of room whilst on the move and it could get wet and draughty at times, but then your trips from place to place were so much quicker! During testing between race meetings it was found that with just the driver aboard the car would cover the standing quarter in 17 seconds and could accelerate from 0 to 50 mph in 6.6 seconds. With its small frontal area and light weight the petrol consumption was particularly good and driven hard on the road the little car would average a shade over 50 mph. Normally, when racing the driver was supposed to keep down to 5,500 rpm in the lower gears and not to exceed 5,900 in top. This gave a top speed of 88 mph but Colin admits to having "seen" 96 mph on the slightly uphill straight of the longer of the two Silverstone Club circuits in use at that time.

With the season over, stocktaking showed that the Mark 3 had been an outstanding success. It had proved itself easily the fastest 750 in the country and had also attained a high degree of reliability. Colin was now completely "sold" on racing, not only for enjoyment but because of the interesting field of learning he was entering. He was now sure that he could do even better than the Mark 3. In this last conclusion he was encouraged by those stalwarts of the 750 Motor Club—Holland Birkett, Bob Yates, Harold Biggs and Dennis Adamson. Another hitherto unforeseen demand had arisen, for now people were asking the three constructors to build replicas of the Lotus for them. One of these people was Adam Currie and, with an eye to raising some capital for his new developments, Colin agreed to completing one of the Allens' chassis for him. So work began on the Mark 3B.

Adam Currie only had a short season's racing before he left for foreign parts but during that time he collected a total of nine awards. Adam was very pleased with this result as he had started with very little knowledge of tuning or competition driving which meant learning the hard way. His brief career with the Mark 3B terminated with his marriage to Colin's cousin, which—in Adam's words—"just shows what a dangerous pastime racing really is!"

Then in November came a turning point in the career of Lotus when Mike Lawson came along to say that owing to trials cars becoming more and more extreme the Mark 2 was now outclassed and he wanted another Lotus.

4.

Trials and triumphs

OBVIOUSLY THERE WAS a business to be built up around this demand for cars and modifications to Ford parts from people who were themselves constructing special cars.

Colin realised that he needed room for this enterprise as he could no longer impose on the facilities offered by the Alexandra Park lock-up, or the Allens' home. But premises cost money, and money was not very plentiful. It was not long, therefore, before he was approaching his father, who owned premises in Tottenham Lane, Hornsey, for alongside the main building was an old stable. To many, the possibilities of creating a workshop here would have appeared almost nil—but not to Colin. Soon he was installed in the rear half of the stable, and the firm of building contractors whose yard was behind the new workshop wondered at the weird noises which emitted far into the night.

The order of a new trials car for Mike Lawson was gladly accepted and Colin began design work immediately on what was to be the Mark 4. Naturally he discussed his plans with the Allen brothers and outlined his scheme to build up a business of manufacturing and converting components for those enthusiasts who were building their own cars. Also he proposed to design, develop and build cars based on the fund of information that had been gleaned from experience with the Mark 3. Michael was very interested, but Nigel, whilst he still wished to drive competition cars, decided to stick to his dentistry career. An agreement was reached by which Colin and Michael became partners in this new venture and took over the two remaining Mark 3 chassis.

Again, January 1st proved to be a convenient date and on this day in 1952 Lotus Engineering Company officially came into being.

The first item on the agenda was the completion of the Mark 3B for Adam Currie—this proceeded swiftly and a car very similar to the first car of the Mark was produced. Adam painted his car black and fitted a "power" bulge instead of a schnorkel to cover the carburettor. Unfortunately the third classis never saw the light of day.

The arrangement between the two partners was that Michael would work full time in the business and Colin would give it all his spare time, still continuing his job with the British Aluminium Company. This arrangement brought long hours for Colin who would often call at the works on his way into London and be toiling well into the night after his day's work. Business was brisk and a great deal of component manufacture was undertaken, the bulk of the customers coming from the ranks of the 750 Motor Club. It was not long before a yellow board appeared on the end of the premises which faced the road, bearing in green the "A.C.B.C" monogram in the odd-shaped triangle. Under the name and address was proudly announced—"Automobile and component manufacturers—racing and competition car design and development".

There were hold-ups in progress on the Mark 4 and Mike Lawson's eagerness to put his new car to use had to be restrained. This new trials car again had the trustworthy Austin 7 chassis frame, "boxed" as before, and was given a body providing a little more room than the earlier trials car. Similar suspension to the Mark 2 was used, but a novel device, which became known affectionately as the "jelly-joint", was fitted at the front. This idea was a method for unlocking the location of the transverse spring and allowing it to pivot at one central point. This gave front wheel travel similar to that used on tractors—ideal for a really bad "section"! An 1172cc Ford engine transmitted power through a Ford 8 gearbox and an Austin 7 back axle. Another novel feature of this car was the hinging cycle-type front mudguards, the idea being that when faced with a narrow tricky climb the driver could hop out at the foot of the hill, tip the mudguards inwards, and so reduce the effective width of the car. Mike Lawson specifically required a dual-purpose car, with full road equipment and good road manners. Unlike the trials cars which were now growing in popularity, the Mark 4 was no freak. It was a fast, safe, road car with a serviceable hood and useful lights. As the opposition became more extreme, Mike Lawson was forced to abandon these comforts in an effort to match the performance of the very light and skimpy contraptions which arrived, often on trailers, to do battle with him. As delivered to him at his garage in Thornton Heath,

Left: The Mark 2 became a star of the comedy film "Brothers in Law" with Ian Carmichael and Nicholas Parsons. Below: Michael Lawson working hard in his Mark 4. Below left: The Mark 4 in its original guise. Bottom: With later squared-up radiator, Lawson takes it to fastest time in a London Motor Club autocross.

LMU 4 had a single carburettor, but this was soon changed to a double—carburettor layout. Another major modification which he made during his ownership of the car was the removal of the "jelly—joint". He had found the suspension too soft for the type of terrain he was being asked to traverse and so fitted a conventional Ford beam axle. This modification also helped in his search for more lightness.

In Mike Lawson's hands the Mark 4 covered itself with glory and the little white car was treated with great respect by fellow competitors. It is interesting to trace briefly the distinguished career of this car from its first major event on March 22nd. This was the Colmore Trophy Trial, a championship event, in which the fourth best performance of the day was achieved and a 1st Class award obtained. These results were repeated in another championship event, the Lancashire, Cheshire and Derbyshire Sporting Trial a month later. This ended the trials season, but in July the car competed in both the London Motor Club and Kentish Border Gymkhanas, and showing its dual nature, was best in its class on both occasions.

September 20th saw the season reopen with the West Hants Motor Club Knott Cup Trials. The Lotus was fifth best and notched up another 1st Class award. At this meeting a "Motorcross" was held—for the first and last time. No doubt the present-day Autocross originated from this experiment but the new version is child's-play compared with the original horror which took place on the Wool Heath tank-testing ground adjacent to Bovington Camp. Cars had to complete a circuit of sandy hills, tank traps, rocks and water holes. In the course of its run the Lotus arrived at a concrete dip which held three feet of water at its bottom, in which there were three cars firmly stranded. More by luck than anything else the white car, now nearly black, scrambled through, and Mike Lawson is still justifiably proud of the Simon Trophy which marks his win at this nightmare event.

More conventional competition followed in October when the cup for the best performance in the Stafford Clark Cup Trial joined the Simon Trophy on the sideboard. Several more minor trials followed, leading up to the eagerly awaited November 15th. On this day the B.B.C. staged its first Television Trial and the Lotus was one of the three-car team from the South competing against teams from the Midlands and the North. Suspense was terrific in many drawing rooms when, after all climbs but one, the Lotus approached the foot of the last hill. If Mike failed then the South would be last, if he climbed half way they would be second, and if he climbed clean then the trophy was theirs! He hurled the car at the hill and with rear wheels spinning madly the Lotus just cleared the "10" marker—Victory!

A signing-on mistake cost the Lotus another best performance in the Kentish Border Sporting Trial on November 30th, but the technical error could not remove a clear class win.

December 6th and the Gloucester Trial saw the Committee Cup add to the groans of the Lawson sideboard. Finally, 1952 was rounded off by the R.A.C. Trials Championship in which the Mark 4 finished 5th.

Mike Lawson competed regularly in the Mark 4 until the end of 1954 when changing conditions in the trials world forced him to change his mount. But the Lotus was by no means spent even then, for on November 20th, 1954, he won the Roy Fedden Trophy in the Bristol Motor Club's event. Outstanding highlights in his 1953 and 1954 seasons were the "runner-up" award on the London Motor Club's French Sporting Trial at Annecy in France, and the second TV Trial, when once again the Lotus helped the South to win against very stiff opposition.

To return from the muddy hills to the workshop at Hornsey, the delivery of the Mark 4 had cleared the decks for development work on a production Lotus which both Colin and Michael were itching to build. Although the demand for components flowed satisfactorily, Colin realised that a great potential existed in offering the components for a complete car which the customer would assemble himself. This pressing need to develop a series model meant that a secret project had to be shelved. The Mark 5 was to have been a 100 mph Austin 7-engined sports car based on the earlier Mark 3. Colin never found the time to build it.

5.

Six sets the scene

EARLIER EXPERIENCE with the Mark 3 had shown that excellent roadholding resulted from a rigid chassis and soft suspension. In the case of the Austin 7 frame, however, the rigidity had been obtained at the expense of weight as the side-members had to be supplemented by a steel "fourth side" and a multi-tubular structure, bolted to the chassis frame.

In designing the first "production" model for Lotus Engineering Company, Colin was no longer tied to the Austin 7 chassis and so set out to produce a multi-tubular frame of great strength and low weight. He was not a believer in the two-large-tube chassis which mathematically is not as rigid as a multi-tube space frame and in any case requires the addition of a body framework. What Colin was after for the Mark 6 was a robust multi-tubular "body frame" which would be rigid enough to locate the various suspension parts, engine and transmission. The whole structure had to be light and critically stressed. If possible there would be no surplus weight—every tube had to do a job, and all brackets and appendages contained in the basic framework.

The resultant spaceframe for the Mark 6 filled these requirements and was to be the basic frame for a long line of future Lotus cars both of the "square-cut" and "finned" variety.

$1\frac{7}{8}$ in diameter 18-gauge lower main chassis tubes were employed with upper tubes of both 1 in square and 1 in round material. Additional rigidity was provided by riveting stressed aluminium panels to the frame to form the floor, scuttle and sides of the car. When completed, Colin was delighted to find that the bare chassis weighed only 55 lb, and with the addition of mounting brackets and stressed panels only 90 lb.

As the Mark 6 was to be offered in the form of a "do-it-yourself" kit, great attention had to be paid to making the various accessories easy to assemble. It was also important that the various components should be easy to obtain. Experience on the earlier cars had shown Ford parts to be very satisfactory and so it was decided that modified Ford front axle, radius arms, brakes, gearbox, torque tube, back axle and wheels would be used.

With the stage set for production of the first cars the company was strengthened by the addition of two employees to work with Michael Allen—John Teychenne and Mike Madan. Colin now found that he saw less and less of his bed, as often he would be in the "office" by 8 a.m. This addition to the premises had been constructed by encroaching slightly on the original space allowance from Mr. Chapman Senior. Colin could deal with urgent matters and still reach his other office by 9.30 a.m. He would be back at Hornsey by 6 p.m., attend to queries, have a high tea, and then get down to manual labour in the workshop until 1, 2, 3 or even 4 o'clock in the morning!

The very first Mark 6 differed from subsequent models as it was for use in trials. This car was built for Sinclair Sweeny ("Todd") and had a solid-beam front axle and lofty ground clearance. This "ugly duckling" later competed with success in trials and rallies in the hands of Arthur Hay.

Progress on the prototype works car was further interrupted when the two Clairmonte brothers placed an order for a racing car to conform with the current Formula 2 of up to 2 litres unsupercharged. This car was to be powered by a 2-litre ERA engine. A chassis was built up and designated Mark 7. Front suspension was by double wishbones with inboard suspension units, rather similar to the later Formula 2 Lotus and Formula 3 Ray Petty. At the rear a de Dion lay-out was fitted with a special step-down, quick-change, rear axle. Unfortunately, before the car was complete, the ERA engine was wrecked and delivery was taken of just the bare chassis/body unit. As the car had not been completed the Mark 7 designation was removed and retained for a future model. Subsequently this car appeared as a 2-litre sports car—the Clairmonte Special—powered by a Lea Francis engine.

At last work commenced in earnest on the first production Mark 6, and after a lot of thought it was decided to use a Ford Consul engine. It was planned that the Mark 6 would accommodate almost any engine up to 1500cc so it was a good idea to start at the limit of the range, but to obtain the required engine was not easy. Colin's father even tried writing direct to Ford's chairman Sir Patrick Hennessy at Dagenham—but to no avail. At this time Sydney Allard was also trying desperately to obtain the same engine to power a new car he was producing, but even through his associated company of Adlards, who were Ford main agents, the Consul engine was not available.

As he could not get an engine the easy way Colin set about it the hard way and went from one Ford dealer to another, buying one part here and another there. Finally, the collection was complete and soon the engine came into being at Hornsey. Imagine Allard's face when it first appeared in the Lotus!

Lotus Engineering Company were lucky in having Williams and Pritchard, of Edmonton, as their body builders, for these practical people co-operated greatly in designing the body. In addition to the stressed parts they produced four neat wings, a propshaft tunnel, nose, scuttle cover, bonnet top and sides. These additional body parts were easily removable and held in position by clips and Dzus fastners. Another careful weight check showed the total chassis/body unit to tip the scales at 120 lb—light by any standards.

As in his earlier models, Colin decided to keep to the divided front axle. His reasons for adhering to the swing-axle were ones of theory and not adaptability, although he was the first to admit that the standard Ford layout lent itself admirably to his purpose. Colin was designing a small and relatively low-powered car and therefore wished to attain maximum cornering speed in order to offset lack of acceleration and top speed. In his experience a great deal of cornering speed was lost by cars with other forms of independent suspension because their wheels tended to lean out on a corner and so developed camber thrust away from the required direction of travel. This camber thrust had to be resisted by an increase in cornering force and to provide this the wheels had to run at a greater slip angle. With the slip angle increasing there was more drag, or roll resistance, and in this way the leaning-out wheels were causing the car to suffer a considerable retarding force, which slowed it down appreciably. In the Mark 3 Colin had experienced several near-misses as he rushed up behind another car in a bend which had suddenly slowed up without a visible sign of the brakes being applied! The finest answer to the problem of keeping the wheels upright was the beam front axle. However, Colin required a soft suspension and with the beam axle this would have induced the unpleasant vices of shimmy and tramp.

A swing-axle would give an almost upright wheel angle if a low enough roll-centre were used. Also, this layout provided the desirable soft ride in conjunction with ample suspension movement. In practice the Ford front axle beam was cut in the centre and two plates were welded on the severed ends into which bushes were fitted. The two bushes pivoted between a bracket attached to the front chassis lower cross-member. The "V" shaped Ford tie rod was cut in half and remade to form two radius arms. The track rod was divided and worked on a centrally-placed slave-arm. A Ford steering box and column were turned on their side and mounted by their base plate, a track rod running from the arm of the Burman box to the slave-arm. By these clever adaptations, Lotus Engineering Company paved the way for their future customers to purchase their own

Above: Jack Richards in his immaculately turned out Mark 6 winning his race at Silverstone in August 1954. Right: The Lotus factory at Hornsey, North London, was nothing if not modest, and belied its prolific output.

Above: The multi-tubular chassis frame of the Mark 6 weighed only 55 lb., or 90 lb. when all brackets and stressed body panels had been attached. Left: Most customers assembled their own cars after receiving their Mark 6 as a kit of parts.

components which could be safely modified to fit the Lotus chassis.

Drive was transmitted by Ford parts, utilising a Ford 10 rear axle and shortening the standard propeller shaft and torque tube. Lateral location of the rear axle was by a specially produced Panhard rod. At both ends of the car, suspension was by helical springs which surrounded Woodhead Monroe telescopic dampers. Ordinary Ford brakes, cable-operated Girling units of 10 in by 1¼ in, were fitted, these being fully capable of dealing with the light weight which had to be stopped.

After a great deal of midnight oil had been consumed, Michael Allen completed the engine and for the first time power unit and chassis made contact. In order to reduce the capacity from 1508cc to under the 1500cc limit the stroke had been shortened. This was achieved by eccentric grinding of the big-end journals which removed "19 thou" off the bottom and .001 in off the top at its original dimension so moving the centre of the journal up by "9½ thou". Standard undersized shell bearings (for worn engines) were then fitted and the swept volume of the engine was reduced by just over the requisite 8cc. The cylinder block had .010 in removed from the top to restore the compression ratio. A special inlet manifold had been fabricated so that twin S.U. carburettors could be fitted. Later in its life this engine was purchased by Laystalls who incorporated a lot of the original cylinder head and manifold ideas in the conversion which they marketed for the Consul engine. On paper there was plenty of power available to provide a very searching test of the new model. In practice it was good torque rather than power at high revs that was produced—excellent for acceleration but giving a rather disappointing top speed. Technically the engine was just about unburstable with its large bearings and generous oil supply.

The trial runs of the new Lotus were most exciting and both Colin and Michael were very pleased with the way the car handled. One immediate modification was necessary—the fitting of an oil-radiator. The car had a definite character when sampled on the road. The steering felt a little unusual and one had to learn its tricks; the Burman steering box gave a light operation and a moderate degree of caster action. However, one soon mastered these peculiarities and was able to enjoy the exceptional cornering power—just enough understeer for stability, and no more. The "back-end" behaved well and could be slid with abandon without fear of a complete breakaway.

Saturday, July 5th, saw the first racing appearance of the car when it was entered at the MG Car Club Silverstone meeting. The new car caused considerable interest in the paddock and was continuously besieged by an inquisitive crowd. Michael Allen drove it in the novices handicap and finished second in his heat. In the final, however, he was plagued by a binding brake. Furious work behind the starting grid enabled Colin to start in the unlimited handicap and he became involved in a fine dice with Peter Gammon in his rather ugly-bodied, but very fast, bored-out MG TC. In the years which followed, Peter was to be a leading exponent with the Mark 6, powered by a very potent MG engine. As the 5-lap race progressed Peter sent up the sand on the corners and Colin banged the oil-drums at Becketts. Finally the Lotus had to be content with second place—very creditable considering its scratch start and gift of 30 seconds to Gammon. For the team relay race, Colin drove the car in the 750 Motor Club team in company with Pat Stephens (Stoneham) and F.B. Taylor (933 Austin). The team had a 2 min. 50 sec. handicap but could not better the steady driving of the TDs of Escott, Lund and Whatmough. Colin tried very hard, hit the drums again—this time at Woodcote Corner—and the team finished second to the MGs.

The little band of Lotus Engineering Company were very pleased with the day's efforts. The new car had behaved very well and the glorious weather had made the occasion most enjoyable. The only unfortunate result was that already the handicappers were treating the car with great respect!

Three weeks later the car was back at Silverstone for the Aston Martin Owners' Club meeting. At this meeting the old Mark 3 was running in the hands of its new owner,

J.B. Davidson. Very cleverly the earlier car had been equipped with a new arrangement of two semi-downdraught SUs, mounted on the same manifold as the original twin-choke Stromberg. Linking the two throttles had called for considerable ingenuity and one of the frame tubes had been replaced by two bowed pieces in order to clear one of the carburettor bowls. The Mark 3 behaved well but unfortunately the Mark 6 suffered from valve gear derangement throughout the meeting which seriously curtailed performance. Nigel Allen drove the car in the team event in company with Freddie Taylor (Nippy-Ford) and Pat Stephens (Stoneham). They comprised the 750 Motor Club number 1 team and justified the title by winning by 12 seconds from the number 4 team. Hazel drove the car in the ladies' race but in spite of great efforts from Colin to urge her on, she could not cope with the rather severe handicap and finished third.

Encouraged by the good showing of the car at its first outing a bold decision had been made and an entry sent in for the 100-mile sports car race at the International Boreham meeting sponsored by the *Daily Mail,* to be held on the next weekend. Very gratifyingly the Lotus was accepted and it was agreed that Michael Allen would drive. Practice took place in the wet, and in order to familiarise himself with the conditions and also the circuit, Nigel Allen went out for some practice when his brother had finished. On his first lap he tried to take Railway Corner much too fast, left the road, and finished up on top of the marker drums. Getting the car back on the road, he tried again and two minutes later, at a slightly reduced speed, arrived back on top of the drums. This performance Nigel repeated four times until finally he managed to get round the corner without spinning. It was an expensive way of learning the circuit as, owing to damage sustained, the car had to be taken back to the workshop in North London. Then, on his way back to Boreham the following morning, Nigel was involved in a road accident and wrote the car off. On a straight stretch of road a van shot out of a side turning; Nigel didn't have a chance and the collison reduced the Lotus to a total wreck. Lucky Nigel

Far left: The author's Mark 6 in a spectacular opposite-lock slide in pursuit of another sports car. Left: Edward Lewis raises a front wheel of his highly-polished Mark 6 at Prescott. Below: POP 444 again, this time competing in a sprint at Ramsgate alongside a Frazer-Nash. The rebodied prototype Mark 8 is behind the Mark 6.

was unharmed but considerably shaken. This was a terrible blow to the band of toilers to have all their hard work destroyed before the car had really begun to show its paces. It was some consolation that there was a comprehensive insurance policy in existence, and the police decided to summon the other driver for "driving without due care".

Something had to be done because the company was now virtually without assets and there were bills to pay and very little in the bank. It seemed that all the conversions and component manufacturing were not paying and so reluctantly Colin and Mike had to dispense with the services of John Teychenne and Mike Madan. A big effort was made to put the little firm back on its feet and the following advertisement appeared in the November issue of the 750 Motor Club Bulletin: "Lotus Engineering Co. At your service for crankshaft balancing, rebores, remetalling, enlarged valves, surface grinding, double valve springs for Ford and Austin, i.f.s. conversions, 7-in. Lockheed brake sets, lightweight wheels and springs, etc. In fact **A COMPLETE SERVICE FOR THE SPECIAL BUILDER.** Call, write or telephone".

Hazel became more and more involved in the secretarial side of the business. She was now helping her mother who had opened a wool shop and all her spare time was spent at Hornsey acting as typist, telephonist, buying department, packing and despatch department and the tea boy to the company! How she hated having to parcel up exhaust pipes and manifolds! The goods clerk at the local railway station came to know her very well as she dashed in with her weird-shaped parcels for all parts of the British Isles.

By Christmas prospects looked a little brighter and in the New Year the insurance money arrived and was just sufficient to meet the outstanding bills. Now that finances were straight again Michael Allen decided to withdraw from the company as on the past results there did not appear to be a very sound living for him in the future. The assets, such as they were, were valued and split 50/50 between Colin and Michael, the Allen share finally amounting to the crashed Mark 6.

Colin was convinced that he could make a

success of producing the Mark 6 in quantity and also continuing his service to special builders, and in his persuasive way he convinced Hazel that things would work out all right. Hazel listened to all the wonderful new schemes for offering a "built-it-yourself" kit to specialist motorists and in the end she made her offering—a loan of £25. With this money, new stationery and office requisites were purchased and the business was formed into a limited company. Initially it was planned that they would run the business themselves—no staff and the lowest possible overheads. So in February, 1953, customers found that their invoices were yellow in colour and bore an attractive green design with the bold heading—Lotus Engineering Co. Ltd., under which were two names, A.C.B. Chapman, B.Sc.(Eng.) and H.P. Williams. The stage was now set for a new chapter in the life of cars and components supplied by the firm with the name of a flower.

The next few months were very hectic, as virtually single-handed Colin built up chassis and components for eight production cars. The system was now working and customers would obtain the various component parts, take them to Hornsey for modification and then assemble them on to their space-frame chassis. The parts for these early cars were completed at the approximate rate of one car per fortnight. This intense activity meant that the body builders were kept very busy and in the cause of efficiency moved from Edmonton to the shed at Tottenham Lane. Panel beating went on by day and Colin took over at night to fabricate the various components.

These production cars were cleaned-up versions of the prototype car. Whilst the customer chose his engine and gearbox, all the other components were the standard proprietary parts specially modified by Lotus. The first production car with Ford 10 engine weighed 8½ cwt, had a wheelbase of 7 ft 3½ in, front track of 4 ft 1½ in, rear track of 3 ft 9 in, overall length of 10 ft 1 in, overall width of 4 ft 3½ in and a scuttle height of 2 ft 6½ in. A very compact, low little car. One of the first was purchased by P.A. Desoutter, who lost no time in fitting a Ford 10 engine and entering the car for competition motoring. At his very first meeting he figured in the results, getting a third place in the 1172 Formula race held at Ibsley on Saturday, April 18. Another early customer was Fred Hill, owner of Empire Garages at Finsbury Park. Fred fitted his car with a 746cc supercharged MG engine which made a most impressive noise. He named the car the "Empire Special" and drove it to good effect throughout the 1953 season. The car was then sold to genial Austin Nurse, who insinuated his bulk into its cockpit throughout the following season. Boxing Day, 1954, the car changed hands again and became the property of David Piper who drove it with great verve during 1955; sometimes he left the track altogether but on other occasions he finished in the money.

A variety of power units were installed in these first eight cars, the most electrifying combination resulting from the very special 1497cc MG unit which Peter Gammon put in his car. Peter did not hurry to get his Lotus on the tracks as he was still finding that his modified MG had winning ways, but when the car did appear at Goodwood for the first B.A.R.C. Members' Meeting in March of the next year, everyone was amazed at the way this

Top left: Mike Anthony in typical form at Brands Hatch. Centre left: Nigel Allen in the prototype Mark 6 at Silverstone. Bottom left: Peter Gammon's quick MG-engined car. Below: The Mark 6 eventually 'grew up' into the Seven.

relatively cheap motor car was able to hold its own against expensive vehicles such as John Coombs' new Connaught. UPE 9 became a well-known participant at race meetings up and down the country, where spectators marvelled at the speed of the little square-cut Lotus. Peter matched the performance of the car with very capable skill at the wheel, and during his 1954 season he won the Performance Car Trophy, having won more awards than any other driver of a 1500cc car during the year. His total bag out of 17 events entered was 14 firsts, 2 seconds and one third place!

Nigel Allen purchased one of the early cars and installed a Ford 10 engine, and he was soon adding more "pots" to the sideboard with wins in the 1172 Formula races. Colin was so busy with his occupation during the day and Lotus in his spare time that he did not get the opportunity to drive any of the first eight cars. However, the customers seemed satisfied and the race reports continuously mentioned the name Lotus, so he manfully put aside the urge to race his product. He was now being helped by Peter Ross and "Mac" Mackintosh, who were a great assistance to him on the design and draughtsman side of the business. Both these contemporaries of his loved the opportunity to put some of their ideas into practice, and being employees of the De Havilland Aircraft Company at Hatfield they had plenty of ideas. It was through Peter and Mac that Colin was able to break his good resolution. One day he mentioned to them how he wished he had the time to build a Mark 6 for himself and so see how the production car really went. In no time a fellow-worker from Hatfield, Mike Costin, heard of this and so took himself along to the 750 Motor Club's May meeting to meet this chap Colin Chapman. On arrival he bumped into Hazel and a few minutes later plans were afoot for assembling Number 9.

The link-up between Mike and Colin was a landmark in the history of Lotus, for from his early spare-time assembly of the Mark 6 Mike became the "Uhlenhaut" of the Hornsey team. He had a great flair for the mechanical side of cars and proved himself to be an untiring worker. His one concern was always the engine or vehicle under his care—it had to have all his attention, despite the

discomfort and long hours the work entailed. Mike was essentially a practical person; he could improvise and often had to! In his hands it was not long before 1611 H, the Chapman Ford 10 Mark 6, was ready for the road. Colin drove the car at Goodwood at the end of July and won a 5-lap scratch race by 3 seconds from Desoutter. In the process he put in the fastest lap at 71.76 mph. Colin shared the driving of the car with Mike Costin and on the latter's first outing at Silverstone a fortnight later he was more tactful and let Desoutter beat him by 3 seconds in the 1172 Formula race. Just to show willing, however, he put in the fastest lap!

The car competed regularly for the rest of the season with very satisfactory results. Colin and Mike were not selfish about the car and at the SUNBAC Silverstone meeting towards the end of the season Colin's father was given a drive in a handicap event. The handicappers were not very kind, possibly because S.F. Chapman looked rather like "A.C.B." in the same crash hat. Mr. Chapman Senior had to start with Nigel Allen on the 48 second mark, which gave them little chance against the heavier metal present.

Hazel drove the car on occasions and had the advantage over the other lady competitors of being told exactly how it should be done by her boy friend. She faithfully followed these instructions, often with gratifying results. One such occasion was the Tarrant Rushton Speed Trial which wound up the season in October. Owing to trouble with Adam Currie's cylinder head gasket on the way down to Dorset the Lotus retinue arrived too late to practise. They were, however, allowed to motor round the course in the Austin saloon. From a straight start the road curved right, there was a short straight then a long bend to the right, dropping away as it finished. Colin whisked the little saloon round and said to Hazel, "piece of cake, flat-out though the gears, keep your foot flat through the second bend and then up to the finish". Hazel did exactly as she was bid and easily won the 1172 Formula class—Colin and Mike were seen to wince at the revs reached on the starting line! It was then Colin's turn in the up-to-1300cc class. All went as he had planned until the second bend when he found that he was travelling so fast he had to lift-off. Result: slower than Hazel! Imagine his surprise when he questioned her about this bend and she replied that of course she had kept her foot hard down—"You said I should"! Colin tried it on his second run, scared himself considerably, and just beat Hazel's best time. He won the class and Mike drove the car into second place.

It was very fitting that Hazel should do so well in her last outing in 1953 as she had put in a great deal of work for the company throughout the year. Her loan to start the company had been repaid by the present of an Austin Chummy for private transport. The present was an absolute necessity as often it was past midnight when the typist began her homeward trek, and Mrs. Williams now lived at Cuffley, in Hertfordshire—quite a step from Hornsey. This change of domicile had been occasioned mainly by her desire for her daughter to forget this mad young man who lived for motor cars and spent every penny he had on them. At first she had enquired about houses in Bournemouth—a town in which she had always wanted to live. Negotiations led to the occasional

Left: Peter Gammon masters the wet at Silverstone. Below: The car which appeared in all the ads; 1611 H was Colin Chapman's 'demonstrator'. Bottom: Nigel Allen in a one-hour speed trial at Silverstone in 1953.

visit to the seaside resorts to inspect a likely house, but always Colin seemed to wheedle his way on to these trips. A few remarks from him about the drains or the foundations would cast doubts and the issue was finally settled when he discovered an aerodrome near the town! So Mrs. Williams settled for Cuffley and resigned herself to the fact that Colin was a determined young man and that her daughter loved him.

The adage "all work and no play, makes Jack a dull boy" doubtless has some merit. Colin has always believed so and even in the hectic days of 1953 he tried to have breaks from the toils of the company. Usually Saturdays were spent at the race meetings but even if work had to be done on a Sunday morning he would endeavour to keep the afternoon free. It was then one could hear the little Lotus singing along out of London making for Cuffley. Whether you went via Potters Bar or Cheshunt, the roads became interesting as you went deeper into Hertfordshire. Colin loved those last few miles where the road curved, dipped and climbed. He was able to dream himself on to the fabulous Nurburgring and as he twitched the little car from bend to bend Hazel could hear the rising and falling engine note growing louder and louder. They had their recreation—it usually consisted of a trip somewhere in the Lotus—but it was purely a pleasure outing and the car was just transport. On the Monday, as they both well knew, they would be up to their necks in the business again.

The Company was considerably strengthened when one summer evening a local enthusiast walked in, picked up a spanner and asked if he could help. The new boy was "Nobby" Clarke. He has heard about the sports cars being produced in Tottenham Lane and so had come along to give a hand. He worked in a small electrical business with his brother but in no time the attraction of manufacturing these special sports cars became irresistible and he spent all his spare time with Lotus. "Nobby" was a great help to Colin and Mike and in a short space of time became an indispensable part of the organisation.

Thousands of eyes were opened on Saturday, September 19th, at the Crystal Palace when they beheld the astonishing sight of Colin with only a side-valve Ford 10 engine under the bonnet fighting it out with some of the hottest 1½-litre machines. The performance of the Lotus was the talk of the paddock and caused *The Motor* to describe the car as "preposterously fast." There was no doubt that the Lotus had come to stay; the number of people visiting Tottenham Lane to place orders proved that. Gradually the business expanded, calls on the time of Mike Costin, "Nobby" Clarke, Peter Ross and "Mac" Mackintosh became greater, and an arrangement for extra welding facilities was made with a nearby firm. The body builders took over the rear half of the store shed and Mr. Chapman Senior was bullied into handing over the rest of the building to the company. The office still remained, but there was now valuable workshop space alongside it. A stores was installed on the rafters above the office.

For the remainder of 1953 and throughout the next two years production of the Mark 6 went steadily ahead. Finally, at the end of 1955, the model had to be discontinued as by then the company were so busy with a later model. In all, just over 100 Mark 6s were built—a remarkable achievement considering the space and labour available. It would require several books to chronicle all the owners and their achievements with this "square cut" model. However, several names stand out from those who built and raced their Mark 6s. Ken Laverton and John Lawry remained faithful to the 1172cc Ford engine and had numerous wins with their cars. The latter, proving that "old soldiers never die", won the 1200cc class of the *Autosport* Series Production Sports Car Championship in 1956. Many racegoers will remember the meteoric drives by Mike Anthony in his beautifully finished, dark green car. Like Peter Gammon, Mike used a 1497cc MG engine and was often engaged in a stirring battle with the similar car. Although a big chap, Mike flung the Lotus about with gay abandon and always managed to come out of "a-mother-and-father" of a slide with a broad grin on his face.

The Mark 6 received all sorts of power units. Already we had seen Consul, Ford 1172 and two types of MG being used, and it was not long before both the 1250cc and 1500cc MG TF engines were fitted by owners. Bill Perkins was very original and insinuated a 2-litre BMW engine into the chassis, this tall unit necessitating a huge "power" bulge in the bonnet. When the Coventry Climax 1100cc engine was discovered one of the people to use it was John Harris. John gave his Mark 6 a very up-to-date specification with a de Dion rear axle and large turbo-finned alloy brake drums. His car proved to be one of the fastest of its type and would often lead later types of Lotus, particularly on the twistier circuits. John loved the rain—in these conditions he excelled, handling his car in a manner rather akin to Mike Anthony! One of the most remarkable "6s" was another Coventry Climax-powered car constructed and driven by Fred Marriott. Although possessing this very fine engine his car retained the live rear axle and cable-operted Ford brakes. The performance was terrific, and the intrepid driver was able to show a clean pair of rear tyres to many other similarly powered vehicles of much more recent origin.

With the number of Lotus cars increasing in this country, it was not long before they began to find their way overseas. The first of these was Colin's 1611 H which was purchased by the Swiss journalist, "Jabby" Crombac. Being resident in Paris, Jabby entered for some of the leading French races and in the Lotus won his class in the Coupe d'Or at Montlhery, which he followed by a class win in the Coupe de Vitesse. When the well-worn engine broke its crankshaft, Jabby replaced it with a Consul unit and at the same time had enveloping wings added to the front of the car, which considerably altered its appearance.

The Mark 6 crossed the Atlantic when Bill Klinck, of Buffalo, New York, purchased an MG-engined version which he soon put to very good use on the track. Another similar car followed when Tom Gilmour, of Toronto, imported the first Lotus into Canada, also an MG-engined vehicle. The Lotus began to figure in the race results "down under" in the hands of Doug Chivas, this Australian car being powered by the Coventry Climax engine and having the de Dion rear axle and large brakes similar to those fitted by John Harris.

With the winter approaching and the hustle of the racing season over, Colin was able to take stock. The picture was a lot rosier than at the start of the year, but he realised nothing must stand still; whilst he could see a ready sale for his present model, he knew that next year things would be much faster and if possible he must have a car ready which would be quicker than all the others. With this aim in view he and Mike went into a huddle.

Below: The first Lotus to be imported into Canada, Tom Gilmour's MG TF-engined Mark 6 was fitted with 'full-width' front wings to conform with local regulations. The first Mark 6 to enter the United States was bought by Bill Klinck of Buffalo, New York, who also used an MG engine. Bottom: John Derisley on the start line for a sprint at Gosport with 3,600 rpm on the clock.

6.

A matter of aerodynamics

FOR ONCE THERE was a gap in the methodical numbering and chronological order of the Lotus Marks. However, the omission of Mark 7 when the new car was considered was no accident. Colin and Mike reasoned that with the experience to be gained from a new prototype, they would probably be able to improve on the Mark 6. They therefore left the "7" designation for this redesigned model. Time proved them right and, with a heavy demand for such a car, the Mark 7 was introduced three years later.

During 1953 the 1500cc sports car racing class had attracted a great deal of attention from the manufacturers which resulted in very closely fought, fast racing. It was for this class that Colin wished to design a car. Already he had made the opposition take notice of his product when using a Ford 10 engine and Peter Gammon in his MG-engined Mark 6 had been having a considerable measure of success. The opposition was stiff and a variety of sports–racing cars were appearing in the class from Connaught, Cooper, Leonard and Tojeiro. But the masters in this particular field were the Porsches and Colin included the Germans in his reckoning.

Finally, after a lot of head scratching, it was decided that a really efficient aerodynamic body might do the trick. Having reached this decision, the little band were lucky in being able to ask assistance from Mike's brother, Frank Costin, an aerodynamist with the De Havilland Aircraft Company. Even though Frank lived and worked in Chester, he was soon infused with the Chapman enthusiasm and began covering sheets of paper with weird shapes and masses of small figures.

Once again a new year had just began, coinciding yet again with a new Lotus project–the prototype Mark 8.

Generally chassis work was now very brisk at Hornsey and under the care of Dave Kelsey. With increased activity promised, John Teychenne was "stolen" back from Arnotts, where he had been working, to help Dave. The band of workers was now overseen by "Nobby" Clarke, who decided to forsake the electrical business and started full-time employment with Lotus on the first day of the year.

Colin worked on the chassis design with Peter Ross and "Mac" Mackintosh. These two were a great help, producing detailed drawings and reams of "worst cases" throughout the design stage. Peter Ross had helped Adam Currie in the final assembly of his car so had first-hand knowledge of "these Lotus things". He had also worked with Frank Costin at Percivals of Luton, and so had a good idea of the lines along which the body designer would be thinking.

The further Frank proceeded along these lines of thought the more worried he became. He realised the tremendous responsibility with which he had saddled himself, and Colin's estimates of 85 bhp, total weight under 10 cwt and a top speed in excess of 125 mph did not help matters. Until this time Frank had been concerned only with shape in the air–he carried this occupational interest into his hobby when he built and flew gliders. Cars, to him, were untidy vehicles of shocking inefficiency. Now he was being asked to design an aerodynamic shape for one of these earthbound carriages and he realised that the lives of the occupants would, to a great extent, be his responsibility. He spent many sleepless nights with the picture before him of the projected lightweight car travelling at something like 130 mph and suddenly receiving a blast from a cross wind—it could be lethal! Meanwhile, Colin was impatient. His chassis design was coming along well and he wanted an idea of the complete car. Dave Kelsey built a model for him at which Frank took one look, shuddered and said "horrible". This was just the incentive necessary for the aerodynamist, and he returned to his slide-rule and wind-tunnel with renewed vigour.

The results of Frank's labours were first let out of the bag by Colin during a meal with some friends in Ruggenis Restaurant in London's Shepherd Market. In fact the head waiter was quite angry about his tablecloth, which finished the meal covered with sketches of a most peculiar object! The Mark 8 was to have a new triangulated spaceframe of 1¼ in, 20-gauge, steel tubing. The aim was, as for the Mark 6, utmost rigidity but without an ounce of superfluous weight. This goal was well achieved when the scales showed only 35 lb for the complete full-width structure. Colin and his helpers designed the frame from the purist point of view; they set themselves the target of a car which would be the lightest, fastest and most stable in its class. There is no doubt that the prototype chassis was excellent in these respects—perhaps the best ever produced by Lotus—but the purist frame had a distinct drawback when it came to accessibility. When complete it was found that 12 man-hours were required to remove the engine, and 24 to reinstall it! The prototype car, SAR 5 as it was registered, was fitted with an MG engine from which certain prominent projections had to be removed. Even then the cylinder-head had to be separated from the crankcase before the unit could be coaxed out of the chassis!

There were now two distinct sides of the Lotus business, one producing components and production Mark 6s with its paid staff under "Nobby" Clarke, and the other engaged on the prototype Mark 8. Colin decided that one must not be allowed to interfere with the other and so he formed Team Lotus, which was to be the amateur-staffed racing organisation for proving the prototype machine. Recruits to this *voluntary* band had come along as the new "dicer" took shape. These enthusiasts gave up their evenings and weekends to be at Hornsey and do a job at the bench. Early volunteers were Peter Singleton and Tony Holder, the latter appointing himself official photographer, as he worked for Kodak's. Team Lotus was strengthened by three more stalwarts who gave their services just for the fun of it—Peter Mayes, Tony "AC" McKusker and John Standen. Tony was a schoolteacher and so was a very valuable asset when school holidays came round. At times during term the "prep" corrections must have been rushed for he gave up his evenings, as did the others, in order to repair or prepare for a fast approaching race meeting. His nickname of course came from a very antiquated form of transport to which he clung with loving devotion! John Standen decided on an even closer association with Lotus and later joined the company in order to look after the stores side of the business.

The specification of the new aerodynamic car had many similarities to the Mark 6. At the front the divided-axle was used, suspended by helical springs and Woodhead-Monroe hydraulic dampers. Great thought had been given to the question of the front end, for Colin was worried that there might be excessive gyroscopic kick at the over-120-mph speeds he was contemplating. Tests however proved the swing-axle to be very satisfactory, and the car handled well, even at top speed. It appeared that the limitations of this type of front suspension were not as strict as originally thought. Steering was by a clever combination of rack-and-pinion and Burman gearbox, the steering column being universally jointed.

At the rear a de Dion type of axle was used, in conjunction with a trasverse helical spring held in tension, and damped by Armstrong piston-type units. The brakes were fitted inboard, each side of the differential housing. This form of rear suspension was chosen mainly to keep down wheel spin and to reduce unsprung weight. A conventional live axle tends to lift under heavy acceleration, as torque reaction tries to lift one rear wheel to induce wheelspin. With the de Dion layout the "diff" housing is bolted solidly to the frame, so obviating the "lift" motion. Drive was taken out to the rear wheels by two separate, short drive shafts. Lockheed brakes with 9 in by 1¾ in drums were fitted all round. The rears being inboard it was feared that they might suffer from the heat generated by the final drive unit, and in order to try to eliminate this possibility, a special lubrication system was devised with a pressure-cum--scavenge pump driven off the propeller shaft which picked up oil from the engine sump and passed it to the differential. In this way the axle casing was replenished with cooled lubricant from the engine approximately every ten seconds. Actual oil-cooling was effected by a heat-exchanger mounted behind the radiator, the normal engine oil pump being retained. Frank Costin had spent a long time on calculations of air flow to the radiator. Air entered through a low slot in the nose of the car, was ducted through the radiator core and then let out downwards under the car.

As the car was to compete in the up-to-1500cc class, an engine was built up of components from the most appropriate power units available in the country. This meant mating MG TC and Morris "10" parts. A Laystall-Lucas light-alloy cylinder head and twin 1¾ in SU carburettors were fitted. Transmission was via a Borg & Beck competition clutch and MG gearbox. Weight distribution had been carefully considered and as a result one 12-gallon fuel tank was positioned in the rear of the car with a further 10 gallons contained in side tanks. The spare wheel was located above the rear axle and could be reached through a hatch.

The shape on which Frank Costin finally decided was quite a departure from the contours of conventional sports cars and had as its main characteristic two large sweeping tail fins. The bodywork was carried out very skilfully by Williams & Pritchard and the semi-monocoque construction looked very purposeful when completed. The car had a low, gradually sloping nose, for good penetration. The low intake supplied air to the radiator duct and also to the front brakes, which were otherwise rather shrouded. The complete nose section could be removed for work on the engine and front

Far left: John Coombs and Brian Naylor fight it out at Brands Hatch. Left: Alan Brown on the line at Avus, Berlin. Below: Colin Chapman seems to be enjoying himself in SAR 5.

Below: Copse Corner, Silverstone, and the Lotus leads. Centre: John Coombs raced successfully but always looked worried! Bottom: The lines of SAR 5 shown to maximum advantage at Oulton Park.

suspension; there was, however, an engine-bay hatch, held in place with Dzus fasteners. The driver sat behind a curved, sloping windscreen and the passenger compartment could be covered by an aluminium panel when racing. Rear wheels were covered by spats and behind these extended the curved tail fins. The purpose of these fins was to extend the side area of the car, so providing greater directional stability. An undertray ran the full length of the car with air ducts to the centrally mounted rear brakes. A semi-monocoque construction was used because for attaching the aluminium body panels to the chassis frame wherever possible greater rigidity was provided without adding to the total weight. In this way an aerodynamic car was produced which weighed less than most conventional sports–racing cars. Unfortunately, experience was to show that this weight advantage was far outweighed by the snags which arose with this sort of construction during routine service, or when repairs to accident damage had to be effected. All Mark 8s produced after the first prototype were given more easily removable body panels which gave much better accessibility.

Lotus made the car's headlamps fully retractable. These hinged flat under the bonnet, and when required could be quickly snapped up into a vertical position, where they protruded through two slots in the engine bay cover. When erect they were extremely ugly and out of place but they were very effective. Overall dimensions of the car were a length of 11 ft and width of just over 4 ft. On paper, SAR 5 appeared definitely promising. There was 85 bhp available to propel just under 10 cwt, which, with a 3.9 to 1 rear axle ratio, would give a maximum speed in the region of 125 mph.

The car was scheduled to have its first outing at the British Empire Trophy race to be held at Oulton Park on April 10th. Work reached fever pitch during the week before the event and the evening toils of the little band of Team Lotus began to stretch far into the nights. As the day approached, bed was forgotten altogether. Finally after three nights' continuous work, the car was ready and at 4 a.m. on the Friday Colin and Mike roared out of the little yard and headed the low silver vehicle in the direction of Chester.

Colin took the first driving spell and the car sang along very smoothly. Behind the wheel you were not conscious of speed of travel; thanks to the good shape you felt no wind rush, but in the passenger seat you got the lot, straight in the face! Colin handed over. As soon as he was behind the wheel Mike was caught out by the lack of speed sensation and wondered why a parked police car pulled out after them in a built-up area. A glance at the rev–counter showed the reason—70 mph! Instinctively Mike began to slow but Colin yelled "clog hard down and we'll lose them". Mike responded and the car shot away. The road ahead was clear and visibility was good. The two occupants of the silver projectile watched the rev counter as the indicator climbed in top gear—115 mph! They were elated and grinned at each other—the first time over "the ton"!

Then it happened, Mike's eyes began to water with the air flow, as he sat a little higher than Colin. He didn't see the roundabout coming up until it was too late, then he tried to brake hard, the wheels locked, and with a grinding bang they shot straight on through a small hedge and up on to the earth centre of the island. Immediately Colin remembered the police car and urged Mike to get the car out of sight, and this he did to the accompaniment of horrible grinding noises. Slowly they backed off the roundabout and hid the car up a small side turning. They were just in time as a few seconds later the boys in blue went screaming past, apparently so intent on getting themselves round the island that they didn't notice the heavy black lines which went straight on!

It was a very sad pair who inspected the battered car. The front end looked a sorry sight and was virtually a write-off. Luckily the radiator ducting had just cleared the kerb when they had left the road and so had not suffered too badly. Mike was kicking himself, but as events were to prove he was only the first of a succession of people who endeavoured to disintegrate the Mark 8 on the road. During its first year of life this car was involved in two more major "shunts" whilst mechanics were driving it—obviously deceived by the good body shape into thinking they were travelling a lot slower than they were.

Behind the Lotus was the rest of the team—Hazel, Tony McKusker, Frank Costin and Colin Bennett—bowling merrily along in a Morris Minor. Imagine their horror when arriving at the black tyre marks Hazel said jokingly, "There's where the Lotus has gone", only to find Colin waving frantically from the side of the road—it was true! Philosophically the position was considered and without hesitation plans were made to rebuild the car. There was no question of not running at Oulton Park, even if it meant working all night—and they had already done that for three nights!

SAR 5 was towed to a nearby garage, which was swiftly commandeered completely by Team Lotus. Colin Bennett, who had come along to act as team manager, very methodically laid out the spares he had brought, but these were hardly adequate for the work that had to be done to restore the Mark 8's beauty. Telephone calls back to Hornsey for wheels, steel tubes, suspension parts, etc., started a convoy of spares on its way north. In the midst of all this activity, Colin was to be found changing into a clean shirt. He had wangled a business appointment at Sankeys in Wellington and so after seeing that all was well in hand, he shot off to his lunch appointment. In the meanwhile, the front of the prototype was completely stripped and Mike started to weld in the new chassis tubes where the originals were beyond repair.

After his appointment, Colin dashed over to Oulton Park and was able to complete three practice laps in Mike Anthony's Mark 6 before returning to see how the repairs were getting along. A very weary crew arrived at the circuit at 8 o'clock that night and with the headlamps of the Morris and a friend's car trained on the "dicer", they continued race preparation throughout the night. It was obvious that somebody must sleep, so it was arranged that four rooms would be taken at a certain hotel in Chester and that the men would sleep in shifts! Hazel and two other girl friends of members of the team, who had now arrived, would stay put, however, throughout the night. Imagine the confusion when at about 2 a.m. a group of dirty, dead-beat individuals in duffle coats booked into the hotel and went to share rooms with other people's wives or girl friends! Luckily one of the first shift realised that as they had all been asked to book-in there would be considerable trouble when it came to making out bills the next morning, so on his way to work at the circuit he quickly found the grubby page in the register and tore it out! To this day the management probably wonder where that page went. As it was, considerable confusion was caused when all the team were present for breakfast the next morning and four people gave the same room number!

The B.R.D.C. kindly arranged a special practice session during the morning so that Colin could put in the necessary qualifying laps. Also taking advantage of this spell was Ken Wharton who had been called on at the last minute to drive the Lister-MG when Archie Scott-Brown had been banned from driving it due to his arm disability. Colin found that the car's handling had not suffered, but he took things easily just in case and found himself on the back row of the grid, beside Ted Lund's MG. At flag fall, John Coombs in the 1½-litre Connaught shot off the line pursued by Mike Anthony. Colin rocketed off from his back row position and shot past half a dozen cars in the first mile. Down the straight on the second lap he flashed past Stirling Moss, who was driving the Leonard MG, to take fifth place. Stirling re-passed after a terrific effort and then Colin became involved in a scrap with Ken Wharton. After completing his eighth lap in 1 min 56 sec, fastest of the race, Colin drew slowly into the pits and sadly the car was retired with a blown cylinder head gasket and boiling fuel. However, the team were rewarded with the very promising performance of the car at its first outing. With a better starting position, Colin would undoubtedly have been up amongst the leaders. His fastest lap was equalled by Peter Gammon, who went on to finish third in the overall Trophy placings in his MG-powered Mark 6 and to win the up-to-1½-litre class.

After the race Frank Costin threw a party at his house—obviously he had managed to get more sleep than the rest of the team in the preceding few days. At midnight Colin decided that it was time for bed and so in an effort to break up the festivities he proceeded to undress and put himself to bed on the sofa! The next day being a fine Sunday, the chance of a little more testing was taken and SAR 5 was driven home via Snetterton. Trouble was being experienced with the valve gear at high revs, and several fast laps of the East Anglian circuit were put in in an endeavour to locate and cure the trouble.

The team were at Goodwood a week later for the Easter Monday meeting where a BRM finished first in the 5-lap Chichester Cup. Lotus were not so lucky as the car went on to three cylinders in its race—a great pity as it had lapped well in practice. The car's first victory came at the Silverstone B.R.D.C. *Daily Express* International Trophy meeting when Colin won the 1100-1500cc class of the 17-lap sports car race, finishing 15th overall. He put up an average speed of 76.42 mph and finished only three-quarters of a lap behind the outright winner, Froilan Gonzales, in the huge 4.9 Ferrari. For the first time SAR 5 showed the way to those successful 1½-litre class contenders, John Coombs (Connaught) and Peter Gammon.

This victory was particularly welcome, for on the next weekend the car was entered for the 17th International Eifelrennen at the famous Nurburgring. As both Colin and Mike had their normal work to do during the week, the trip to Germany had to be planned to a very tight schedule. Colin took SAR 5 to work with him on Friday and the car, now resplendent in British Racing Green, was parked all day in St. James's Square. At 6 p.m. Mike arrived and together they dashed for the night boat. They had some sleep during the Channel crossing, then straight away drove the 350 miles to the famous German circuit, arriving at midday. The organisers decreed that as Colin was inexperienced on the very tricky, 22.8 kilometre circuit a German driver would have to handle the car. This was fixed with Erwin Bauer from Stuttgart. Final preparation took most of Saturday night and on the Sunday the two Britishers were well rewarded by the sight of their green car finishing fourth behind two works Borgwards and an Osca, vanquishing a third Borgward, two Oscas and all the Porsches. Directly the race had finished, the petrol tank was filled to the brim and the Lotus was driven flat-out to the boat, only to arrive an hour late. However, the

Above: Brian Naylor locked in close combat with his MG-engined Mark 8 at Goodwood. Below: Dick Steed prepares for the Dolomite Cup race in Italy with his car, one of the first to be fitted with a Coventry Climax engine.

Test pilot 'Fifi' Fifield and other aviation experts helped with a series of invaluable aerodynamics tests on the Mark 8 at a disused airfield near Chester.

boat was also late and after much yelling in English and French, SAR 5 was allowed aboard.

Five minutes later the ship sailed. Colin's and Mike's excitement kept them awake, yet they had only had about three hours' sleep since Thursday! Just after 9 a.m. the green car was back in St. James's Square and Colin was down in the "Gents" changing into clean clothes, left there over the weekend in a suitcase. At 9.30 nobody would have dreamed that the young man sitting behind his desk on the first floor had driven a sports—racing car to the Eifel mountains for a race meeting during the weekend!

At its next outing the Mark 8 decided to go agricultural and in the rain at Aintree tried to take the horse jump at Becher's Brook. A little panel beating followed back at Hornsey. However, with the determination which marked the progress of Lotus, the car was back to win its class at Goodwood a week later at the Whit-Monday meeting. This was the weekend that Peter Gammon, in his earlier model, had a fantastic run of successes—five firsts and a second at Silverstone on the Saturday and an outright win in the 20-lap, 1500cc race at Brands Hatch on the Bank Holiday Monday.

With one race meeting following hard on the heels of another, the disadvantages of the Lotus construction were being felt by the Team Lotus mechanics who were called upon to work on the car. This particularly affected engine work. One Monday night, or was it early Tuesday morning, Colin went home to bed having arranged that the engine would be removed from the chassis for an overhaul. The luckless mechanics dismantled the power unit but try as they would the crankcase would not come out of the frame. As day dawned they crawled off home, leaving a pitiful little note to say that they tried for two hours and the "monkey puzzle" was beyond them. Apparently there was a knack—and if you lifted, pushed and twisted in the right degree, at the right time, the unit would suddenly pop out like a champagne cork!

At about this time, Frank Costin was able to persuade Colin that he should spare the car long enough to make some aerodynamic tests. He wished to do this because the body had been designed on pure aerodynamic principles as applied to aircraft and he wanted to see how it actually behaved on a car. Luckily, Frank had a friend who owned a farm at Poulton, near Chester, on which there was a disused airfield. So early one morning the car was taken there and specially equipped with the paraphernalia for recording the facts that Frank was seeking. Mike went with Colin, and Frank brought along Bruce White and Tony Chalk, both de Havilland aerodynamics experts. Another friend, "Fifi" Fifield, a Martin-Baker test pilot, came along to watch the fun and give help with his experience. Much useful data was obtained about boundary layer behaviour and the general efficiency of body contours. In order to study air flow in the well behind the front wheels, Frank was very brave and allowed himself to be strapped to the bonnet so that he could peer into the arches and watch the behaviour of wool tufts he had fixed there. Many runs were made in this fashion at speeds up to 110 mph! Here again his findings were most interesting—the tufts were virtually stationary up to 80 mph, after which the air flowed in a forwards direction. The practical study of air flow was most helpful to Frank, who hitherto had been forced to work on theory alone in this new field of cars. His practical discoveries were to give him much food for thought when it came to the shape that future Lotus models should take.

By coincidence it was at Crystal Palace again

that Colin really made people sit up and take notice of his new car when, in mid-June at the B.A.R.C's meeting, he shattered the sports car lap record. In the sports car race he rocketed past all the 2-litres and put in a lap at 70.88 mph—bettering the previous figure by 2.4 sec! Unluckily, on the sixth lap a half-shaft sheared coming out of The Glade, and that was that.

The car was definitely on top of its form now, and at the next meeting at Brands Hatch, in early July, Colin lowered the sports car record there as well, leaving it at 70.63 mph—very similar to his speed at Crystal Palace. Brands was a fine day for Lotus with Peter Gammon winning both the 1500cc sports car races with Colin second in both cases. Mike Anthony came third in one of the races in his Mark 6. These three were now entering as Team Lotus, and a very formidable team they made, too!

There was no doubt that SAR 5 was now the fastest 1½-litre MG-powered machine anywhere in the country. Colin proved this, and more, when he triumphed in the 1500cc class of the sports car race at the British Grand Prix meeting at Silverstone on July 17th, when he vanquished the 4-overhead-camshaft Porsche 550 of Hans Herrmann, so achieving a secret ambition. Gammon also beat the Porsche, and Mike Anthony finished ninth, to earn them the team award. A great day for Lotus—one that caused the Germans to go home and think.

But Lotus did not intend the Germans to think too long and were preparing an onslaught of three Mark 8s for the sports car event due to precede the German Grand Prix to be held in a fortnight's time. Two of these cars were the first of the Mark to be built for private owners—Nigel Allen and Dan Margulies. They had a slightly altered chassis layout in order to provide better engine accessibility and were fitted with 1467cc MG engines. As the German race took place on the Saturday of the August Bank Holiday weekend, Colin had planned a busy programme, not wishing to miss the meetings at Crystal Palace or Brands Hatch on the Monday! However he did not bargain for the hectic time which was to ensue.

He took the car to Wales on the preceding Saturday to compete at the Fairwood circuit. All went well in his first race, which he won, easily beating Archie Scott-Brown in the Lister MG. However he bit off more than he could chew in the 2½-litre race and had to give best to Archie, now in the Bristol-engined Lister. Colin's efforts to hold the bigger-engined car left their mark when, in the next race, a connecting rod suddenly popped through the side of the crankcase, wrecking the block. Then the panic started. The car was towed home immediately and work began on the engine on Sunday morning for on Wednesday the car was due to cross the Channel for Germany. The task was Herculean, for the engine was now very special, with welded cylinder liners, special pistons and an unusual version of the Laystall-Lucas cylinder head. The power unit had to be completely rebuilt, including balancing and polishing the internal parts. Only the evenings were available, and the little band of mechanics, Mike, Tony McKusker, Peter Mayes and John Standen worked through with about two hours sleep each night as Colin dashed hither and thither collecting the requisite bits and pieces. Finally all was ready, the Wednesday night boat was caught—just—and the car arrived at the Nurburgring on Thursday evening in time for practice on the Friday. But the troubles of Lotus were not over because having arrived early Nigel Allen had practised on Thursday and had blown-up his engine, wrecking the special cylinder head. A cable was sent home for a replacement to be sent out and the engine was removed from the chassis for attention. The head had not arrived by Friday morning when the officials required all cars for scrutineering. There was only one thing to be done. Colin wired up all the loose petrol and oil pipes and the bonnet was firmly shut and the car pushed into the scrutineering bay; imagine the sigh of relief when the officials cleared the car without checking to see if there was an engine!

In the race the three streamlined cars fared very badly, none lasting the distance. Dan Margulies shared his car with Colin's earlier driver Erwin Bauer. SAR 5 was going very well until it was put out with a broken de Dion tube. This was welded up and then on the dash back to the coast a suspension link broke. Colin dashed round a local town and in what he thought was good German, asked for a "welder". Apparently it was not so good, as he was directed to the nearest "convenience"! Finally the link was welded, and the car reached the coast in time to catch the Sunday night boat. The second trip to the Eifel mountains had not been so successful.

SAR 5 kept its "date" at Brands but could only manage fourth place in its heat in the 1500cc national sports car championship. Colin then drove the car to the Crystal Palace and arrived just in time for his race. Again, the car was not behaving properly and he was forced to retire on the second lap. The fault was obvious—the carburettor had been tuned to run on German fuel at 2,000 feet above sea level. There had been no time to alter the settings and test them, so the performance was bound to suffer on different fuel and at approximately sea level. Colin rushed back to Brands and borrowed Nigel Allen's car, but this was afflicted with the same carburation trouble as his own, and it was left to Mike Anthony to uphold the Lotus name in the final, which he did by finishing third behind Alan Brown (Connaught) and Archie Scott-Brown (Lister). So ended a very busy Bank Holiday for Colin and the Mark 8—it had been very enterprising but he was the first to admit that perhaps he tried to do rather too much!

For the rest of the season Colin had to restrict his racing a little as the business called for a lot of attention. Orders for Mark 8s had to be completed. One of the private owners for the new car was John Coombs, who fitted it with £850-worth of Connaught 1½-litre engine. This car soon proved to be the fastest 1500cc car in the country—always immaculately turned out and very skilfully driven. However, SAR 5 did manage to show it the way home during one of its first races, at Castle Combe in late August; Colin ran clean away from John and set a new class lap record of 81.18 mph. However a week later John started on his winning ways at Brands Hatch where he had Archie Scott-Brown in the Lister to contend with.

Mark 8s were also built for Dick Steed, "Tip" Cunane and Brian Naylor. Steed fitted an 1100cc Coventry Climax engine in his car—the third engine to be supplied by Climaxes for use in a car. Kieft had pioneered this adaptation of the "fire pump" engine when they had entered a car so equipped for the Le Mans 24-hours race earlier that year. After teething troubles, Dicky had successes with the car both at home and abroad. He later removed the engine and sold the car to Dave Kelsey, who installed the trusty Ford 10 engine out of Colin's original 1611H, Mark 6. Cunane and Naylor both fitted 1467cc MG engines to their cars and the latter raced his car extensively but seemed to receive more than his fair share of bad luck. "Tip" Cunane entered all sorts of competitions, embracing circuit racing, sprints, rallies and hill climbing. In spite of the largish aerodynamic body, he had many successes in the exacting hill-climbing field.

As the season drew to a close, Colin already had new plans in mind for the next year, not the least of these being his forthcoming marriage to Hazel. SAR 5 therefore was sold to Austin Nurse. Austin had already completed a season with the "Empire Special" Lotus, having graduated from 500s, and he now wished to speed up his Lotus motoring! SAR 5 behaved very well for him throughout the next season and he amassed many wins. In 1956 the car was purchased by Roy Bloxam who shared it with his wife Jean. Mrs. Bloxam competed in it regularly until one day at Mallory Park she tried to demolish a row of posts and a bank—not through any fault of her own. When SAR 5 reappeared the tail fins had disappeared and the colour had changed to a deep red—perhaps in shame.

On October 16th the wedding bells rang out at Northaw Church, in fact they rang rather longer than intended. Hazel was changing in a nearby house and thought that she should let the bells finish before she left for the church. With the non-appearance of the bride the bellringers dutifully began another peal. As zero hour passed Colin began to pace up and down, mumbling that "she could be on time, just this once". Hazel realised her mistake and arrived at the church, a little breathless, ten* minutes late. All was well and soon Mr. and Mrs. Colin Chapman were receiving the congratulations of their relatives and friends. The Lotus boys had turned up in force in the transporter, the destination board showing "the last lap". * No, fifteen! – Colin.

7.

Town and country planning

MONKEN HADLEY is just north of Barnet. It was here that Colin and Hazel had bought a little house, converted very charmingly from an old stable. The situation was excellent with a lovely view over a nine-hole golf course. If Colin wanted seclusion in which to work on his next year's plans, Gothic Cottage was ideal. It took a skilled rally navigator, together with some very detailed instructions to find the narrow driveway which was bounded on one side by a high fence. Care was needed in this passage as trees had encroached here and there, so narrowing the already small space still further. Directly the fence finished you turned right and there you were—right by the front door.

It was Hazel now who had to put up with Colin's humming and efforts at singing whilst he worked on his new schemes. He still favoured the bath for inspiration, but luckily did most of his drawing at a large board in one corner of the lounge. As this room was directly under their bedroom, Hazel had to be very firm about noise when she went to bed and left Colin at work, but the warning was often unheeded and she would wake to hear the soft, but rather tuneless, rendering of a popular song rising from the floor below.

Colin realised that 1955 promised to be more hectic than ever for Lotus Engineering Company. The Mark 6 was still in demand and had to be built, people were considering installing larger engines in the Mark 8, and he wished to redesign this latest model and bring out a new version. He discussed the matter at great length with Mike Costin and Hazel—should he and Mike take the plunge and start working full-time with the company? Mike was keen as he loved the work, and Hazel thought that for his health alone Colin would be advised to do so. To her it was incredible how he had survived so long without cracking under the strain of continual lack of sleep. If he was with the business all day, surely he would not need to be there half the night as well! It was quite amazing how Colin appeared to exist without the normal quota of sleep—perhaps at 26 there were a few grey hairs, but married life was beginning to make him quite fat!

Finally the die was cast, and in Lotus tradition, Colin and Mike started full-time employment at Tottenham Lane on January 1st, 1955. Mike was to look after the development side of the business, and already the production side was well cared for by "Nobby" Clarke. A separate company, called Racing Engines Ltd., was formed with Mike as one of the directors. This off-shoot would specialise in engine development and tuning, together with axle, brake and gearbox conversions. The earlier business of components for the "specials" builder was no longer very popular with Lotus Engineering Co. Ltd., as they were now hard-pressed to produce the chassis and modify the components for customers who were constructing their Lotus cars.

Mike Anthony for some time had been worrying Colin about installing a Bristol engine in the Mark 8. The matter had been carefully considered and with slight modifications it was found that the chassis would be suitable. The main alteration was the enlargement of the engine bay to accommodate the bigger power unit. Peter Scott-Russell and Cliff Davis were also interested in cars of this nature so it was decided to effect the necessary alterations to the Mark 8 frame and lay down a new model—the Mark 10. Colin was already working on a smaller-engine successor to the Mark 8 for which he retained the "9" designation.

For interchangeability it was decided to have a similar rear-axle layout on the 10 as would be used on the 9. A de Dion system was still favoured, but now the suspension was by the familiar Lotus combination of coil springs and dampers, the differential housing being a special alloy casting. Colin was very interested in the possibilities of disc brakes, and this new model seemed to call for them. Here was to be a lot of power propelling little weight—good brakes would be essential. In shape the Mark 10 was exactly similar to its forerunner, except that the engine cover bulged slightly to clear the high Bristol engine. In order to get the power unit as low as possible, the whole transmission line was lowered. This was achieved by using a Salisbury hypoid final-drive, for which ratios of 3.75, 4.125 and 4.56 to 1 were readily available.

As the engine was much heavier than those used before in this type of chassis, it was found necessary to locate plenty of weight at the rear of the car, so the fuel tank was positioned behind the rear axle, as were two "pusher" type fuel pumps and the battery. The power/weight ratio was definitely promising, as the very potent Bristol was only being called on to propel an all-up weight of 11 cwt.

Mike Anthony's was the first car completed, and Mike lavished much care and attention on it and obtained a very high standard of finish. The car had mixed fortunes, starting badly by crashing in its first race—perhaps this was because Mike insisted on a registration number 13—but he competed regularly with it and achieved a fair degree of success, though often being put out by petty troubles. Unfortunately, Mike's interest in the 10 came to an untimely halt when he was shunted from behind by another competitor during a tour d'honneur lap at Brands Hatch. The car was rebuilt and then sold to Dimitri Kasterine of the Six Miles Stable.

Bill Short, with 4,500 rpm on the clock, prepares to take his Bristol-engined Mark 10 off the line for a sprint at Gosport.

Left: Disc brake assembly of the Mark 10. Below: Mike Anthony pressing on in his Bristol-engined car. Bottom: Anthony's drysump engine was canted over in the chassis and equipped for a time with side-draught carburettors. Right: The same car being driven by B. Bowman in a sprint. Below right: And in its owner's hands making a good start in the sports car race preceding the 1955 British GP at Aintree. Note the vertical carburettors.

Both Cliff Davis and Peter Scott-Russell raced their cars regularly, the former's for a long time remaining in unpainted polished aluminium, as had his well-known earlier cars JOY 500 and LOY 500, and the latter's resplendent in light green. Cliff attained fourth place at his first outing with the car in the over-1900cc race on July 4th at Brands Hatch. These three drivers had a good tussle at Snetterton in August—Mike led until he holed a piston (possibly due to the very high compression ratio he used), then Salvadori won the race in the Cooper-Maserati, but was closely followed by Peter Scott-Russell in second place and Cliff in third. With Reg Bicknell as co-driver, Cliff ran his car in the nine-hour race at Goodwood and finished a very creditable second in the 2-litre class, having led the class for much of the race. But although these three Mark 10s had their successes, their performance was overshadowed by the fantastic results being achieved by the smaller-engined version of Lotus.

Possibly unknown to many, thousands of cinemagoers were treated to the sight of Cliff's car in naked form in the J. Arthur Rank production "Checkpoint". In the film the car was supposed to be a "special" built, cared for and driven by Anthony Steel, an impecunious racing driver whose financial predicament was not borne out by the delightful mews flat at which Mr. Steel was shown titivating the Lotus. Cliff's car was definitely photogenic as it also appeared as the "star" in a play about a motor car manufacturer on Independent Television when it was driven by actress June Whitfield. All this posing must have turned the car bashful, for at the beginning of the 1957 season it turned up at Goodwood resplendent in a coat of red paint! Another Mark 10 intended for stardom was the one ordered by the young American actor James Dean. This car was shipped to the States without an engine as it was proposed to install an Offenhauser unit, but unfortunately the actor met his untimely death before the car could be completed and delivered to him.

A fifth Mark 10 was ordered by Dr. Vaughan Havard, but sadly he was taken seriously ill before the car was finally assembled. On his recovery he drove it on occasions in hill climbs and sprints in company with its constructor, Bill Short. Later in 1955 Mike Young took delivery of a Mark 10 into which he installed a 2-litre Connaught engine, and another make of engine was used to power this Mark when George Nixon purchased one to be driven by the experimental 1500cc, fuel-injected Turner unit.

The line of Mark 10s was not long, because people's attention began to swing away from the bigger engines in favour of the fantastic Coventry Climax power unit. In making their plans for 1955, Colin and Mike had kept this amazing little 1100cc engine very much in mind, but at the same time they were not going to give up their development work on the 1467cc MG unit. On the face of it the larger engine should have been the more effective as it produced approximately 15 bhp more—surely enough to overcome its weight disadvantage. Undoubtedly there was going to be very interesting racing in the 1100cc class, but Lotus was still thinking of international competition in the popular 1500cc category.

8.

A pair of Nines

THE MARK 9 HAD ITS debut in March, the first two examples being shipped to American owners for the Sebring 12–Hours sports car race. Both these cars were fitted with the new Coventry Climax 1100cc FWA engine.

This new model of the marque was a direct descendant of the Mark 8, but in the light of experience the design had been "cleaned-up" considerably. The chassis frame was still a triangulated multi-tubular structure, but by effecting economies on overall dimensions and tube sizes in certain places the total weight was reduced. Strength was not impaired by these reductions, in fact the resultant frame was stronger than its predecessor. The wheelbase remained at 7 ft 3½ in, but the car was shorter than the Mark 8.

Now that Frank Costin was becoming a little more at home with shapes on four wheels he had been able to endow the new car with even more graceful lines. The bodywork was still fully aerodynamic, and featured the low, penetrating nose, but because of the reduction in overall length the tail fins were dumpier, and to ensure that there should not be a loss of side area, the fins were swept up a little higher than on the earlier model. The lessons of accessibility had been well learned, and it was now possible to remove the top half of the whole front of the car, so laying bare the engine, instruments, front suspension and cooling system. For routine engine attention there was a bonnet hatch, complete with slots through which the headlamps could be erected. The car was still very much a sports car and had hinge-down doors on both the driver and passenger sides, and for racing the passenger's compartment could be covered by an aluminium cover. Following further aerodynamics tests, the plastic windshield had been reduced in height and now wrapped round and down each side of the driver, small portions being fixed to the door and the metal tonneau cover. Good accessibility to the rear axle and centrally mounted brakes was provided by a removable panel at the rear, the spare wheel fitting under this cover.

As there were now customers purchasing complete cars—initially these were mostly overseas buyers—a full retail price had to be quoted. With the 1100cc Coventry Climax engine fitted this was listed at £1,150, although in Great Britain the crippling burden of Purchase Tax had to be added. Because of their lack of space and their desire to enable the enthusiast to construct his own car, Lotus were still very keen on supplying the Mark 9 as a chassis/body unit and then modifying and producing the other components for the customer to assemble himself. As most of the chassis built were for completion this way the Hornsey firm had to put up with a great deal of specialised work for people who wanted their car to be different.

Later in 1955 this demand for different specifications had led to two distinct types of Mark 9 being offered—the Club and the Le Mans. The two types used similar chassis/body units and front suspension, but in the case of the Club, which was intended for road use and club racing in Great Britain, a modified Ford 10 back axle was suspended on coil springs around telescopic shock absorbers, and the power unit could be either the Coventry Climax 1100 or the Ford 10. When the

Climax engine was used a special adaptor ring mated it to an MG TC gearbox; the Ford engine used its own gearbox. Final drive ratios of 4.125, 4.4 and 4.7 to 1 were available for the Club model and 10 in by 1¼ in standard Ford drum brakes were fitted with a specially modified linkage. The Le Mans model was announced after the first Lotus appearance in this world-famous race, and was intended for serious international sports car competition. The Coventry Climax 1100cc engine and MG gearbox were fitted, and drive was transmitted to an elektron-cased final-drive unit, with large ribbed sump mounted rigidly to the frame. A de Dion rear axle was used, suspended by the same spring medium as on the Club model. Five final drives were available – 3.9, 4.2, 4.5, 4.9, or 5.125 to 1. Colin had spent a lot of time on the design of the de Dion layout for the new car, and had evolved a much stronger form of rear hub and articulated half-shaft. The half-shaft tube now formed the Rudge hub and live stub axle, with no changes of section. The hub carrier was a special elektron casting and radius arms ran forward from points at the top and bottom to anchorage positions on the chassis.

One of the outstanding items of the Le Mans were the brakes, which were enormous, being 11 in diameter and 2¼ in wide. The drums were elektron with steel liners, and had deep radial fins which increased in depth as they continued to the very edge of the drum. Ingeniously, the fins of the front drums used the wheel rims as shrouds, fitting snugly into 4.50 by 15 Dunlop wire wheels. The Lockheed actuating cylinders were mounted on special light alloy back plates which only masked a small portion of the back of the brakes, so leaving the shoe exposed.

The new brakes were not ready for the two cars destined for Sebring, and these had to leave with the earlier type of 9 in brakes fitted. However, these smaller "stoppers" proved to be quite satisfactory, and after eight hours of the race, run in typical Florida sunshine, the owners of the two new cars, Frank Miller and Norman Scott, were trading first place with each other in both Class G and the Index of Performance. But at 7 p.m., co-driver Samuelson took over from Scott, and after a few laps had a stroke of bad luck. The sun

Below: Colin Chapman holding off Ivor Bueb's Cooper, an Elva and another Cooper to win another sports car race at Brands Hatch with his Mark 9. Bottom: Len Bastrup scoring his first victory with his newly acquired Mark 9 at Thompson Raceway in 1955.

was right on the horizon, and going into a corner he was blinded by it; the Lotus left the road, hit a rock and holed the sump. The other car kept going like a train, leading Class G, but in the last hour the Lotus pit crew became confused and thought that the Porsche lying second was overhauling their car, whereas it was several laps behind. They hung out the signal "Go, go, go", and Miller responded, but in his haste clouted a straw bale. He returned to the pits, found the damage was only minor, and handed over to his co-driver George Rabe. George was promptly black-flagged for a faulty light, which was repaired, Miller jumped back in again, and the engine would not start! As there was little of the race left, the owner pushed his silver car to the finishing line, and as the flag fell crossed the line on his starter motor. Unfortunately, the officials took exception to this, and the Lotus was disqualified—very hard luck after such a fine effort.

Back home at Hornsey the usual pre-season rush was at its height endeavouring to complete a works car for the British Empire Trophy race to be held at Oulton Park on April 2nd. The ultimate plan was to build two Mark 9s for Team Lotus, a 1500cc MG-engined car for "gaffer" Colin to drive and an 1100cc Climax-engined car to be driven by Peter Jopp. For Oulton Park the MG-engined car was given top priority, and as a weight-saving experiment was fitted with an MG J2 gearbox.

The specification of the new model had been consolidated and the result was a sturdier but lighter car than the earlier edition. In starting-line trim the works car weighed 9¼ cwt. As in his earlier models, Colin had paid great attention to weight distribution, and with the lighter Coventry Climax engine he had moved some of the tail weight forward by positioning the petrol tank alongside the passenger seat; three sizes of tank, giving 7, 11 or 19 gallons capacity, were offered. The battery was still kept at the back of the car, but the positioning of the petrol tank amidships had the advantage of minimising changes in handling characteristics as the fuel was used up.

The radiator, of the cross-flow type, was only eight inches deep and was fully ducted, and the same frontal slot in the bodywork of the car supplied air to the radiator and the front brake

Below: Colin Chapman in a well-balanced drift with the works MG-engined Mark 9. Right: Same car, same driver, different view, this time with the Lotus understeering into a corner. Below right: The ingenious form of 'pop-up' lighting on the Mark 9, which was later frowned-upon by the Le Mans organisers.

Below: Team Lotus prepares for the 1955 nine-hours race at Goodwood. Centre: Peter Lumsden's Mark 9 in pole position on the same circuit. Bottom: Canadian Tom Gilmour after a race victory at Harewood, Ontario, in 1957.

drums. Water for the cooling system was supplied by a header tank mounted on the scuttle behind the engine. Although the capacity of this tank was quite satisfactory for the 1100cc engine, it did not appear enough for the MG engine at its first outing.

In its primer coat of paint, the first works Mark 9 arrived at Oulton Park too late for practice and so was relegated to the back row of the grid alongside Peter Jackson's Cooper-MG. Right from the start of the race Colin began to carve his way through the field and he was soon up in fourth place. Then on the seventh lap he had to pull into the pits with the water temperature gauge "off the clock". Consolation came in the fact that the new car had put in a lap at 77.66 mph—a speed which was only bettered by Les Leston, who won the up-to-1500cc heat, in Peter Bell's Connaught.

The 1955 season now started to get under way in earnest and initially the new model from Hornsey had more than its share of bad luck—retirement at Goodwood after two laps with engine troubles and retirement at Ibsley after hitting a concrete post while trying to pass another competitor. But the Ibsley meeting did have the reward of fastest lap in 1 min 26.6 sec—very satisfactory as the field included the new "Manx"-tailed Coopers with Coventry Climax engines driven by such people as Ivor Bueb. The bad luck continued at Silverstone in May where the MG crankshaft broke after only a few laps.

After this final failure of the MG power unit, Colin and Mike decided that something must be done as engine breakages were robbing the new car of a chance to show its undoubted superiority in roadholding and braking. The engine was completely rebuilt and converted to dry-sump lubrication, an oil tank being positioned where the passenger's feet should have been. I well remember this modification because at that time I was paying frequent visits to the works to collect various bits and pieces for the Mark 6 I was constructing. One Friday evening I happened on a knot of mechanics busily putting the finishing touches to the conversion. As completion of the Coventry Climax-engined Team Lotus car had been occupying most of the mechanics for the past few days, it was not surprising that my components were still "not quite ready". So, perhaps rather unwisely, I offered my services for running-in the 1500. Colin was pleased to accept, for the following day the car was due to compete at the Whitsun Snetterton meeting. At 1 a.m. the car was finally finished and with Peter Mayes driving and myself jammed behind the new oil tank, the Lotus nosed out into a very dark and very wet night. A stop was made at Peter's flat for eggs and bacon in the hope that the rain would relent, but by 2 a.m. it was worse than ever and reluctantly we decided that the running-in really ought to start. The rest of the night was very uncomfortable—water attacked you from all sides and in no time you sat in a very cold puddle. To get 6 ft 3 in behind pedals built with Colin's shorter stature as a measure necessitated sitting on a pair of gumboots, and this put your face up in the air stream so that the rain drops hit you like bullets! As dawn broke the skies cleared, and having put nearly 200 miles on the clock a snack was taken at a pull-up-for-carmen. What a relief it was to prop ourselves against the tea urn and watch the steam rise! Running-in continued on and around the Norfolk circuit until the Team Lotus transporter hove into sight and the "dicer" was returned, rather travel stained, to the paddock.

The nocturnal motoring was all made worthwhile when the Mark 9 won its first race in the 5-lap event for sports cars up to 1500cc. Colin steadily drew away from the field and put in the fastest lap at 84.23 mph. For me the journey back to London was probably even more uncomfortable than the trip north, for now the "dicer" was in the transporter and I was perched perilously in one of the side bunks. John Standen was driving the Bedford and appeared keen to keep up with Colin's laden Ford Anglia, which resulted in quite a high-speed procession, and as the transporter swayed on the bends, the occupant of the bunk very nearly pitched headlong into the bonnet of the Mark 9.

Overnight the back axle was changed so that Peter Jopp could drive it at Brands Hatch on the following day. This outing was also successful, and Peter pressed Les Leston's Connaught throughout the Fawkham Trophy race and was only beaten into second place by half a length!

The Lotus run of success was consolidated at Goodwood on the Whit Monday when Colin won again after a stirring battle with Reg Parnell in a Connaught-powered Cooper and Ken McAlpine in his new 1500cc Connaught. Again Colin put in the fastest lap. The new Mark 10 also came into its own at this meeting, Mike Anthony winning the up-to-2-litre event with Peter Scott-Russell third.

These successes were very welcome to the boys from Hornsey, and gave them renewed hope for their next big step with the new Climax-engined car—*les Vingt-Quatre Heures du Mans et Grand Prix d'Endurance,* to give the French classic its full title. Although the Lotus was disqualified at Le Mans, the story of preparation and participation in this world-famous race is of great interest and is covered in detail in the next chapter.

After their sojourn in France, the Team Lotus mechanics had to help with production matters at the works, for increased demand for cars was making deliveries fall well behind schedule. Life was very hectic indeed, for the Mark 6 was in steady demand, there were Mark 10s such as Cliff Davis' to complete, and now there were customers clamouring for the new Mark 9.

Lack of space was still the big bottleneck. Colin and Mike had foreseen this when they made their decision to give the business their full time and had taken steps to rectify matters, but a cold and frosty winter and spring had rather upset these plans. They had been able to obtain a piece of land at Tottenham Lane behind the gardens of the adjacent public house, and after the usual protracted negotiations they had received the necessary permission to erect an assembly shop on this land. Colin was able to put his earlier training to good use in contracting for the erection of the new building, and he kept a knowledgeable eye on the progress when work commenced. Originally they had hoped to have the shop in use by the start of the season, but the bad weather had delayed the builders and now, in July, the work was only just completed.

The biggest possible building had been put on the ground available but with the increase in business it was already beginning to look too small. As well as an assembly shop the new premises housed a small office where Colin had his desk and Hazel her typewriter. Outside the office a small flight of stairs led up to the stores built just under the roof—at one end of the stores John Standen could just stand upright but at the other end things were definitely cramped.

The B.R.S.C.C. meeting at Brands Hatch in early July saw Team Lotus back on the entry list, this time with Colin driving the 1100cc and Peter the MG-engined car. However it was Cooper's day, and in the up-to-1500cc race Peter finished fourth behind the rival make of car, and in the smaller capacity race Colin dead-heated with Ivor Bueb for second place behind Jim Russell's Cooper-Climax. These defeats were softened by the news that on the day before in County Wicklow, David Piper had won the Leinster Trophy on handicap in his Mark 6.

Colin set the terraces buzzing with excitement in the sports car race at the British Grand Prix meeting at Aintree a week later. In the little MG-engined car he was duelling with the big boys, and finally finished ninth overall and easily winning the 2-litre and 1500cc classes! The eight cars ahead of him were the four works Aston Martins, three D-type Jaguars and Abecassis' H.W.M.—and in 17 laps he was not lapped by winner Roy Salvadori.

Returning to the scene of his earlier successes, Colin won the 2-litre sports car race at Crystal Palace on August Bank Holiday Saturday in the MG-engined car. He appeared to be going to repeat the performance at Brands Hatch on the Monday, but after winning his heat and leading the final for 12 laps his engine tired and he finished third. However, he had left his mark—a lap at 71.54 mph which was a new class record.

By the time the International meeting at Snetterton came round on August 13th, one or two customers had their Mark 9s ready for the fray. One of these was Ken Smith, who had previously constructed and driven 500cc racing cars, but for Ken the 13th was definitely unlucky, and on his first lap he "lost" his beautiful car and damaged it extensively amongst the marker barrels. Luckily he was not hurt himself. The 1955 season had closed by the time the car was rebuilt

With the front body section removed, the Coventry Climax 1,100cc engine was readily accessible on the Mark 9. Note the very large finned front brake drums and the central mounting for the oil filter.

and then, owing to business commitments, Ken temporarily had to give up racing. He used the Mark 9 as an everyday road car, and by the end of 1956 had covered over 15,000 miles in it. Another private owner at Snetterton was John Coombs, now with his second Lotus. His Mark 9 had a special tail from which the fins had been removed, so giving the car a longer and more rakish appearance. John won the 1301–1500cc class at his first outing after Colin broke a drive shaft on the MG-engined works car.

Team Lotus entered both their cars for the Goodwood Nine Hours race, Colin and Peter driving the 1500, and Ron Flockhart and Cliff Allison the 1100. John Coombs entered his car and had John Young as co-driver, and another new private owner, R.A. Page, entered his car with Paul Emery. On the very first lap Tony Gaze's DB3S Aston Martin spun and came into violent contact with Ron Flockhart's Lotus. The front suspension was completely wrecked and the mechanics manfully began to rebuild it in front of the pits. The car ran again but was finally put out with a slipping clutch caused by oil seal failure. The 1500cc car was running beautifully and after seven hours was leading the 1500cc class, ahead of the Moss/von Hanstein Porsche. Colin was really making the little push-rod-engined car motor amazingly quickly, then, just as darkness fell, the wonderful run came to an end with an unusual malady—the engine flywheel came adrift. With 234 laps completed John Coombs' car broke a wheel mounting and shed a wheel, John Young bringing it to rest without incident. The Page/Emery car continued to run regularly, after one stop for chassis attention, and at midnight had completed 268 laps, placing it eleventh overall and fourth in the 1500cc class.

Oulton Park a week later was not really a good day for Team Lotus as Cliff Allison crashed the 1100cc car at Old Hall corner, luckily escaping with minor cuts. The 1500cc car fractured a steering arm, and then Colin was forced out with an oil-soaked clutch on the 24th lap. Consolation came from Peter Scott-Russell's first and Mike Anthony's second in their Mark 10s in the up-to-2000cc class of the *Daily Herald* International Trophy race.

Colin drove brilliantly at Aintree a week later to win the 51-mile race for sports cars up to 1500cc from Tony Brooks in a Connaught. The MG-engined Lotus set up a new lap record of 79.18 mph. Another new private owner of the Mark 9 figured in the 1100cc class results—Edward Lewis, who finished third. Peter Jopp had the MG-engined car at Brands Hatch the next day, as the 1100 was still being rebuilt after its Oulton Park accident, and he won the up-to-1500cc, 12-lap race from Peter Gammon, now driving a Cooper-Climax.

Two aspects of the works cars had for some time been receiving a lot of thought from Colin and Mike. They concerned the two extremes of performance—increased power and increased braking efficiency. It was found possible to increase the maximum output of the 1100cc Coventry Climax engine from 75 bhp at 6250 rpm to 83 bhp at 6800 rpm. This increase was brought about by utilising a higher-lift camshaft and improving the air-flowing of the induction manifold. Coventry Climax themselves were very interested in the development work which Lotus and Cooper were carrying out on their engine, and working with these two firms they brought out a Stage II conversion for customers to modify their engines up to the more powerful form. There is no doubt that the increasing interest in small-capacity sports car racing was being brought about by the wonderful performance of this relatively cheap and reliable "off-the-peg" engine.

The cast elektron brake drums were found to be far from trouble-free, and so an alternative and equally efficient form of retardation was being sought. The faults with the large finned drums were in manufacture, where there was a very high reject factor caused by liners which did not bond satisfactorily or castings which cracked on bonding. In operation these drum brakes were fantastic, and pulled the car up very rapidly and always evenly. The substitute had to be as good and the answer appeared to be a disc brake. Here Girlings were most co-operative, and two of their technicians practically lived at Hornsey while they sorted out the teething troubles. Ultra-light, hydraulically operated 9½-in discs were fitted to the works cars, outboard at the front and inboard at the rear. Initially there were plenty of bothers with these new "stoppers", and some nasty moments were experienced with locking brakes or brakes which did not "lock" at all. Bigger master cylinders were fitted and the dodge of soaking the discs in oil was resorted to in order to get even braking!

As has always been the case with Lotus—and is no doubt the same with all high performance car manufacturers—the testing and proving of these new modifications had to continue in public amidst competition with others who were also striving to improve their product. One such occasion was the Tourist Trophy race in September, where Colin Chapman and Cliff Allison in the 1100cc car dumbfounded everyone by leading all the 2-litres by nine minutes and being miles ahead in the Index of Performance until an oil pipe fractured. After the pipe was replaced at a cost of 11 minutes, the car continued to put up a fantastic performance, regaining all but 7 seconds of the deficit round the tricky Dundrod circuit, hanging on to such cars as Swaters' 3-litre Ferrari, and finally finishing 11th overall and second in the 750cc-1100cc class.

Colin took the car to Goodwood the next weekend and made up for the bad luck in Ireland by easily winning both the up-to-1250cc and up-to-1500cc scratch races. A sign of the times at this meeting was the fact that no fewer than five other Lotuses, all privately owned, figured in the results.

Lotus ended the 1955 season on a high note with three "tail of the year" meetings, at all of which Colin, driving the 1100cc car, had stirring fights with Ivor Bueb in the works Cooper. In the first, at the International Castle Combe meeting on October 1st, he had to give best to Ivor in the Bristol Aeroplane Company Two-Litre Trophy after an excursion off the track. The result was the same in the 15-lap invitation sports car race, but here Peter Jopp in the MG-engined car supported Lotus fortunes with third place. The tables were turned at Brands Hatch a week later when Colin won the up-to-1200cc sports car race with Ivor Bueb in second place. During this race the 1100cc Lotus set up a new record for the circuit with a lap of 72.47 mph! Then on Boxing Day another tussle took place between these two on a very wet track at Brands Hatch in the up-to-1200cc, 15-lap sports car race, from which Colin emerged victorious by six seconds.

As the year had passed, more and more privately owned Mark 9s had been appearing on the circuits. The 1100cc Coventry Climax engine was the favourite power unit, and cars with this engine installed were built by Peter Lumsden, L.I. Bramley, Dick Steed, Tom Barnard, Edward Lewis, Peter Ashdown, Bryan Hewitt and many others. All these cars were raced regularly and had their successes. Peter Lumsden's dark green car had a splendid 1956 season which culminated in his winning the BARC Brooklands Trophy. This car then changed hands and became the property of jazz-band leader, Chris Barber. Peter Ashdown had many a fight with his namesake and raced his car regularly throughout the last half of 1955 and all of 1956. A trip to Sweden was very rewarding for him as he won the 1500cc sports car race at Karlskoga at the end of his ownership of the Mark 9. His consistent performance was rewarded at the Club Lotus dance in 1956 when he was awarded the newly presented John Coombs Lotus Trophy for the most outstanding performance by a private owner during the year. Bryan Hewitt spent the winter of 1955/56 fitting disc brakes, similar to those being used on the works cars. He experienced many delays in effecting the conversion as his was the first privately owned car to be so equipped, but the resultant performance was well worth the waiting period.

Michael MacDowel chose the "Club" specification for his car and had many successes in the 1172 Formula, racing his Ford-engined, axled and braked car. This car later became the property of another regular 1172cc competitor—J. Anstice-Brown.

As well as the two early cars shipped for the Sebring race, other Mark 9s crossed the Atlantic. Len Bastrup of Connecticut was an early customer and raced his car regularly, and two other American owners who used cars of the marque to good effect were Duncan Black and G.D. Buchanan. One Mark 9 found its home in Canada, the proud owner being Jerry Polivka of Toronto.

By the middle of 1955 it had been very plain that Lotus Engineering Co. Ltd., were now in the car business in a big way—no longer was the activity confined to the modification of components and the building of a few chassis frames. Complete cars were now assembled for customers and valuable dollars earned for the country. With an eye to even further increasing sales, the company applied for membership of the Society of Motor Manufacturers and Traders. They were accepted and enrolled, initially, as accessory manufacturers. The little band from Hornsey could now take the big plunge and display their wares before the world at large, and this they did in October at the Earls Court Motor Show.

Whether strings were pulled, or it was just luck, the Lotus stand, No.61, was not in the gallery with the accessories, but on the ground floor, rubbing shoulders with the other full-scale manufacturers, and very conveniently alongside the entrance to the Grill Room and Alpine Tavern. The stand was small, but the gleaming exhibit of a Mark 9 minus its body panels kept crowds milling under the yellow and green banner. The finish on this "show" chassis was outstanding, and the polished aluminium fuel tanks shone like mirrors. After the show, this masterpiece adorned the Piccadilly showrooms of Coventry Climax Ltd. for a long time.

There was no doubt that Lotus had "arrived" The staff, looking rather different in well-pressed suits instead of the more customary overalls, were kept very busy answering the multitude of questions fired at them, handing out brochures and booking orders! It was a very hectic time for everybody as the wheels at Hornsey still had to be kept turning, and visitors to the show would find Hazel typing away on a square inch whilst Colin dictated with one eye on the queue of people who "just wanted a few words with Mr. Chapman". The results of the Earls Court "shop window" were very encouraging, and gave Colin, Hazel, Mike and their band of helpers added incentive for the winter months of planning and experimental work, some of which was to result in the design and construction of what was to prove to be by far the most successful Lotus sports car yet conceived.

9.

Reverse at Le Mans

FOR MANY YEARS Colin had nursed a secret ambition to drive in the classic 24-hour road race at Le Mans, and in 1955 his dream was realised. The advent of the 1100cc Coventry Climax engine gave Lotus a power unit well capable of withstanding a full day and night's fast motoring. This fact did not pass unnoticed by those other small British constructors—Cooper, Arnott and Kieft—who also entered 1100cc cars in the same year.

There was great jubilation at Hornsey when the Automobile Club de l'Ouest accepted their entry, and immediately plans were drawn up for the type of car to be built for the French classis. Le Mans is a very special type of race—a fact of which Lotus were fully aware. Therefore they went into the whole thing with their usual thoroughness, checking and re-checking the regulations and studying reports and opinions of others who had raced on the Sarthe circuit. Situated just south of Le Mans, the circuit measures 13.429 kms, or 8.35 miles. It incorporates just over three miles of nearly dead straight Le Mans/Tours road and then, just before the village of Mulsanne, turns sharp right on to the undulating and twisty road which runs out towards Arnage. At the junction of the Monce en Berlin/Le Mans road the circuit turns sharp right again and continues up hill, through the snake known as White House and up to the permanent pit area. Just after the pits a specially constructed road sweeps away to the right, dives down into the trees through an "S" bend and then rejoins the straight down to Mulsanne at another sharp right-hander known as Tertre Rouge. For the whole distance the surface of the road is perfect—as smooth as a billiards table.

With a circuit of this nature it was thought that the light, responsive Mark 9 should be just right. The perfect surface would not be too hard on the chassis and should give plenty of opportunity for the good roadholding to show up to advantage. As a precaution the Le Mans car was built on the heavy side and was panelled in 22 gauge aluminium instead of the lighter 20 gauge elektron which had been used on the MG-engined car. This second works Mark 9 was the car later driven by Peter Jopp. For the 24-hour race Colin had teamed up with the Scots driver Ron Flockhart, and Peter was to go along to get as much experience as he could.

With the fast straights and three dead slow corners, Le Mans is very hard on brakes. This, it was hoped, would be catered for by the new Girling discs. Much midnight oil was burnt over the perfection of these new brakes—work which all proved well worthwhile, for after the French race, disc brakes became the fashion at Hornsey. Initially, the mechanics had to install a brake actuation system which might have caused certain competition managers concern. As there was insufficient height available to install Girling master cylinders which had the fluid reservoir above them, they fitted a Lockheed unit and connected it up to the Girling system! However, this "marriage" was only temporary, and the master cylinders were eventually lowered to allow a pure Girling installation.

The event was due to start at 4 p.m. on Saturday, June 11th, and it was only by round-the-clock work at Hornsey that the car was presented for the official scrutineering on the preceding Tuesday. Mike Costin, accompanied by John Standen and Peter Mayes, took the car via the Dover/Dunkirk crossing in the transporter. Colin, Hazel and Peter Jopp used the same route in Colin's Ford Anglia. As Mike had worked for three nights without sleep prior to the crossing, he tried to snatch some as the transporter trundled across France. He found the bunk in the interior above the driving cab to be stifling—a fault he soon remedied by punching a ventilating hole through the "Motor Racing" advertisement.

Team management was to be in the hands of John Eason Gibson, then editor of *Autocourse* and later to become Secretary of the British Racing Drivers' Club on the retirement of Desmond Scannell. He was to be assisted in his task by Ted Lawry and Bob Gibson Jarvie, the latter appropriately being a director of Laystall Engineering Company. These "back-room boys" travelled in a Rover and met up with the others in Le Mans. Headquarters for the pre-race preparation was to be 18 miles south of Le Mans, out on the Tours road, in the little town of Mayet. Here the team were to be accommodated by M. and Mme. Mica at the Auberge de St. Nicholas.

Ron Flockhart at the wheel of the Le Mans Lotus Mark 9, the front of which bears evidence of contact with the bank at Arnage.

The small hotel could provide just enough beds for the *equipe,* and had an ancient garage in the courtyard behind, where the car could be prepared. Nothing was too much trouble for M. and Mme. Mica, who made every effort to make the Lotus boys comfortable. They were called upon to import vast supplies of Coca-Cola—a beverage not often requested in the Auberge de St. Nicholas!

Scrutineering brought its headaches, the most serious of which concerned the car's lights. The officials did not like the retractable spot lights which were to be brought up through the bonnet for night driving. These lights were only to supplement the headlamps which were now neatly faired into the wings behind Perspex covers. After much argument the officials insisted that the spot lamps be fitted each side of the air intake grille—a task which proved far from easy and kept Mike, John and Peter hard at it up to the time of the first practice session. There was much detailed work still to do on the car and the three mechanics began to forget what a bed looked like.

Practice also had its share of troubles, commencing with Peter Jopp receiving a shunt from behind by a Porsche. As the public roads are used for the Le Mans circuit, the practice sessions took place from 6 p.m. until midnight. This caused a minimum of disorganisation to normal traffic and allowed drivers to learn the circuit in the light, dusk and dark. Peter Jopp practised with Ron Flockhart and Colin in order to gain experience and also help with the running-in of a new engine. A great deal of trouble was experienced with oil getting through the rear main bearings and into the clutch—an early fault of the 1100cc Climax engine. This resulted in a visit to the Cunningham headquarters on Friday afternoon at the invitation of the great American enthusiast, Briggs Cunningham, who had noticed that the Lotus was in trouble during practice. Here, work was a lot easier than in the cramped confines at Mayet, and the spares available were unbelievable. That year only two Cunninghams were running, but there was 16 tons of spares accompanying them—the year before it had been 39 tons! They had everything and it was all put at the disposal of Lotus. Mike found it incredible when in answer to a request for just a short piece of $\frac{5}{8}$-in. tubing for an oil breather a mechanic sorted over roll after roll of different diameter tubing and then cut 1 foot of the correct diameter from a roll which must have been six yards long!

After working all through the night the Lotus and its weary mechanics were back at Mayet on the Saturday morning ready for the fray. It was here that I joined the team after flying out from Blackbushe Airport to the small 'drome beside the Le Mans circuit. The exhilaration of the flight was paled by the "low flying" of Peter Jopp in the Anglia between the circuit and Mayet! As there

were not enough official passes to go round, the journey into the pits was made under cover of the bunk bedding in the transporter—peering out through Mike Costin's ventilation hole! Gendarmes were everywhere when the pits were reached, but they proved to be poor at mental arithmetic, for three mechanics unlocked the transporter doors and four came out with the Mark 9.

The rules and regulations at Le Mans are many in number, in fact they occupy a thick booklet. They must all be observed or else a fine is imposed; in cases of infringements of a serious nature you are disqualified as well as fined. For four hours before the race the various rituals were gone through—draining of tanks, refuelling and sealing, listing of spares, checking of engine and major component numbers, and the final verification of faults found at scrutineering. This last item is most important, for if the faults have not been rectified satisfactorily, then there may not be sufficient time before the start of the race to put things right, and all the efforts of the

Colin Chapman leads a DB-Panhard into Tertre Rouge early in the race. Later on, a handful of sand was 'borrowed' from the banking at the exit from the corner in an attempt to cure clutch slip!

previous weeks may be wasted in a last-minute disqualification.

At last the spares are all stowed, small items strapped under the passenger seat and larger items in the tail of the car beside the spare wheel. The drivers had their last briefing. The two timekeepers took up their positions with charts and stop watches. The mechanics looked remarkably fresh and one could not blame them if they all had their fingers crossed! John Eason Gibson checked that the signalling equipment was where it should be, and at 4 p.m. there was a scamper of feet and with a deafening roar the race was on.

Initially, the Lotus led the 1100cc class, followed closely by John Brown in the Cooper. After the first hour Colin was still leading the class, being 7 seconds ahead of Duntov's Porsche, the car which was destined to win the 751-1100cc class and finish 13th overall. At this time the crowd present were being thrilled by the terrific scrap between Castellotti (Ferrari), Mike Hawthorn (Jaguar) and Fangio (Mercedes). At 5.15 p.m. this trio screamed through the pits in line ahead formation and Colin shot into the pits to try to remedy a slipping clutch. Mike smartly pumped half of the contents of the pit fire extinguisher into the bell-housing and Colin rejoined the race. As it appeared that clutch slip was to be prevalent throughout the race, a search was made for further supplies of fire extinguisher fluid, and once again Cunninghams came to the rescue with a huge tin accompanied by instructions from Briggs Cunningham to "keep her going at all costs".

The Cooper now led the class following the pit stop and still the crowd thrilled to the duel between Hawthorn and Fangio which brought back memories of their fantastic struggle at the French Grand Prix at Reims in 1953. On the 28th tour the Jaguar put up a new lap record of 122.393 mph and then at 6.30 p.m. there occurred the most dreadful accident in the history of motor racing when Pierre Levegh's Mercedes crashed amongst the spectators, killing and injuring a great many people. In the Lotus pit it was not possible to appreciate the serious nature of the accident, although the pall of smoke obviously signified a serious crash. Just before 7 p.m. Colin stopped again at the pits to have a front wing straightened after hitting the sand bank at Arnage. This excursion had cleared the clutch slip, and when later the malady struck again, Ron Flockhart, who was then driving, was despatched to Tertre Rouge with instructions to surreptitiously stop and throw a handful of the stuff through the holes into the bell-housing!

Soon after 10 p.m. (quarter distance), with Colin back at the wheel, the car slid off the road at Arnage just where Don Beauman was vainly trying to dig out his works Jaguar. Without hesitation Colin reversed out and rejoined the race.

It was with consternation that the pit staff heard an irate official demand that the car be brought in as it was disqualified. Arguing was no good. John Eason Gibson put out the signal and the Mark 9 stopped at the pit for the last time. Pleading was futile as the decision was final and the Lotus was out of the race. No doubt the terrible accident earlier in the evening had severely scared the organisation, and when they saw a Lotus driven backwards against the direction of the race without awaiting a signal from a marshal, it was too much for them. It was a cruel blow for such an innocent infringement to eliminate a car which was running perfectly and was well placed in its class and on the Index of Performance.

A very tired and very unhappy team returned to Mayet to catch up with some of their lost sleep. At eleven the next morning they were back at the circuit to see the build-up to the Jaguar overall victory and watch their rivals the Cooper finish, after running for hours during the night with "pop" purchased at the Hippodrome cafe keeping up the level of a leaking water system!

There was no celebration on the Sunday night; instead, the still tired mechanics had a whole night's sleep in readiness for the long trek home on the Monday. Bright and early on the Monday morning the transporter left on the journey across the north of France to Dunkirk and, after one stop for a meal, just caught the night boat. It had been an unfortunate experience for Team Lotus, but a great deal of information had been gleaned. As Colin said farewell to M. and Mme. Mica, he vowed that in 1956 he would be back—and would win.

10.

The First Eleven

THE HEADING OF THIS chapter is not intended to imply that the Lotus Engineering Company had by now grown so large that the members began to form teams for football and cricket! The number of employees would have been just sufficient, but the spare time on weekends and evenings was definitely not available. The reason for the departure from the earlier practice of calling each model a "Mark"-something-or-other was one of personal preference on Colin's part. He could see the habit continuing year after year, and the numbers becoming quite astronomical. It was decided, therefore, to call the new car for 1956 just plain "Eleven".

The previous year had been very hectic by reason of the multiplicity of models and specifications being offered. In order to simplify production and ease the stores position, Colin and Mike decided that in 1956 there would be only one basic model. Varied specifications would still be available, but the only chassis frame would be the Eleven—a design directly descendent from the Mark 9. Mike Anthony was keen to build another Bristol-engined Lotus but Colin was firm in his decision that Mike would have to do this with the basic chassis—no special cars would be built, so his would have to be a Mark Anthony!

At the Earls Court Motor Show I had sounded out the reactions of owners and Lotus enthusiasts to the idea of forming a club for them. The interest was most encouraging, and so in November we formed Club Lotus. Meanwhile, directly the Motor Show was over work began on construction of the prototype Eleven. By the time this was complete, it had been decided to offer the new model in three definite types so that the requirements of a greater number of potential customers could be satisfied. The shape of the new model was even smoother than the Mark 9. The scuttle was the same height as on the earlier model but the bonnet and tail sloped down more steeply, and the tail fins had all but disappeared, only a slight finning effect remaining. For serious competition work, where a higher degree of stabilisation was required, the Eleven could be fitted with a head fairing which appreciably increased the side area of the car.

The new chassis frame followed the general principles of the Mark 9, having main steel tubes of 1 in diameter and subsidiary ¾ in. in 18- or 20-gauge section according to the work they had to do. In order to reduce weight, the transmission tunnel on the new model was made into a stressed member, produced from 20-gauge strong aircraft alloy sheet. This stressed section was to take the final-drive torque reaction, part of the floor load, and give support to the rear engine mounting.

The front suspension followed in the usual Lotus tradition, swing axles being fitted, but with a lower pivot than previously in order to give less frontal weight transfer. A new rack-and-pinion steering unit was fitted with a short rack to bring the ball joints into the correct position for the suspension geometry, and specially cut steel steering arms were fitted. The Girling helical spring units which encircled hydraulic telescopic dampers were shorter than those used on the Mark 9 and had less travel, being mounted closer to the centre line of the car.

Much experimental work had resulted in the

fitting of an even lighter radiator, which was fully ducted and fed from a very small air entry. The nose of the car was kept very smooth by the housing of side and headlamps being specially shaped Perspex covers.

Great attention had been given to the electrical system in view of the annoying and petty troubles that could arise in this department. A special lightweight 12 volt, 31 amp-hour battery weighing only 24 lb was positioned in the tail beside the spare wheel. The fuse box was mounted on the dash panel for easy access, and provision was made for 7 in headlamps, separate side lights and a full complement of twin stop lights, tail lights, etc.

As this model was intended for a variety of roles, there had been more attention to detail, and items such as map pockets in the drop-down doors, a covered dash panel to match the upholstery, and lighted instruments were provided. In order to provide unhindered accessibility, the complete nose and tail body sections could be lifted up on cam-hinges and, if necessary, removed althogether.

Knock-on 15 in wire wheels, with identical rims at the front and rear, were fitted with 4.50 by 15 tyres on the front and 5.00 by 15 tyres at the rear, the spare wheel with 4.50 by 15 tyre being mounted under the rear panelling. Dimensions were wheelbase 7 ft 1 in, front track 3 ft 10½, rear track 3 ft 11 in, overall length 11 ft 2 in, overall width 5 ft, height to top of tail fin 3 ft 1 in, height to top of scuttle 2 ft 3 in, and minimum ground clearance 5 in. Approximate dry weight was 7½ cwt.

It is interesting to see how the three alternative types were evolved from this basic specification. Firstly, the Le Mans model was offered to those people who wished to race in top-line events. This model could either be fitted with the 1100cc Coventry Climax engine or the new 1500cc version of the same engine which was now available. This new four-cylinder engine had a bore of 3 in and a stroke of 3.15 in, giving a cubic capacity of 1460cc. Basically the engines were very similar, the new version giving 100 bhp at 6,200 rpm on an 8.6 to 1 compression ratio. These engines were carried on two rubber mountings at the front and a single rubber mounting at the rear around the gearbox. They were tilted sideways through approximately 10 degrees to reduce frontal area and to permit a carburettor arrangement with horizontal induction tracts. At the rear a de Dion layout was used which saved 10 valuable unsprung pounds from the layout used in the Mark 9. The tube was pierced to allow the half shafts to pass through, so giving them much greater length and less deflection for the universal joints. The short tubular shafts were still extensions from the Rudge-type hubs, but were now carried on a pair of taper roller races in a light alloy housing. As earlier, a pair of radius arms located the axle on each side, but now one of them was triangulated into an A-frame to absorb lateral forces. Ultra-light, hydraulically operated 9½ in Girling disc brakes were fitted outboard at the front and inboard at the rear, the calipers of the rear brakes being carried ahead of the axle to reduce overhung loads, whilst at the front the calipers were behind the discs in order to reduce wheel bearing loads. A horizontally mounted hand brake operated the rear calipers through inner and outer cables. Transmission was via a single dry plate clutch of 7¼ in diameter, mechanically operated, and a four-speed gearbox. During the early part of the season this gearbox was specially built up at Hornsey and incorporated special gears in the Austin A30 casing, but later a switch was made to the MGA gearbox. Final drive was through a hypoid unit, and five different axle ratios were available, ranging from 5.125 to 3.89 to cover a speed difference of over 4 mph per 1,000 rpm, when using standard 500 by 15 rear tyres. For racing purposes a head fairing and wrap-round windscreen were available, together with a metal tonneau cover for the passenger compartment. The basic price of the Le Mans 75 model was £1,337 ex works, and this increased to £1,387 if you required the Stage 2 tuned engine—this latter model being known as the Le Mans 85. When the 1500cc single cam engine was fitted, approximately another £250 was added to the basic price.

Secondly, there was the Club model, which was intended for the person who only intended to enter competitions of a more minor nature and could not afford the Le Mans model. As the same basic specification applied to all models it would be possible at a later date for the owner of a Club model to incorporate the more expensive specification, as and when he could afford it. The Club model differed from the Le Mans in that a proprietary make of live rear axle was used in place of the de Dion layout. It was located by parallel trailing arms and held laterally by a diagonal member. Springing and damping were similar to the Le Mans model. The other difference in specification was to the brakes, the Club model having drum brakes fitted outboard both front and rear, which were hydraulically operated by two leading-shoe units. Cast iron drums were used of 9 in diameter at the front and 8 in diameter at the rear. Separate front and rear master cylinders were fed from a single hydraulic fluid reservoir containing separate front and rear compartments. A full-width windscreen was available, with screen wipers if necessary, in conjunction with a hood and framework. The basic price of the Club model was £1,083.

The third variation was the Sports model. This specification had been devised for the enthusiast who required a fast yet economical sports car for road use and perhaps the odd competition outing. The model was soon officially recognised as a standard production sports car, and as such quickly became popular for use in competitive events for that type of car. The only difference from the specification of the Club model was that the more expensive Climax engine was replaced by the Ford 100E, 1172cc side-valve, four cylinder engine. Complete with gearbox, this unit enabled a much cheaper car to be built which still gave excellent performance. The standard engine would produce 36 bhp at 4,500 rpm—a figure which could be increased easily by a little "breathing on". With all the benefits of low weight, low drag and a basically economical engine, the Sports model gave the fantastic petrol consumption of 65 mpg at moderate speeds. The basic price of this model was £872.

Although Lotus were now limiting their models to the three strict variations on the one theme, they were as keen as ever for their customers to construct their own cars. Not only did this help to

Two variations on the 11 theme. Below: The Club model was equipped with a live rear axle located by parallel trailing arms and fitted with outboard-mounted drum brakes all round. Bottom: The more sophisticated Le Mans version had a de Dion layout with inboard-mounted disc brakes at the rear. A third variant, the Sports model, was produced for road use and was in effect a Ford-engined version of the Club 11.

ease the problem of space scarcity, but it also helped the customer as he did not have to pay Purchase Tax on a car which he had genuinely constructed himself. When constructing cars in this way, the customer was still required to obtain some of the components himself, but this was a small price to pay for the large saving of Purchase Tax.

Early in 1956 there was a new face behind the typewriter in Colin's office because Hazel had left in anticipation of a coming happy event. Susan was born in May—not quite in the Lotus tradition with regard to weight as she scaled 9½ lb on arrival!

Two new Elevens appeared in public for the first time in Great Britain for the Goodwood Easter Monday meeting on April 2nd. One of the cars, to be driven by the new Team Lotus driver Reg Bicknell, was powered by the 1460cc Coventry Climax engine. During practice on the Saturday, the cars were rather a handful, weaving on the straight in an alarming manner, but Colin Chapman arrived back from Sebring on the Sunday and soon began to sort out the troubles. Reg Bicknell ran on the Monday, but the car was too new, and he could only manage fourth place in the up-to-1500cc sports car race.

Hard work at Hornsey during the next ten days produced three well-prepared Elevens for the British Empire Trophy race on April 14th—two Team cars to be driven by Colin and Reg Bicknell, and a third car purchased by Ivor Bueb and to be driven in this event by his Le Mans partner, Mike Hawthorn. Irrespective of engine capacity, Colin recorded the fastest practice lap, and in Heat 1 for cars up to 1500cc he went into the lead pursued by Moss, Russell and Salvadori, all in Coopers. In the course of his progress Colin equalled Reg Parnell's sports car record of 1 min 58 sec established in the works Aston Martin the year before. Mike Hawthorn began to duel with the Coopers and Reg Bicknell passed Russell, and the race finished with Colin first, Mike third and Reg fifth. In the final, the 1½-litre cars fought it out right from the start, with Stirling Moss leading Colin for the first 12 laps, after which Colin forged ahead and built up a seven-second lead until he had an unfortunate spin at Druid's corner, which

Left: Record-breaking with a difference with the 1956 Le Mans car. Below: Journey's end, and the author has set a new time for the cross-Britain journey. Bottom: It must have been around this time that Colin Chapman gained the nickname 'Chunky'!

let the Cooper through to win the trophy by ten seconds. Colin's second place was backed up by Mike Hawthorn, who finished fourth, and consolation came in the fact that the leading Team Lotus car had shared fastest lap with Moss and Benoit Musy in his 3-litre Maserati at 84.96 mph.

A week later, three Team Lotus cars were at Aintree for the B.A.R.C. International meeting. The third car was powered by an 1100cc Climax engine, and was to have been driven by Cliff Allison, but unfortunately he crashed one of the 1500cc cars in practice, so Colin took over the new car, and after working through from the back row, won the 1100cc class. Mike Hawthorn had now really got the hang of "these Lotus things", and won the race outright from Roy Salvadori in the works Cooper with Reg Bicknell third. The Eleven was showing its paces right from the start of the season, with Colin recording the fastest 1100cc lap at 79.65 mph and Mike the fastest 1500cc lap at 82.82 mph. A rather interesting modification had been necessary to the car Mike Hawthorn was driving in order to accommodate his large feet and long legs; wells were made in the undertray into which he could fit his heels. Without this modification he was apt to push all three pedals at once!

On the following weekend another member of Team Lotus covered himself with glory—this time at Brands Hatch in the 1100cc car. Graham Hill was the name on many tongues as the spectators left the Kent circuit. Graham for years had put in as much racing as he possibly could, but had been handicapped by the lack of finance to purchase his own car. However, his enthusiasm and ability was such that he soon became noticed, even when driving indifferent 500cc racing cars. In order to keep close to the racing scene he took a job as a mechanic at Hornsey, and following a fine practice display in the Mark 9 after the 1955 season Colin gave him his chance at the end-of-April Brands Hatch meeting. Graham made excellent use of it, winning the up-to-1200cc sports car race, and then finishing a very good second to Reg Bicknell in the 1500cc Team Lotus car in the up-to-1500cc race. In spite of giving away 400cc Graham recorded the fastest lap in this latter race at a speed of 72.23 mph—a 1500cc class record! Another privately

owned Eleven appeared at this meeting and was well driven by another great enthusiast—Bill Frost.

At Silverstone, on May 5th, the Cooper of Salvadori triumphed and Colin had to be content with second place. Then at Snetterton on May 19th the results of much hard work were visible in the shape of several new Elevens in the hands of private owners, including Peter Taylor, Keith Hall, J. A. Somervail, Jack Richards and David Piper. It was also noticeable how popular the Stage 2 turning had proved, for nearly all the Coventry Climax engines present appeared to have received "the treatment". This meeting, organised by the West Essex Car Club, included an innovation in the shape of a Lotus Only Handicap race, with handicaps supplied by Club Lotus. Mark 6s, 9s an 8 and the Elevens competed alongside each other, using Climax, Ford and MG engines and the event was won by R. N. Prior in his 1250cc MG-engined Mark 6 with Keith Hall second.

On Sunday, May 20th, Colin Chapman startled everyone by setting up a new absolute sports car record at Brands Hatch with a lap of 73.42 in the 1500cc Team Lotus car. He won his race as he liked, with Les Leston and Jack Brabham in Coopers second and third. Elevens filled the next three places, fourth being Archie Scott-Brown, fifth Alan Stacey and sixth Keith Hall. In the race for cars up to 1200cc, Cliff Allison won from Alan Stacey.

On the Bank Holiday Monday, the B.R.S.C.C., rushed across to Crystal Palace to organise their second meeting in two days, and in both the Anerley Trophy and the Norbury Trophy Graham Hill finished third in Tommy Sopwith's new Eleven. Also on the Whit Monday an epic struggle took place at the B.A.R.C. Goodwood meeting between Colin Chapman and Mike Hawthorn in the up-to-1500cc sports car race. They passed and repassed on Woodcote and Madgwick corners, their Elevens appearing to be tied with a short piece of elastic, until following a brief contact on the 12th lap. Mike had to dash into the pits for bodywork repairs which enabled Colin to win. Between them they set a new class record with a lap at 88.71 mph. Team Lotus had a good day as Cliff Allison won the 1100cc class, finishing fourth overall. Then in the unlimited Whitsun Trophy race Mike Hawthorn went like the wind, after Colin had stripped a timing gear. Mike finished second, only 1.8 seconds behind Desmond Titterington in a D-type Jaguar. During his meteoric progress he bettered his earlier class record and raised it to 89.26 mph!

At Aintree on June 2nd, another new private owner of an Eleven figured in the money. This was Brian Naylor, who won the 7-lap scratch race for sports cars up to 1500cc from Keith Hall. Brian Naylor's car was unique as he had managed to endow it with the engine from his 1500cc sports Maserati. Two hours after winning at Aintree, Brian was at Oulton Park busy winning the up to 2-litre race!

Club Lotus blossomed out on June 10th and organised their first event at Brands Hatch in conjunction with the 750 Motor Club. Unfortunately the weather was dismal, and it rained throughout the afternoon, but a good-sized crowd watched the varied programme of races. John Harris in his Mark 6 with de Dion rear end and Coventry Climax engine was undoubtedly the star of the meeting after winning three races and coming second in another.

An Eleven took to the hills on June 16th when, in pouring rain at Shelsley Walsh, Edward Lewis came third in the up-to-1500cc sports car class. Then, just to keep up the variety, the works 1500cc car was fitted with a detuned 1100cc Climax engine and lent to Mr. and Mrs. Charles Bulmer for the Mobilgas Economy Run. This turned out to be 650 miles in the most appalling weather! The torrential rain was hardly ideal for an open car, and great credit is due to the crew, who finished second in the Allcomers Class with an aggregate performance of just over 60 mpg! According to Mike Costin, the engine had been tuned to run "on the smell of the stuff"!

On the same weekend as one works car was getting drenched by the British climate, Reg Bicknell was sunning his in Portugal at the City of Oporto Cup motor race where he finished a very good third, leading home a Porsche Spyder.

The Hornsey cars were outstanding at Aintree a week later. In the 1500cc race Colin won as he liked after a stirring first-lap battle with Roy Salvadori in the works Cooper; Scott-Brown was

Top left: Alan Stacey takes the lead in an 1,100cc sports car race at Goodwood. Centre left: And gives Innes Ireland a lift home at the end of it. Bottom left: Ireland sits lower as he leads Peter Ashdown through the chicane. Below: Keith Hall leading Cliff Allison on his way to winning the Autumn Trophy race at Crystal Palace in 1956. Bottom: Lotus line-up at San Diego. Ignacio Lozano, Bill Knowles and Frank Monise in 11s. Harvey Mayer in a Mark 9, John Timanus in a modified Mark 8, and Jean Oddous in his Mark 6.

driving Tommy Sopwith's car and finished third behind the Cooper. Keith Hall and Cliff Allison took second and third places respectively in the 1100cc race, sharing a new class record lap at 81.08 mph. Graham Hill was driving the first of the Sports models in the standard production sports car race, which he won, putting in a lap at 71.24 mph—a spanking speed for a Ford 10 engine.

The month of June was rounded off with an orgy of motor racing at Reims where Colin Chapman was to have his first chance in a grand prix at the wheel of a Vanwall. But Colin had very bad luck in practice when, due to ineffective rear brakes following a relining operation, he crashed the car into a concrete post. He found the speed of the 2½-litre, fuel-injected racing car quite fantastic on the long straights and was beginning to get the feel of things when his crash put paid to his chance of competing in that particular *grande epreuve*. Colin himself had put in a lot of work on the Vanwall, and it is interesting to trace the origin of this connection. It all went back to a friend of his named Derek Wootton who, after a season as mechanic to Peter Whitehead, joined the Vanwall team as assistant to the team manager, David Yorke. On his suggestion, Frank Costin was employed to design a new body for the cars, which showed up well at an outing at Oulton Park. On being asked his opinion, Frank said he was well pleased with the aerodynamics but he thought that perhaps the chassis ought to be redesigned by Colin Chapman. That was how the Vanwall came by a new spaceframe at the end of the 1956 season, and how it started the 1957 season with a new suspension very similar in layout to that used for the Eleven. In 1957 Colin was also called in as a consultant to the BRM racing car, and he gave this assignment his usual devoted attention and spent much time with the Bourne people testing and working on the car.

To return to Reims, although Colin was not driving a Lotus, the marque was represented by Ivor Bueb's car in the 12-hour sports car race. His co-driver was the American, Herbert Mackay Fraser, and between them they put up a remarkable performance, having a ding-dong battle for many laps with the ultimate class winner. After holding the lead for a short while, they had to retire when all but top gear disappeared from the modified A30 gearbox and the engine expired from the flogging it received from a 3.2 to 1 top gear ratio. Colin was very impressed by the driving of Mackay Fraser, an impression which led shortly to "Mac" joining Team Lotus as a works driver.

The boys at Hornsey were now working at top pressure. The orders for the Eleven were rolling in, and it was becoming very plain that once again the business had outgrown its premises. It was very heartening to see the orders arriving from the dollar countries, but as July came round, each new order brought the headache of where and when could the car be built. The payrool had been increased to cope with the growing demand for cars, but now the business of repairs and modifications to older models had to be looked after. In every respect life was very busy and Nobby Clarke had a heavy burden as foreman of the outfit.

On Saturday, July 7th, Reg Bicknell drove his 1500cc car to a fine victory at Mallory Park in the sports car race for cars of that capacity, and then proceeded to hold Bruce Halford's G.P. Maserati at bay for six laps in the unlimited race. Graham Hill drove his Ford-engined model brilliantly in the 24-lap race counting for the *Autosport* Series Production Sports Car Championship and had a race-long duel with Shale in an "S" type Austin Healey—what the Eleven lacked on the straights, it more than made up for on the bends! Although Graham had to give best to Shale, and to Dalton in another "S" type, he did have the pleasure of recording the fastest lap of the race at 76.18 mph. Whilst the Elevens battled at Mallory, S.D. Nicholl had taken his brand new Club model to the famous Rest-and-be-Thankful hill climb in picturesque Glen Croe, and on his first outing came second to hill climb champion Tony Marsh in the up-to-1500cc sports car class.

Team Lotus took two cars to Rouen for the Coupe Delamare Debouteville meeting, and were backed up by Tommy Sopwith's car, to be driven by the Franco-American, Harry Schell, and Ivor Bueb's (Ecurie Demilitre) car to be driven again by

Mike Hawthorn. This onslaught resulted in Mike Costin proudly displaying the signal '1-2-3' as the three leading Lotuses flashed by on their last lap, completely eclipsing Cooper, Porsche and Masarati. Run on the magnificent Les Essarts circuit, which dips and climbs through the forest, the event was much to Colin's liking. He revelled in the fast downhill sweeps to the hairpin then the twisting uphill climb through the trees. Schell led the race initially, but spun on the fourth lap and then Colin took the lead. Cliff Allison in the 1100cc car was going magnificently, easily leading the 750-1100cc class. Mike Hawthorn had to drop out with gearbox trouble, and after one and a half hours of racing Colin took the chequered flag, followed by Harry Schell and then Cliff. The local beauty queen presented the garlands and the French press went mad about "le Lotoos".

The team dashed back home, cutting short the celebrations, as the next weekend was the 9th R.A.C. Grand Prix meeting at Silverstone and on the programme there was a race for the new Formula 2 racing cars of up to 1500cc capacity, unsupercharged. A single-seater racing car for this formula was on Colin's drawing board, but it would be 1957 before it was raceworthy, and so the Lotus cars for Silverstone were all lightened sports cars, with such items as lights, batteries and spare wheels removed. Only one monoposto car faced the starter's flag, the works Cooper with Roy Salvadori at the wheel. For ten laps Colin led the Cooper, setting fastest lap of the race at 97.93 mph, but Salvadori managed to scrape past on the eleventh lap and with a rather tired engine Colin finished 30 seconds behind in second place. Reg Bicknell in the second Team Lotus 1500 had dropped out, but Cliff Allison was driving a third similar car and he kept the flag flying by coming home fourth. Graham Hill had been going like the wind in Jack Richards' immaculately turned out 1100cc car and he finished a fine seventh—the first 1100cc car home. It was interesting to note that the leading Lotus' fastest lap was no "flash in the pan", as down Hangar Straight the streamlined car was timed at 123.71 mph against the Cooper's 119.21 mph.

For some time David Piper and Bob Hicks had been carrying the battle into the enemy's camp by taking their Elevens abroad to race. On the day following the Silverstone meeting they led the 1100cc sports car race at Sables d'Olonne from start to finish, David winning by a small margin from Bob.

A week later Brian Naylor took his Eleven to County Wicklow in Eire and returned with the Leinster Trophy for the best performance on handicap. Another new Eleven owner figured in the results—Malcolm Templeton, who finished fifth on handicap in his 1100cc car and then came second in the up-to-2000cc scratch race, which Brian Naylor also won. In this latter event Cliff Davis finished third in his Bristol-engined Mark 10—Lotus 1-2-3 again, with engines of 1500cc, 1100cc and 2000cc!

John Coombs just completed the construction of his third Lotus in time for the Vanwall Trophy meeting at Snetterton. He had fitted a 1500cc Coventry Climax engine to the car and he lent it to Cooper driver Roy Salvadori for the event, and Roy promptly won the ten-lap 1500cc sports car race with Archie Scott-Brown second in a similar car. Private owners Bill Frost and Jack Richards had a private battle in their Elevens in the 1100cc division of the race—Jack won the battle, Bill set the fastest 1100cc lap—but they both finished behind Peter Gammon's very fast 1100cc Cooper.

The Elevens were really getting around now, and on July 26th the Hon. Edward Greenall took his new car to Jersey for the Bouley Bay international hill climb and returned with the 1500cc sports car class in his pocket. Two new Scots owners, Tom Dickson and A. Birrell, had their new Elevens at the Crimond race meeting on the next weekend and between them collected a first, two seconds and two thirds.

Whilst the Aberdeen and District Motor Club held their meeting in Scotland many miles south Team Lotus were preparing to go into action at their second Le Mans. This year, three cars were entered, and hopes were high for two class wins and perhaps a win in the highly-prized Index of Performance, but fortune was a little unkind and the nett result was a win in the 751-1100cc class, fourth place in the Index of Performance, and a qualification for the 1956/57 Biennial Cup. The

Left: The Lotus 11 cockpit epitomizes functional simplicity. This is the Sports model with full-height screen and studded bodywork to accept a soft hood and framing. Below: Len Bastrup practising for the 1956 Sebring 12-hour race in his 1½ litre Lotus just a lap before rolling it.

story of this second journey to the Sarthe circuit is told in the next Chapter.

Tommy Sopwith returned to the wheel of his shining dark blue Eleven with 1500cc Climax engine at Great Auclum hill climb on August 4th. Following a very unpleasant crash in his Cooper at Oulton Park the year before, Tommy had been forced to bow to the parental request for no more circuit racing, but he was able to let himself go on the little hill near Reading to obtain the very satisfactory result of a win in the 1301-1800cc class, in the course of which he set up a new sports car record of 22.97 seconds—just beating my own record achieved the year before in the Mark 6. A year later the same car did well at this venue in the hands of its new owner, Sir Gawaine Baillie.

On the Bank Holiday Monday, Mike Hawthorn appeared at Brands Hatch with an experimental 1290cc Coventry Climax engine under the bonnet of an Eleven. Mike drove brilliantly on a wet track and won his heat from Jack Brabham in the works 1500cc Cooper, but the track dried for the final and Mike found his lack of 200cc too much of a handicap. However, Reg Bicknell kept the Lotus flag flying by winning in his Team Lotus 1500 and then went on to take second place in the Formula 2 race. Graham Hill's Sports model appeared in a coat of bright yellow paint for the production car race, but it was not Graham's day, and over-exuberance led to rather too many spins and culminated in his receiving the black flag for his efforts.

Over at the Crystal Palace on the same day, Keith Hall showed how a private owner could beat the works by leading Cliff Allison in both the heat and the final for 1100cc cars. Keith's car was very fast indeed, due in no small measure to the fact that two twin-choke Weber carburettors now nestled under the light green bonnet instead of the usual SUs. Two more new Eleven owners made their mark at this meeting, "Tony" Ellis winning the second heat of the 1100cc race, with Marke Zervudachi second.

Elevens in the hands of Brian Naylor, John Coombs, Alan Stacey and Edward Greenall did well at the two meetings organised by the Nottingham Sports Car Club at Mallory Park and Silverstone. The drivers of the newer cars had their work cut out at the latter meeting due to the fine driving of Peter Ashdown and Bryan Hewitt in their Mark 9s.

Club Lotus was by now a flourishing organisation with a membership exceeding 100 and growing steadily, and the R.A.C. had given it official recognition. In view of its solidarity the Club was able to enter a team consisting of two Mark 9s and four Elevens for the six-hour relay race at Silverstone, the drivers being Peter Ashdown, Bryan Hewitt, "Tony" Ellis, Marke Zervudachi, Dennis Parker (driving Jack Richards' car as Jack had slipped off to get married!) and another new Eleven owner, Tony Bik. The Club chairman, Alan Smith, was team manager, and auditor Mike Smyth and committee member Peter Jepson helped with the timekeeping and lap scoring in the pits. In spite of some very fast driving, slick handovers, and some excellent work by John Playford, mechanic to Jack Richards' car, the very severe handicap of only one credit lap from the scratch team proved too tough—fancy having to give away 43 laps of the Club circuit in six hours to an 1172 Ford team! Finally the Club team finished sixth—not a disgrace—and everybody present agreed how very much they had enjoyed this rather different form of racing.

Whilst the Club raced at Silverstone, poor Mike Hawthorn had a most spectacular crash in the Eleven at Knicker Brook on the Oulton Park circuit in the up-to-1500cc *Sporting Life* Trophy. Mike's crash allowed Stirling Moss to win the race in the Willment Speed Shop Cooper, but second and third places were taken by the 1100s of Keith Hall and Cliff Allison—Keith in front again.

Nothing daunted, David Piper ran his 1100cc Eleven in the Pescara Sports Car Grand Prix for cars up to 2 litres. Run on the very fast 16-mile circuit on the Adriatic coast of Italy, the event was hardly suitable for the low-powered Lotus, but David put up a fine performance and finished 18th overall. Whilst David battled in Italy, an Eleven was figured in the results in America, where at Montgomery Airport, Charles Cunningham finished third in the class G race behind Len Bastrup's Mark 9.

Just for a change John Coombs took his car to Brighton Speed Trials on September 1st and set up a new record of 28.4 secs in the 1101-1500 class for the standing-start kilometre.

Down in Southern Italy the following day David Piper and Bob Hicks faced strong opposition from Stanguellini and Osca with such drivers as Cabianca and Siracusa for the 1100cc sports car race at Cosenza for the Sila Cup. This race took place over 70 laps of the picturesque 2.2 kilometres street circuit through the town making a total distance of 150 kilometres, and after a fine drive David emerged victorious, with Bob a good second.

Frantic work had been going on at Hornsey to produce a special record-breaker Eleven for Stirling Moss to attack International Class G records at Monza on the day after the European Grand Prix, September 3rd. The rush was due to a last-minute change in the availability of the high speed track, and because of the hurry a purely standard car was used to which the head fairing was welded in instead of being held, as normal, by Dzus fasteners, and a completely enveloping "bubble" cockpit cover was added. Weber carburettors were fitted to the engine, which was brought up to Stage 2 tune. The car was rushed to Italy on a trailer behind a Vanguard van while Stirling won the Grand Prix.

The record attempts started in the early morning and soon a 50 kilometre record at 135.54 mph and a 50-mile record at 132.77 mph had been established. The attempts were halted when, owing to the roughness of the bankings, the rear sub-frame fractured and the tail of the car parted company with the rest of the vehicle at high speed!

Following participation at the Shell Grand Prix of Imola in Italy on September 30th, Team Lotus returned to Monza with the record-breaker. Two attempts were made on October 2nd and 9th with Mackay Fraser driving, and these resulted in a fine crop of new records—50 kilometres at 138 mph, 50 miles at 130 mph, 100 kilometres at 137.2 mph, 100 miles at 137.5 mph, 200 kilometres at 137.5 mph and 1 hour at 137.5 mph. The fastest flying lap was put in at 143 mph—an incredible speed for an unblown 1100cc sports car.

The September Goodwood meeting saw Keith Hall again beating Cliff Allison in the Madgwick Cup race for cars up to 1100cc. The ten-lap Woodcote Cup was for racing cars up to 2 litres (the old Formula 2) and again Colin had to give best to Roy Salvadori in the single-seat Cooper. The other Team Lotus 1500 driven by Reg Bicknell finished fourth. Later in the day there was a race for the new 1½ litres Formula 2 and here again the order was 1 Salvadori, 2 Chapman.

The next day Team Lotus moved over to Brands Hatch where the 1500cc race was won by Reg Bicknell with Cliff Allison second. Colin had an easy win in the Formula 2 race, as the new Cooper was not present owing to a contretemps in practice.

On the following Sunday at Silverstone two more new Elevens appeared, G.R. Baird's to win a 5 lap handicap and Peter Ross', one of the Lotus design team, to finish third in a similar handicap.

Gordon Jones was at the wheel of an Eleven at Mallory Park on the following Saturday to win the up to 1200cc sports car race, with the Hon. E.G. Greenall second and another new Eleven driver, L.I. Bramley, third.

At the final Goodwood members' meeting of the season a week later, a new name was added to the list of promising Lotus drivers—Innes Ireland. He had only completed his Eleven during the early hours of the morning of the race, but still managed a second and a fourth place in his brand new car.

Up at Oulton Park on the same day, much "lolly" was being offered in the race for the new Formula 2. The race was dominated by the new single-seater Coopers—Rob Walker had now taken delivery of his new car to be driven by Tony Brooks. On the starting grid there were 11 Lotuses and 14 Coopers. The opening laps were very hectic and poor Reg Bicknell finished up in the lake with the 1500 when a brake locked on. Ron Flockhart was driving John Coombs' Eleven and Mackay Fraser was in Tommy Sopwith's car, and being gently roasted as the result of a blown exhaust gasket. The Coopers of Salvadori and Brooks were first and second, but Ron and Colin finished a gallant third and fourth, easily winning the concurrently run sports car class. Cliff Allison was seventh in the 1100cc car, comfortably winning the 1100cc award.

A beautiful blue Eleven appeared at Silverstone

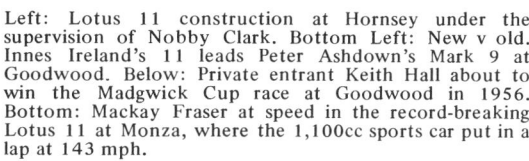

Left: Lotus 11 construction at Hornsey under the supervision of Nobby Clark. Bottom Left: New v old. Innes Ireland's 11 leads Peter Ashdown's Mark 9 at Goodwood. Below: Private entrant Keith Hall about to win the Madgwick Cup race at Goodwood in 1956. Bottom: Mackay Fraser at speed in the record-breaking Lotus 11 at Monza, where the 1,100cc sports car put in a lap at 143 mph.

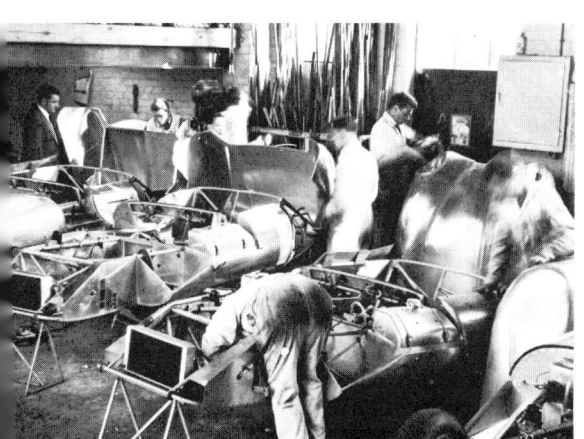

Left: The epic duel between Colin Chapman and Mike Hawthorn in their Lotus 11s was a feature of the 1956 Whit Monday race meeting at Goodwood; Chapman was the winner. Below: The versatility of the 11 revealed by the Ford-engined Sports model alongside the Coventry Climax-engined Le Mans car.

a week later—proud owner H. Deschamps, but unfortunately the new car began to belch white smoke on every corner and had to be abandoned.

Innes Ireland really got into his stride at Aintree and set up a new lap record for the Club circuit at 81.55 mph. The light green Eleven, of very similar shade to that of Keith Hall, was going very fast now, and Innes was thoroughly enjoying every moment of the fastest motor sport he had so far indulged in. In 1957 Innes also had a very successful season with the Lotus, particularly at

Goodwood, which ended in his receiving the *Motor Sport* Brooklands Memorial Trophy—the second year running that a Lotus had been connected with this award.

It was on the Sunday of this weekend that Team Lotus journeyed to the public park of Castellaccio, near Bologna, for the Shell Grand Prix of Imola. The event took place on the picturesque 3.12-mile circuit and saw "Mac" Fraser driving for the first time as an official member of the team. Initially, Cliff Allison led for 12 laps from Castellotti in an Osca but then went off the road when a hub fractured. "Mac" was going steadily in the other 1500cc car and finished a good fifth—he wished to impress but not to the extent of bending the car on his first outing!

Following his successful visit to Monza, "Mac" was now firmly installed in Team Lotus, and just to show he deserved the position, he wound up the 1956 season in grand style on the 4.09 kilometres circuit at Castelfusano, just outside Rome, by winning the 1100cc sports car race. David Piper came second but could do nothing about Mac's fastest lap of 160 kph. Ron Flockhart and Cliff Allison had also made the journey to Rome with the 1500cc Team Lotus cars, but both retired with stripped fibre timing gears, the former when lying third behind the Oscas of Castellotti and Musso. Brian Naylor upheld Lotus prestige, however, in the 1500cc race by finishing second to Musso in his Maserati-engined car.

Whilst the team were in action in Italy, there was great activity at Hornsey as the second visit to Earls Court was imminent. Lotus were now fully fledged members of the S.M.M. & T. and as such, could display their wares amongst all the other full-scale manufacturers. During the year a friend of Colin's, Alfred Woolf, had become P.R.O. for the company and it was on his shoulders that the burden of preparing the Lotus stand rested. It was a difficult task because with only hours to go to the official opening, the exhibits were still being completed. However, when the show opened, everything was in place beneath the yellow and green banner, and the tremendous interest caused by the three cars on display kept the crowds milling round the Lotus stand throughout the show.

A great deal more room was available than on the stand of the year before, and two versions of the latest full-width Eleven were displayed. These were built to the specification of the models specially constructed for the Le Mans race and complied with the new international sports car regulations. One was a beautifully finished chassis, complete in every respect except for the addition of body panels. The second was a complete car sporting the new full-width windscreen and bucket-type seats—this car had a fully trimmed interior and brought a great deal of praise for its high degree of finish. The third car was one of the surprises of the show—the hitherto unseen Formula 2 single-seater racing car. This slim, low, green projectile looked magnificent as it gleamed under the powerful lights of the auditorium. Under its bonnet nestled the new twin overhead camshaft Coventry Climax 1500cc engine, and behind the seat was the very special Lotus combined five-speed gearbox and back axle unit, although both items were so new that their internals were missing!

Visitors from far and wide came to the Lotus stand and the busy staff had to cope with a variety of strange languages. One very welcome caller was Jay Chamberlain from Burbank, California, who had been appointed distributor for the U.S.A. Jay had been racing an Eleven very successfully during the latter part of the year and this very popular personality was building up a fine reputation for Lotus in the States.

It was a very weary group who returned to their offices at Hornsey after the show to assess the results of their second "public sale". There was no doubt as to the result—1957 was going to be even more hectic than ever! An interesting fact had arisen from an item of advertising at the show which mirrored the gigantic increase in activity and numbers of Lotus cars both in the home country and abroad. As secretary of Club Lotus, I had compiled a list of all the first, second and third places gained by Lotus cars during the 1956 season. At the time of the motor show this gave the amazing total of 132 firsts, 121 seconds and 91 thirds achieved by 98 different drivers at 106 meetings—and this list was no doubt incomplete! By the time the last race of the season had been run, the grand total had increased to 148 firsts, 134 seconds and 99 thirds.

For myself, 1956 had a memorable ending when, early in November, a friend Tim Martin and I were lent one of the Le Mans 1100cc cars for an economy run from Lands End to John O'Groats. This resulted in the little car covering just over 2,000 miles in four days and completing the 892 miles from one end of Great Britain to the other at an average speed of 51.06 mph and an average fuel consumption of 38.525 mpg.

Production continued into 1957 when many Elevens were shipped to America, and more and more of them were built to the Sports specification for either road use or competition as a production car. In the latter category, owners such as Tom Barnard, John Lawry, Dick Prior, Mike Parkes and Geoff Williamson had many successes with their cars. Ian Walker purchased Graham Hill's "yellow peril" and with a Willment Powermaster inlet-over-exhaust cylinder head on the Ford engine proved to be fantastically fast and easily capable of racing on level terms against all the other standard production sports cars of any capacity. A most successful 1957 season with this year-old car resulted in Ian winning the *Autosport* Series Production Sports Car Championship by three points from Ken Rudd's AC Ace-Bristol as well as the newly instituted Lotuseer Cup. I had donated this latter award to Club Lotus for annual presentation to the newcomer to the marque who had put up the most meritorious performance during the year, and Ian was the obvious choice for 1957.

The success story of the Eleven continued throughout 1957. Many of the first owners of 1956 Elevens retained their cars for competition use for a second season, some were sold to new enthusiasts and still more people continued to assemble their own cars. In total 150 Elevens were produced—64 of these going to American owners. But during the winter of 1956, Colin and his design team were preparing a new sports car for Team Lotus for the coming season; they had the new Formula 2 car as a test bed for new ideas which they hoped to be able to incorporate in an improved version of the Eleven.

11.

Return journey

DESPITE THE ADVERSE criticism in the daily press following the tragic accident in 1955 and gloomy forebodings about the future of Le Mans, the classic 24-hour race was held a year later on Saturday and Sunday, July 28th and 29th. A great deal of work had been carried out on the circuit in order to improve the safety factor—the pits had been rebuilt and set back so as to increase the width of the road at that part, modifications had been made to the fast corner under the Dunlop bridge just past the pits and also to the turn at Arnage. There had also been considerable resurfacing in the "Maison Blanche" area. Very strict rules now existed concerning entering the pits, and drivers had to pull in well before the pit area to the right of a yellow line painted on the road—any infringement of this regulation would entail immediate disqualification. In order to reduce high speeds, the engine capacity of Prototype cars was limited to 2½ litres and fuel tanks to 130 litres, refuelling being barred between intervals of at least 34 laps. One item of interest to team managers arising from the modification was a decrease in lap distance of 8/100ths of a mile—just over 140 yards.

Team Lotus had decided to go all out to make up for their bad luck of the year before and had entered three cars. Two of these were of 1100cc capacity and the third was powered by the 1500cc version of the single-overhead-camshaft Coventry Climax engine. All three cars were accepted—a pleasing indication of the high esteem in which the marque was held by the French organisers.

It was obvious from the requirements of the new regulations that considerable modification would be needed to make the existing Team Lotus cars eligible for the race, the main alteration of increasing the interior width of the cockpit being virtually impossible without completely rebuilding the cars. There was no alternative, therefore, but to build three new cars.

Basically the special cars were very similar to the production Elevens, but the chassis frames were wider at the centre section and swept in abruptly just ahead of the rear wheels, so that the track remained at the standard width. Bucket seats were fitted, as were twin sport lights, each side of the frontal air intake. These additional lights were fixed behind plastic covers which kept the front contours of the car perfectly smooth. The new regulations called for a full-width windscreen of a minimum depth and a windscreen wiper. The screens fitted to the Team cars sloped backwards so as to maintain the aerodynamic shape of the car and they also wrapped round on each side to provide extra protection for the driver, the side portions being fitted to the drop-down doors.

It is no exaggeration to say that when completed the three new cars looked beautiful. Their turnout was immaculate, and they sparkled green in the sunlight, proudly displaying their large numbers 32, 35 and 36, with a thin yellow line on their flanks which broke on the door section to show the words TEAM LOTUS.

A very favourable impression was created at scrutineering; the French press began to ponder on the chances of a Lotus win in the Index of Performance and the Porsche team became very interested in the perfectly streamlined little cars. The official "verification" did not bring many headaches, certainly nothing which was to cause the mechanics much trouble, and Colin Chapman must have felt very proud as the three cars passed along the row of scrutineers' tables. His pride, however, did not help him at the drivers' medical where, for the second year in succession, the presence of a pretty nurse was too much for him to be able to oblige in the bottle provided!

Team management was again in the hands of John Eason Gibson, aided by his timekeepers of the year before. A new regulation concerning signalling was to add still further to the burdens of the team manager, for now all signalling had to be carried out from special pits just after Mulsanne corner. These secondary pits were connected by telephone to the main pits and anyone who has used a French telephone might well be excused having doubts about the effectiveness of this arrangement. However, Team Lotus found the system satisfactory, thanks in no small measure to Lotus driver John Lawry, who ran the signalling pit with great efficiency.

Colin was to drive the 1500cc car with "Mac" Fraser, and the 1100s were in the hands of Reg Bicknell and Cliff Allison. Last year's member of the team, Peter Jopp, rejoined the fold to partner Reg, and private owner Keith Hall was invited to partner Cliff. Again the Auberge de St. Nicholas was Team headquarters, and M. Mica was called on to supply even more Coca Cola for the enlarged equipe. The courtyard behind the hotel was too small for three cars, so the team virtually took over a small garage at the opposite end of the little town. This provided excellent working space but had one drawback—a glass roof. How the sun beat down during the days before the race, and how the mechanics sweltered!

Unfortunately the fine weather did not hold, and at 4 p.m. on the Saturday a light drizzle was falling as Stirling Moss rocketed into the lead in the Aston Martin and only the blue Talbot-Maserati was left motionless on the line. At the end of the first lap people in the crowded pits were amazed to see Colin flash through in 16th position, just behind Cornet in the 1500cc Maserati and leading Behra's Talbot-Maserati. The 1500 was going magnificently and Colin was well up with the works Porsche coupes. At 5 p.m. he

Left: Colin Chapman shared the 1½ litre Lotus 11 with Mackay Fraser in the 1956 Le Mans race, but the car retired with big-end failure. Below: Team Lotus all set for their second assault on Le Mans, complete with faithful Bedford transporter. Bottom: Peter Jopp with co-driver Reg Bicknell scored the team's first Le Mans success, by winning the 1,100cc class.

was 17th overall—lying fifth in his class behind three Porsches and the Maserati. Cliff Allison was driving very well and was in 22nd place, leading the 1100cc class. Then the Maserati dropped a valve and the Team Lotus 1500 moved up a place in its class, with the works Porsches in line-ahead formation in front.

The first refuelling stops were all completed without any undue loss of time, and the three "number two" drivers were soon settled down on the damp, slippery, circuit. As the light began to fade, valve trouble struck at the Storez/Polensky Porsche, which meant that "Mac" Fraser had only the Herrmann/Maglioli and Frankenberg/Trips cars ahead of him in his class. After the second pit stops, the lone American-entered Cooper, of Hugus and Bentley, was just ahead of the two 1100cc Lotuses, which were now six laps behind the flying 1500.

At midnight the weather was worse, and a cold wind accompanied by continual showers had thinned the crowd who now huddled in the shelter of the booths, stalls and tents which make up the unique atmosphere of Le Mans. The bad weather could not stop all the fun of the fair with its blaring hurdy-gurdy music, the shouts of vendors, and the clatter of dishes trying to compete with the gabble of the public address loudspeakers and the roar of the cars on the circuit.

Driving conditions were terrible. Cars shot through the pit area in a wall of spray and the three Lotus drivers became wetter and wetter. They were enduring a nightmare ride, for their cars were travelling at "in between" speeds—a very hazardous experience under bad conditons. It meant a continual look-out for the tail lights of a slower car ahead, and the ever-present worry that the headlamps behind were of a much faster car which must be given plenty of room to overtake. Tough though they were, both Colin and Mac later admitted that the conditions were frightening. As he drove through the night into the lashing rain Colin began to long for an excuse to visit the comfort of the pits, but nothing happened, and so on he had to go, fighting back the nagging desire to invent trouble and pack it in. Soon after he took over during the night "Mac" experienced bad cramp in his right leg—the cramp was genuine and most painful. As he tore down the Mulsanne straight, counting the markers on his right so he knew when to pull over the wheel to take the invisible swerve at the end of the straight, he fought the desire to call at the pits. His reasoning was rather the reverse of Colin's—he dare not stop as he was sure everyone would think he had invented the cramp in order to quit the cockpit!

As day began to dawn and the tricky mist which always settles on some part of the circuit in the early hours of morning began to drift and drop in patches, Cliff Allison came swooping down the straight from the Hippodrome cafe and without warning a large dog rushed into the road. Cliff did not have a chance—he killed the dog stone dead and badly crumpled the front of the Lotus. On inspection it was found that the damage was extensive, and so the car had to be retired—a cruel blow as it was running perfectly.

With the coming of full daylight the rain ceased and the road began to dry. The remaining 1100cc car was still locked in combat with the Cooper. The leading Porsche had retired and so now the 1500cc Lotus was in second place in its class but a long way behind the remaining works Porsche, which was still lapping very fast. Then, just after midday, with under four hours to go, fate struck again and the 1500 coasted to a halt. A big end bolt had broken—tragic luck after its brilliant progress for 172 laps.

Consolation came in the fact that the remaining 1100cc car was steadily winning its duel with the Cooper. With three hours to go the Lotus passed the Cooper, moving into eighth place overall. Peter Jopp was now at the wheel and slowly he drew ahead of the Cooper. A pit stop by the latter put Peter just over a lap ahead, but then the Cooper began to catch up again. John Eason Gibson and his timekeepers were convinced that Peter was a lap ahead of the Cooper, but Colin Chapman was not so sure and insisted that the "Faster" signal be given. Peter tried to increase speed but this only resulted in a spin so with just over an hour to go, the car was brought in and without oil or fuel being added, Reg shot back into the race. Refreshed by rest, the new driver began slowly to draw away from the Cooper. The chase was on—a chase which was not necessary. The little green car flew round faster and faster, and soon the stop watches in the pit showed that he might catch the Cooper, but it would be a close thing. As the two cars flashed past the pits just before 4 p.m., there was still quite a gap between them. At the start of the Mulsanne straight, Reg suddenly saw the Belgian-entered Jaguar of Laurent and Rousselle in his mirror. By frantic arm waving he conveyed to the driver of the larger car that he wanted a tow past the Cooper in front of him, and the response was immediate. The little Lotus tucked in behind the tail-finned car and was sucked along down the long straight, the driver of the larger car being very careful not to get too far ahead of his charge. It was a shock to the Cooper driver to be passed at speed at the end of the straight by the Lotus—still nudging the tail of its benefactor!

The pit personnel could hardly believe their eyes when the Lotus crossed the line well ahead of the Cooper, but they did not stop to reason why for they were too busy congratulating each other. So, after two unfortunate retirements, the third car "brought home the bacon" with a win in the 750-1100cc class at an average speed of 87.97 mph, taking fourth place in the Index of Performance and seventh place on general classification. The little car had completed 252 laps in the 24 hours and had enabled Colin to keep his promise of the year before that he would be back again to win. It transpired that both the charts and the timekeepers had been correct, and that the last hour's drama had not really been necessary, as was confirmed later by John Cooper, who couldn't understand why the Lotus—a lap ahead—should suddenly start racing as if it were a 5-lap club event.

A very elated team returned to Mayet, and M. Mica, after 24 hours at the circuit providing for the entourage, worked miracles again and provided a wonderful celebration dinner. The drivers and mechanics were tired and dirty after all their hard work in horrible weather, but the wine that flowed that Sunday evening soon revived them.

The second visit to "Les Vingt-Quatre Heures" had added much to the experience of the team in long-distance racing. When the official figures were published, they told the pleasing story that over the measured kilometre on the Mulsanne straight, the 1500 had averaged 128.2 mph and the class-winning 1100, 119.44 mph—concrete proof of the aerodynamic efficiency of the Hornsey cars. However, Colin and Mike were looking at the 138.09 mph recorded by the fastest Porsche, and were wondering if the new 1500cc engine being developed by Climax's would enable them to comfortably exceed that figure in 1957.

There was no need for Colin to assure M. Mica of his return the next year—that was obvious. The proprietor of the Auberge de St. Nicholas was very proud of his visitors from England and already was assuring his friends and the local press that next year Lotus would return to win even more prizes.

Another 1956 winner. Less than three months after scoring their first success at Le Mans Team Lotus were record-breaking at Monza with this 'bubble-top' 11, which caused quite a stir when it appeared on the roads near the Hornsey factory.

12.

Room for one only

THE ADVENT IN 1957 of a new International Formula 2 for racing cars of up to 1500cc unsupercharged was of great interest to Lotus. This new formula would give a chance of continuing development of all that had been learned on the 1100 and 1500cc sports cars without the encumbrances of a full-width body and other road equipment such as lights and wings. To Colin Chapman it presented a grand opportunity for a full-scale design exercise, although he realised only too well that racing a team of single-seaters as well as the sports cars would stretch Team Lotus resources to the limit. One of Lotus's main rivals, Coopers, had already shown the paces of their new single-seater at the end of the 1956 season with very satisfactory results, and if rumour was correct there was an F2 Ferrari on the stocks for the 1957 season.

These prospects acted as a spur to Colin, who went to work at his drawing board with the aim of producing an exceedingly light car which would hold the road better than anything the opposition could devise. The result of his labours, aided considerably by Harry Mundy, was the sleek green form that appeared on the Lotus stand at the 1956 Earls Court Motor Show. So short had been the design stage of the car that it was far from complete—neither engine nor gearbox having any internals!

The Eleven, of course, had influenced the new F2 car, but in many respects the design was strikingly new. At the front the swing axle had disappeared but the new layout was arranged so as to retain the characteristics of a swing axle of 40 inches effective length. In a static position the front wheels had a 1 degree positive camber and 5 degree castor angle. The new suspension was controlled by a double wishbone system with the front member of the top wishbone doubling up as an anti-roll bar, the springing and damping still being controlled by direct-acting combined spring and shock absorber units. It was realised that the high speed potential of the single-seater would produce a further increase in gyroscopic loading if the swing axle had been retained, and so feeling that the limit must nearly have been reached Colin had decided to adopt a fairly conventional wishbone layout. A proprietary king-post assembly was used, but a heavier than standard stub-pin was fitted which permitted a wider bearing spacing in the wheel hub. This, in its turn, enabled the wheel bearings to deal with the slight increase of load brought about by fitting the disc brake calipers ahead of the king-post in order to assist the cooling.

Originally, a de Dion rear axle assembly was fitted, of very similar design to that used on the Eleven, but with one radius arm only each side and a central location for the de Dion tube instead of the earlier Panhard rod. The layout was so designed that the lines of action of the fore and aft location (radius arms) and the vertical location (suspension unit) passed through the wheel hub axis, thus relieving the tube of all major loads other than side bending loads. However, following tests and early competition with the new car it was found desirable to incorporate a rear suspension in which the camber angle altered slightly with the load imposed and so reduced handling changes to a minimum. With the main fuel tank in the tail of

Above: Cliff Allison, pursued by Stirling Moss's Cooper, on his way to victory in the F2 section of the Glover Trophy race at Goodwood in 1958. Below: Graham Hill holds a tight, understeering line in the single-seater Lotus.

Above: The prototype Formula 2 car was fitted with a de Dion rear axle, although this was soon replaced by the Chapman strut suspension. Below: The twin-ohc Coventry Climax engine was a tight fit in the pencil-slim body.

the car the load change over the rear axle was quite appreciable between a full and empty tank and this requirement was met by the clever Chapman independent strut-type suspension.

This newer type of rear suspension proved very satisfactory, and following the correction of rather awesome teething troubles, such as knotted drive shafts, it was fitted to all the cars. In the strut system there were three basic members—the drive shaft which located the wheel laterally, a forward-facing radius arm, and the strut member comprising coil spring and damper. These three members converged into an aluminium casing just behind the wheel in which there were two wheel bearings. The radius arm was attached to a lug containing two small bearings, with a distance piece between them, projecting from the front of the casing, and the suspension unit was shrunk into a circular housing at the top of the casing. This latter unit leant inwards and was attached to a lug high on the side of the tail of the car. The drive shaft, with universal joints each end, was inclined upwards by 3 degrees towards the wheel end when static, so giving the wheels a slight negative camber. The arrangement of the geometry allowed the contact point of the tyre with the road to move in a near vertical path between the limits of usable wheel deflection. So, for instance, as the wheel moved inwards on the arc described by the axle on bump it was compensated by the outward movement from this arc at the point of tyre contact with the road. The results of this strut suspension were very satisfactory, drivers reporting that the handling of the cars was virtually identical whether the fuel tank was full or empty. A weight advantage was also gained over the de Dion layout.

The new front and rear suspensions were attached to a chassis frame very much in the Lotus tradition. The unit was a welded, multi-tubular structure, and together with attachment brackets only weighed 47 lb. The lower main longitudinal members were 1 in square 20 s.w.g. tubes, and the upper members 1 in diameter tubes of the same gauge; ¾ in diameter tubes of similar gauge were used for bracing members. With a racing car the chassis members are naturally disposed nearer to the polar axis of the chassis frame and consequently Colin Chapman found it more difficult to obtain the same degree of stiffness for any given weight as was possible in the wide-framed sports car. He overcame this by making use of the very strong crankcase of the Coventry Climax engine. This was mounted rigidly in the chassis in the form of a torque box so greatly supplementing the torsional stiffness of the unit. To do this a rear engine plate of 10-gauge strong alloy was made up and incorporated as a chassis bulkhead at four attachment points, and the front engine bearers were bolted straight to the chassis with 5/16 in high-tensile bolts.

The power unit on which all British constructors were pinning their faith for this new formula was the twin-overhead-camshaft Coventry Climax F.P.F. unit of 1475cc. Basically this unit was designed to produce 142 bhp at 7,200 rpm but it was not long before the "boys" were extracting over 150 bhp. Initially the engine was run on twin-choke Weber carburettors, but these were replaced by the new twin-choke 1¾ in bore SU carburettors directly they became readily available. With an all-up weight of 280 lb this dry-sump engine obviously had great possibilities, but initial experience with the power unit was disappointing. Piston and valve failure were an all-too-common experience in the early part of 1957, several engines being seriously damaged by a dropped valve. However, by the end of the season the teething troubles had been overcome and a good degree of reliability obtained. There was plenty of power, as was proved when the Lotus was driven round the Oulton Park circuit at a speed in excess of the lap record set up by a 1956 works G.P. Maserati.

Drive was taken via a twin-plate 7¼ in diameter Borg and Beck clutch to a two-piece propeller shaft. As the engine was mounted in the front of the car this shaft had to pass beneath the driver's seat, and so in order to keep the seating position low it was kept small in diameter. A hollow steel shaft of ¾ in outside diameter was used, any tendency to whip being taken care of by a centrally-placed steady bearing.

In order to obtain a low seating position it was decided to build a special combined gearbox and back axle unit—no small task for a concern the size of Lotus. In this work Colin was greatly assisted by Harry Mundy, A.M.I.Mech.E., M.S.A.E., at that time technical editor of *Autocar,* and by Richard Ansdale, who did the detail design work. The constant-mesh unit that this trio produced was a masterpiece of compact design and provided four essential advantages. First, a 5 in step-down in the transmission line was achieved by using a hypoid crown-wheel and pinion, of about 1 in offset, and virtually five pairs of transfer gears, which ran between the normal pinion bearings and at 4 in shaft centres. These pairs of transfer gears were all similar in general dimensions except for the number of teeth, and were readily interchangeable to permit alternative top gear ratios and changes of intermediate gearing to suit different circuits. Secondly, there was a reduction in the power loss of the transmission and in heat generated by having only one meshing point on the indirect gears. Thirdly, with a combined unit having a rather high rotational speed (top gear was an overdrive) and wide gear centres, a reduction in loading and a considerable saving in weight was achieved by comparison with a more conventional layout. Also, the weight, only 49 lb without brakes, etc., was in the right place—over the back axle. Lastly, the gear ratios were quickly interchangeable with the box in position—a great advantage when racing. In fact it only took about ten minutes to remove the propeller shaft, couplings, centre bearing and front cover of the box in order to expose the gears.

It was not possible to get the gears cut quickly enough in Britain so Colin had to order these from the German firm of Z.F.—a limited-slip differential of this company's manufacture also being incorporated. Although it was inconvenient to have components coming from so far the order to Germany did provide Colin and Hazel with a good excuse for a short trip in early March to see how the gears were coming along and also to look in at the Geneva Motor Show. At the latter, Ghia were exhibiting a special sports body on the Mark 9 chassis displayed at Earls Court in 1955. The original intention had been a closed coupe, but shortage of time had dictated the open version.

To return to the F2's "revolutionary" gearbox. Great attention was paid to the oiling arrangements for both the gear train and also the

Graham Hill, surrounded by Coopers, makes a good start in a Formula 2 race at sunny Goodwood.

final drive unit. A pressure and scavenge pump was driven off the input shaft of the gearbox, the main oil supply being kept in the lower half of the differential casing. From there the pressure pump fed oil through the centre of the selector sleeve and out of holes direct on to the backs of the mating teeth. This oil was then picked up by the scavenge pump to feed the bevel pinion, the crownwheel lubricating itself by dipping in the main supply. But oiling troubles beset the unit directly it was tested. For a time everything would function perfectly, then suddenly the crownwheel and pinion would fail, and each time inspection showed the failure to be due to an apparent lack of oil, although the level in the differential housing was quite adequate. As race meeting followed race meeting with the same unhappy results all manner of remedies were tried, resulting in the unit being exhaustively tested by Buck and Hickman Ltd on a special rig which measured vibration, distortion and temperature. Their final report still further added to the puzzle, for they found the unit to be mechanically perfect.

With the possibility of case distortion ruled out full attention was turned to the oiling side again and a unit was run in the engine test house under conditions similar to racing—high revs and much gear changing—then suddenly the answer presented itself. Whilst the power was being transmitted the level in the differential casing was inspected and found to be well below the crownwheel. Directly the revolutions dropped the level went up and the crownwheel once again dipped in the lubricant. Tests proved that at high revolutions as much as two pints of oil was being held in suspension in the gear-train. The remedy to this elusive fault was quickly found by speeding up the delivery of the pressure and scavenge pump and redirecting the flow. A deflector was also fitted to ensure that any oil in the vicinity of the crownwheel would be thrown on to the rotating teeth. Throughout all these trials and tribulations the gearbox itself gave no trouble—a credit to the ingenuity of its designers. One feature of this gearbox which made it so suitable for racing requirements was the fact that with only one additional pair of gears it was possible to get six different top gear ratios and a comprehensive selection of intermediate ratios; overall ratios varied between 3.2 to 1 and 10 to 1. Actual gear-changing had its difficulties and drivers had to learn the art of pulling to the right for an upward change or pressing to the left for a downward change; the "gate" for the five-speed was a succession of "Zs", with a gear at the bottom of each "Z".

Engine lubrication did not present any difficulties, and the dry sump was fed from a two-gallon tank mounted on the extreme rear chassis tubes. Originally it had been planned to transmit this oil in the lower chassis tubes, but this proved impractical and pipes were fitted instead. Two petrol tanks were fitted, the main one in the tail carrying 15 gallons and an auxiliary one above the driver's legs containing 12 gallons.

Brakes were 9 in diameter Girling discs with quick-change segmental pads. The rear units were centrally mounted each side of the differential housing, and at the front they were mounted outboard. Steering was by rack-and-pinion with two equal-length track rods connecting the rearward-facing steering arms. Two universal joints were incorporated in the steering column so as to by-pass the engine mass.

Outwardly the most striking difference between the F2 car and earlier Lotuses was the wheels. These were cast disc-type magnesium alloy units which bolted on and so dispensed with the heavy knock-on assembly. Colin chose this design as he required the lightest and strongest possible type of wheel since unsprung weight represented a major problem with such a lightweight vehicle. In order to keep weight down the web of the wheel had to be as thin as possible, consistent with strength and for ease of manufacture—the foundry liking uniform thickness. In order to satisfy these two requirements and yet obtain the required variation in bending strength throughout the wheel the "wobbly web" principle was employed. With this the peripheral distance at various radii from the hub is kept approximately constant, which results in quite deep folds near the hub where great strength is required. These folds fade out to quite shallow waves at the rim where loads are less. Another advantage of this continuous-web wheel is that fatigue life of the wheel is greatly enhanced by the absence of "holes" cast between the "spokes", so removing the chance of rough edges which might provide starting points for fatigue cracks.

Another aspect which arose during the design stage of the new bolt-on wheels was that of wheel-changing during a race. First, with an estimated dry weight of 620 lb for the complete car, it was unlikely under normal conditions that the tyres would wear out during a race of up to grand prix distance of 300 miles. Secondly, Colin reckoned that in the new formula the racing was going to be so competitive that a wheel change would put you "out of the money" anyway. With these thoughts in mind he was quite happy to attach the wheels by a six-bolt fixing. At the front of the car the hubs were integral with the wheels and the bolts held the brake discs in place. The six bolts in each rear wheel actually located them to the axle.

A final point in favour of the "wobbly web" wheels concerned cooling of the front brakes. Although there was plenty of air about with a monoposto racing car body the convolutions of the wheel created air turbulence around the brake disc, so further improving cooling.

Great attention was paid to the question of airflow and cooling, and here Frank Costin was well primed for he had already designed the successful single-seater body for the Vanwall grand prix car. In the usual Lotus fashion the radiator, with its built-in header tank, was fully ducted. This unit was leant backwards just behind the anti-roll bar so as to reduce the height of the bonnet line and keep the weight of water in the header tank at the top of the radiator over the front wheel centres. The body of the car was designed to produce a minimum frontal area whilst still preserving a reasonably clean shape overall. As the body was not of the all-enveloping type it was not as efficient aerodynamically as the Eleven. This removed the necessity to provide a tail fin or head-fairing to stabilise centre of pressure movement. In order to increase driver comfort the cockpit was surrounded by a generous wrap-round screen and a tail of approximately the same height as the top of a driver's shoulders.

Early experience with the Mark 6 dictated the treatment given to the carburettor air intakes.

Below: Cliff Allison at Spa for the 1958 Belgian GP, which he might have won had the race been one lap longer. Bottom: The simple, functional cockpit with the novel 'zig-zag' gear-shift quadrant on the left.

created by the exposed front suspension parts and wheels caused a dead area behind them. The moving part having the most profound effect on this situation is the top of the wheel, which, when on the move, is travelling forwards at twice the speed of the car and is tending to throw forward the air that it carries around with it, and this air spills into the rearward airflow past the car so making the relatively calm pocket. It was into this area that the air intake carburettors of the F2 car protruded, with a small cowling covering their tops.

When the internals for the engine and gearbox were available the completed dry weight for the racing car was found to be just under 6½ cwt—an extremely light weight for a car measuring 10 ft 11 in overall. Other dimensions were wheelbase 7 ft 4 in and front and rear track 4 ft.

Unfortunately, castings and gears for the gearbox took a long time to materialise, so early in March, 1957 a car was fitted with a conventional proprietary gearbox which was mounted behind the engine and fitted with a gearchange in the approximate position that the correct one would occupy. This car was extensively tested at Silverstone by Colin Chapman and Ron Flockhart.

Easter saw the debut of the F2 car in the hands of Team Lotus driver Cliff Allison at Goodwood. Initially the car went very well, displaying good road holding and very impressive, wheelspin-free acceleration, but alas the "drive" failed when Cliff was lying a good third behind two Coopers. There were two cars ready for the Formula 2 races at the Whitsun Brands Hatch meeting—Cliff's now being fitted with the strut-type rear suspension. The other retained the de Dion axle and was driven by team driver Mackay Fraser. Back axle trouble still hampered the Hornsey cars, Cliff retiring with high gearbox oil temperature when dicing with the leaders in both the races. "Mac" managed to finish third and second to give him a combined second place behind Jack Brabham in the very fast works Cooper. Mac could only find two gears in his box towards the end of the second race, and in order to save flogging his engine he made for the pits, only to be hounded out again by the Lotus mechanics who realised he had a chance of a good placing.

Team headquarters at Hornsey. One single-seater gets a new set of wheels while a later chassis frame is hoisted awaiting completion.

Numerous tests with wool tufts on the square-cut car with wings removed had shown that the air close to the bonnet sides was virtually stationary, the tufts certainly not blowing back along the body. The reason for this was that the turbulence

There followed a period of rest from Formula 2 for Team Lotus as they were very busily engaged at Le Mans, Rouen, Reims, Roskilde and Spa. During this interval extensive tests went on the locate the reason for the back axle failures. Then on Saturday, September 14th, the team were at Silverstone for the BRDC *Daily Express* Trophy race with much higher hopes, armed with three cars, all with strut-type rear suspensions and back axles that worked! There was to be a Formula 2 section of the Trophy race for GP cars and the event was to be run in two heats and a final. Cliff Allison was in the first heat, but after stalling on the starting grid and being pushed off, the car retired amidst a cloud of smoke at Copse Corner, but not before gaining the lead in the F2 category. Sports car team driver Keith Hall was driving an F2 car in the second heat and the third car was given to Henry Taylor. Keith Hall had an unlucky first race with the car when something broke in the rear suspension and he had to abandon the car at Club Corner. Henry Taylor went very well and then was called in to hand over to Cliff Allison, who then proceeded to travel at a terrific speed in an effort to catch the race leaders. This resulted in Cliff gaining a place in the fifth row of the starting grid for the final, one row ahead of Dennis Taylor in his privately owned F2 Lotus. The field for the final consisted of three makes of British cars facing five GP Maseratis, the two Lotuses having as compatriots three BRMs and no less than 16 Coopers. On lap 12 Cliff sailed past Roy Salvadori's works Cooper to lead the Formula 2 race, and on lap 13 set up a new Formula 2 lap record of 99.41 mph—a fantastic speed for a 1500cc car. With three laps to go the Lotus was miles ahead of the Formula 2 opposition and the only signal from Cliff's pit was "EASY". Perhaps this instruction was his undoing, for he made an error at Becketts Corner—a rare occurrence for this fast, steady driver—charged the barricades and damaged the car too badly to continue. Luckily the driver was not hurt, just fed up; very bad luck after such a brilliant drive.

Spurred on by the performance of the cars Team Lotus entered their three cars for the Formula 2 race at Goodwood a fortnight later. This time the third car was driven by the new Team Lotus recruit, Graham Hill. The race turned out to be the fastest ever run at Goodwood, being won by Roy Salvadori in the works Cooper at an average of 94.43 mph. Jack Brabham in the other works Cooper fought all the way and set the fastest lap at 96 mph. Cliff was baulked at the start by Brooks when his gearbox failed, but made up ground to finish a good third, while Graham Hill quickly acclimatised himself to the new car and drove very well. Poor Keith Hill had the radius arm locating bolt shear in the rear suspension and parked his car in the protective ditch at Fordwater. At this meeting Team Lotus had forsaken Dunlop tyres and had fitted their cars with Continentals. The new tread pattern appeared to suit the lightweight cars, for drivers improved on earlier lap times and reported that the handling of the cars appeared to be improved.

All Formula 2 eyes were on the Gold Cup and £1,000 first prize to be won at Oulton Park a week later. Team Lotus entries were the same as at Goodwood and initially the three cars went excellently. Unfortunately, petty troubles robbed both Graham Hill and Keith Hall of the finishing positions they deserved, and they finished eleventh and twelfth. Graham, however, put in the fastest lap of the race at 87.81 mph—a new class record and equal to the all-out lap record previously held by Stirling Moss in his GP Maserati! Cliff Allison strove valiantly to catch race leader Jack Brabham, but failed by just over half a minute. Cliff's second place and the efforts of the other two team members gave them consolation, however, in the form of the team award.

So ended the initial season of the first Lotus racing car—not perhaps so dynamic as the successful sports car, but nevertheless rewarding, particularly in the technical field. During 1957 seven single-seater cars had been built, all eventually sporting the "strut" rear suspension. In Britain the three team cars were backed up by private owner Dennis Taylor, who perservered with his car and although he had his troubles put up some good performances. The other three cars went to Messrs. Brooke (of Brooke Bond Tea), Voegler and Tadgell, but did not feature much in competition motoring, the last of these three cars being shipped to New Zealand.

103

13.

Improving a winner

DURING 1956 THE ELEVEN had proved most satisfactory so it was decided to leave the design basically unchanged for 1957. Orders from both home and abroad were rolling in so production was able to continue through the winter months and Colin and his design team were left free to concentrate on the racing car and a very special product that was to be constructed behind closed doors.

As 1957 began Lotus had a "spring clean" in anticipation of the busy season ahead. The body building firm which had occupied the rear part of the original stable moved to new premises in Edmonton and Team Lotus were able to take over their old premises for a racing department. Walls were painted, benches built and tool racks erected. The front part of the old stable now became a repair shop, still leaving two minute offices between the two workshops. In these two small spaces three and sometimes four people had to work. The occupants of these offices were additions to the staff brought about by the growth of Lotus Engineering Company Ltd. Colin Bennett occupied the front office with a secretary and set up a sales headquarters. For some time Colin had given part-time help to Lotus on export sales matters and now that the volume of work was sufficient he was able to join the company on a full-time basis. Colin's association with Lotus went back a long time to the days when he was team manager to the Peter Gammon, Michael Anthony, Colin Chapman trio, and to his credit at that time went the origination of "TEAM LOTUS". The second office was the domicile of "Accounts" presided over by Ron Clover, who quickly realised that his stamina was to be sorely tested in this exacting branch of Lotus activities!

There was not enough room now to carry out engine tests and work on components such as gearboxes and back-axles in the main assembly shop so a special engine shop was constructed beside the new Team Lotus workshop. Speed was essential in the construction of the new shop as council permission was a little unsure and so building had to be executed quickly whilst a pile of chassis frames camouflaged activities from prying eyes! Graham Hill was put in charge of the engine shop, with John Campbell-Jones as his assistant.

A further addition to the staff was draughtsman Ian Jones who had already been working with Colin Chapman in his spare time. It was not possible for Ian to work at Colin's home all the time so somewhere had to be found for his drawing board. The solution was the old attic above the stable where spare parts had previously been stowed. So Ian was installed with a vertical ladder as his only means of contact with the outside world—nobody could accuse Lotus of wasting space! It soon became very evident that the provision of a full-time draughtsman on the staff was providential, for the part-time help from Colin's old team of Peter Ross and Mac McIntosh became less and less. Apparently Lotus had only themselves to blame for this for they had helped these two to construct their own Elevens at advantageous terms in recompense for their hard work. The result of this was that Peter started to race, and spent all his spare time tuning his car, and Mac went courting and ended up by getting married!

In America Jay Chamberlain was becoming more and more active as Lotus after Lotus passed through his hands. He was conducting extensive experiments with special camshafts for the Climax engines which met with most rewarding results. All of this information he passed on, of course, to Mike Costin and his band of mechanics. Jay also provided the new engine shop with a magnificent roller dynamometer which enabled horsepower readings to be taken from the rear wheels. The gadget consisted of double rollers which were set in the floor of the workshop and an instrument panel consisting of a mass of dials. In all, this item of equipment supplied at a special price by Jay, cost close on £1,000! Typically Lotus were too busy to find out how it worked and for months resorted to their "round-the-block" method of testing a car. It was not in fact until after the tragic Reims race in July that the dynamometer was first used. Jay called at the works and although still very stiff from his unpleasant crash insisted on getting the equipment working. This he did and quickly showed the Lotus mechanics what a valuable piece of mechanism it was for providing accurate comparisons of engine power when tuning cars. Items such as distributor settings could be done in a few minutes with the rear wheels of the car driving the rollers whilst the distributor was rotated and one watched the dials of the dynamometer for the best setting.

A most unexpected surprise gave a good start to the year when on February 13th Colin Chapman was awarded the Ferodo Gold Trophy for the most outstanding British contribution to the sport of motor racing in 1956. The presentation by John Eason Gibson, Secretary of the British Racing Drivers Club, took place in front of the B.B.C. Television cameras and the official citation to the award read: "Mr. A.C.B. Chapman is responsible for the design and construction of Lotus sports cars and made an important design contribution to the advancement of the design of a British Grand Prix racing car". This latter car was, of course, the Vanwall. The presentation was most aptly timed for on the following night the president of Club Lotus was able to show the magnificent gold trophy and the equally fine gold replica to the members attending the Club's first annual general meeting.

Although the 1957 Eleven was to resemble the 1956 car very closely Colin was keen to incorporate the wishbone front suspension as fitted to the F2 car and to make detailed alterations to the rear-end so that the power of the twin-cam 1,500cc Climax engine could be accommodated. The main alteration made to enable the latter was to increase the 18-gauge de Dion tube from 3-in diameter to $3\frac{5}{8}$-in diameter. This not only strengthened the assembly but allowed 1300-series Hardy Spicer joints to be used at the outboard end where they passed through the tube instead of the earlier 1100-series. A prototype chassis was started on these lines just before Colin left for Mexico to co-drive with Joe Sheppard and Dick Dungan in an 1,100cc Eleven at Sebring. The trip was successful as the car won the 1,100cc class and came third in the Index of Performance. Colin extended his stay a little and went on a tour of agents handling Lotus cars with distributor Jay Chamberlain.

On his return he found that the prototype car was completed and he gave it a thorough test. It is interesting to note that this new car bore chassis number 300—proof of the remarkable number of cars the small factory had produced in the four years since the first production Mark 6. The new car differed very little in handling characteristics from its predecessor, although one apparent advantage of the wishbone front suspension was the elimination of the tendency to wander at high speeds on bumpy surfaces. Plans were immediately put in hand for the production of "wishbone" cars for Team Lotus, for Colin was still very keen that the sports cars should be able to match anything the opposition had to offer. Sports cars were the main business of Lotus, and his hope was that the new racing car would help to improve these sports cars. Colin had used much of the Eleven to design the F2 car, and he now hoped that in return the single-seater would benefit the 1957 sports cars.

On a basic chassis it was now possible to offer a range of four distinct Elevens, whereas there had been three models in 1956. First came the Sports 45 (b.h.p.) with Ford engine, live rear-axle and drum brakes, next the Club 75 with Climax engine

105

replacing the Ford, then the Le Mans 85 with the de Dion and disc brakes and finally the newcomer, the Le Mans 150 with twin-overhead-camshaft engine. As larger tyres were required on the latter car the body contours of the standard car were altered slightly to provide bigger wheel arches. In the case of the Sports and Club models the original swing front axle was retained and the back axle produced by BMC for the Nash Metropolitan replaced the Ford unit used in 1956. The nose-piece of this new hypoid final drive unit was also used in the de Dion assembly on the two Le Mans cars. The standard ratio fitted was 4.875 to 1, but there were six other alternative ratios available—5.375, 5.125, 4.55, 4.22, 3.89 or 3.73 to 1. Typical speeds per 1,000 rpm on standard 5.00 by 15 rear tyres with the more popular of these various axle ratios were 3.89 to 1—19.52 mph, 4.22 to 1—18 mph, 4.55 to 1—16.7 mph and 4.89 to 1—15.55 mph. The basic prices of these four models when purchased complete were: Le Mans 150—£2,885, Le Mans 85—£1,690, Club 75—£1,309, Sports 45—£1,021. When the car and various proprietary components were obtained and assembled by the owner himself a saving of about 17 per cent on these prices could be made.

As in the case of the final 1956 cars the new Eleven complied fully with Appendix C—the international regulations governing this type of car. This was a most essential requirement for both Team Lotus and individual customers were now competing more and more in international competitions.

Following animated discussions in such congenial surroundings as the Steering Wheel Club or at the many Club dinner and dances which took place during the closed season the Team Lotus drivers were announced. There were to be two teams for 1957, the first consisting of Mac Fraser, Cliff Allison and perhaps Colin himself, with a second team of private owners receiving works support, of Keith Hall, Peter Ashdown and Alan Stacey. Work began immediately on building three 1,100cc cars for the last three drivers, together with a further 1,100cc and 1,500cc single-cam car for Team Lotus. Whilst these were in the course of construction orders were received from Dan Margulies, Brian Naylor, John Coombs and Bill

Below: Lotus 11 line-up at Hornsey outside the new showroom. Bottom: Mike Costin driving the Le Mans 11 at Brands Hatch on Boxing Day 1957. Right: The Le Mans 11 laid bare. Below right: Graham Hill and Alfred Woolf showing off the 1956 Le Mans 11 to the television cameras.

Frost for the new car. The former required an 1,100cc car in a great hurry for continental racing and was promptly sold the prototype car. Brian Naylor again wanted a car for a Maserati engine—this time a 2 litre unit. Although really against the new principles of Lotus, Colin agreed to build such a car having extracted the promise from Brian that at times he would run his 2 litre under the name of Team Lotus. John Coombs wanted to fit the new twin-cam engine while Bill Frost was getting together a single-cam 1500 for his car. This spate of orders for the "wishbone" car meant much round-the-clock activity at Hornsey as everybody wanted delivery in time for the BRDC Empire Trophy Race on April 6th—an impossibility.

The new season began in earnest on March 31st and immediately the earlier Elevens continued their winning ways. However, the works 1957 Eleven did not appear until the Empire Trophy race at Oulton Park, powered by a single-cam 1,500cc Climax engine and sporting the magnesium alloy wheels. Colin Chapman drove the car and in Class B of the Trophy race had a magnificent duel with Ron Flockhart in John Coombs' 1956 1,500cc car, but he spun at Cascades corner and Ron went through to win.

Brian Naylor also had his car ready in time for this race, but a spin at Esso Bend ended his progress on the 20th lap. Brian had fitted knock-on wire wheels to his car—a fashion that was to prove more popular than the rather more expensive disc wheels.

John Coombs had his new car ready for the Goodwood Easter Monday meeting but regrettably troubles in practice made the car a non-starter. However, Ron Flockhart was not deprived of a drive as John had not parted with the single-cam car. Mac Fraser drove the Team Lotus 1500 in the Formula 2 race, but after lapping very fast he locked his brakes in the chicane and went straight on into the barrier, causing a considerably dented nose. Probably this was just the answer that the B.B.C. cameraman was requiring when he asked before the race "how fast do they go through the charades?"! As quick as a flash the Team Lotus mechanics had ripped the bonnet off John Coombs' new car in the paddock in order to

Traffic jam at Brands Hatch as Chris Bristow gets into a spot of bother at Druids Hill Bend in his 11. Note the preponderance of Lotus cars in this sports car race, which typifies the marque's domination in the fifties.

replace the one crumpled by Mac. Colin Chapman was in the repaired car in no time, and whistled it off on a warming-up lap to stop the scrutineers noticing a considerable degree of toe-out on the front wheels. The Chichester Cup became a repetition of Oulton Park with a fine battle between Colin and Ron after Roy Salvadori in the Cooper sports car with twin-cam 1500cc engine had dropped out. Colin made no mistake this time, and led Ron over the line by a bare two seconds. Brian Naylor rounded off the day by winning the 2 lite class of the 21-lap scratch race for sports cars exceeding 1,500cc.

On the Saturday following Goodwood the new car scored its first victory abroad at the first race meeting to be held in Austria since the war. The meeting took place at Aspern on one of Vienna's main airfields and one or two of the local drivers showed the spectators a new and mechanised version of the Viennese Waltz! Tony Hogg was driving Dan Margulies' new car and after a very steady drive he won the 1,100cc class of this "Flugplatzrennan Wien-Aspern". Peter Ross had his new Club model at the meeting, and after some sharp spins on the bumpy surface in the early part of the race he followed Tony home in second place.

The works 1500 received its baptism on the hills in early May in the hands of Edward Lewis at Prescott. Edward was waiting delivery of a special "square-cut" car and so had been loaned the Eleven in order to keep his hand in. This he did very well by winning the 1,101–1,600cc class, setting a new class record for the climb in 46.90 secs.

A week later three Team Lotus cars were taking part in major continental events. An 1,100cc car had been completed and Brian Naylor was running as a team member. The 2-litre car went to Spa together with Mac Fraser and the 1,500cc car. Gregor Grant, Editor of *Autosport*, took over the 1100 for a saunter round Italy, more commonly known as the Mille Miglia! At Spa, Mac drove brilliantly in the 132-miles sports car race, put in a fastest lap at 103.36 mph, and finished a complete lap ahead of his class which included two Porsche Spyders. His meteoric drive gave him seventh place overall, ahead of two DB3S Aston Martins, a D-type Jaguar and a Cooper-Jaguar. Brian Naylor won his class comfortably, disposing of 2 litre Ferraris and Maseratis. Poor Gregor Grant was not so fortunate as he was plagued with a leaking fuel tank which eventually burst when he was only 70 miles from the finish. His retirement was a great pity for at the time of the tank failing he was lying second in the 750-1,100cc class—a class dominated by OSCAs, which finished 1-2-3 Gregor tells his story of this race in Chapter 22.

With only a week's rest Brian Naylor was at Silverstone on May 18th to win four 10-lap races with his 2 litre car. Bill Frost had his new 1,500cc single-cam-engined car at this meeting and notched up a win and a second place. A day later at Snetterton Cliff Allison in the works 1500 won the 1,100-2,000cc race as he liked—the car proving much quicker than all the 2 litres.

Another week's respite and Brian Naylor was at Oulton Park. Result—wins in both the 2,000cc and 3,000cc races. A fortnight's gap followed before Brian continued his run of successes with a win in the 2 litre class at St. Etienne. Dan Margulies drove his new car at this event in the 1,100cc class of the 1,500cc event, and finished third behind earlier Elevens of Bob Hicks and Eugene Hall.

Whitsun saw Colin Chapman back at the wheel in the 10-lap 1,101-2,000cc sports car race at Brands Hatch, which he won from Roy Salvadori in the works Cooper, with Bill Frost third. Team Lotus had a very slick 1-2-3 victory in the 1,100cc sports car race with the private owner/team drivers using their new cars to good advantage; Keith Hall won with Peter Ashdown second and Alan Stacey third. Ivor Bueb now had a new 1,100cc car and he brought it home fifth on its first outing at this meeting. Over the holiday weekend Brian Naylor journeyed to Chimay in Belgium and put up a new circuit record at 107.30 mph, but after setting the pace in the early part of the race he was forced to retire with a broken oil pipe.

Whit Monday, and Colin met Roy Salvadori again, this time at the Crystal Palace in the 1,100-2,000cc sports car race. Despite being slightly down on power with his single-cam 1,500cc engine against the Cooper's twin, Colin hung on grimly to the manx-tailed car, often drawing alongside on braking. By a supreme effort he slammed past Roy on the last bend, and by some artful dodging amongst the tail-enders managed to win by a nose. Colin drove the 1,100cc car which had been loaned to Gregor Grant in the 1,100cc race and found the extra weight built into this car in order to cope with a thousand miles of Italian roads rather a disadvantage. He had to give best to fellow team member Keith Hall, who won the race and gave as good as he got! During his efforts to keep ahead of the "gaffer", Keith set up a new class record at 77.22 mph. Peter Ashdown and Alan Stacey were upholding the Team Lotus name at Goodwood on the same day and Alan was able to "bring home the bacon" by winning the 1,100cc event after Peter had packed up with electrical bothers and race leader Innes Ireland in his 1956 Eleven broke his camshaft on the very last lap!

With the Whit weekend over, feverish activity began at Hornsey as there were five special cars to build for Le Mans in under a fortnight's time. In fact there were only six days available in which to build these cars before they were due to be shipped across the Channel. During those six days and nights the electricity meters at 7 Tottenham Lane did not cease to turn for one moment, but the results achieved at the classic French race were more than recompense for all this hard work—four out of the four cars started finishing first, second and fourth in the 1,100cc class and first in the 750cc class, with the additional achievement of first and second in the coveted Index of Performance. The story of this wonderful victory is told in the next chapter.

After Le Mans the Team Lotus cars had gone straight to Rouen in preparation for the sports car races on the Rouen-les-Essarts circuit on Sunday, July 7th. Cliff Allison in the 750cc car dominated the small class of the Delamere-Deboutteville Cup and easily vanquished Panhard and Stanguellini opposition. Colin Chapman drove the 1,100cc car in the 751-1,100cc section of the race and had a terrific duel with de Tomaso in the new OSCA. It was a magnificent dice which took the two protagonists way ahead of the field, but near the end Colin had to dash in for water for a very hot engine, which allowed the OSCA to win easily. This bad luck was countered by Ron Flockhart driving John Coombs' twin-cam 1500 in the up-to-1500cc race, which he won easily, setting a new class lap record at 92.68 mph. Jay Chamberlain, fresh from his success at Le Mans, was driving the single-cam "non Le Mans" 1500 team car, and he finished second just ahead of Goethal's Porsche. Mac Fraser in the "Le Mans" 1500 had the bad luck to fracture a wheel-hub and leave the road when going very well after a bad start. Bill Frost was also out of luck, being put out with timing-wheel failure.

The meeting at Reims the following weekend was a tragic one for the team. First, in practice Jay Chamberlain received nasty injuries to his head, shoulder and ribs when his 1,100cc car left the road and was completely written off. Then Cliff Allison had a brush with the police over a road accident and landed in gaol! Colin was so busy trying to get Jay transferred to a Paris hospital and Cliff out of clink that he overlooked the regulation about presenting the cars for fuel-draining in the "parc ferme" before the 12-hour race. This caused the team to be disqualified. As the FIA had chosen to homologate the 1,100cc car as a Grand Touring machine under Appendix J prior to the event there was really no foundation to the grumbling indulged in by the Alfa Romeo Guilietta drivers during practice. However, the organisers insisted on the disqualification, and so Team Lotus were left with Saturday in which to prepare the two F2 cars and one 1,500cc sports car for the Formula 2 race on the Sunday. Mac Fraser drove the streamlined car and for 30 laps kept amongst the single-seaters, right on the tail of the Coopers of Jean Lucas and Tony Marsh in sixth place. Then on the way to Garenne it happened—the car left the road on a patch of oil dropped by another car when it "threw a rod", and turned over and the popular American driver succumbed to his serious injuries. Tragically, Marga Fraser, Mac's wife, was watching the race, having travelled up from their home in Bonassola on the Italian coast near Genoa. To her went everybody's sympathy as a very sad Team Lotus made their way back to England.

The 1957 Elevens dominated the 1,100cc section of the sports car race prior to the Grand Prix of Europe at Aintree a week later. Keith Hall won with Alan Stacey second, Ivor Bueb third and Peter Ashdown fourth.

Edward Lewis borrowed the 1,100cc works car for Great Auclum hill climb on July 27th, his new car still not being ready. Again he was successful and won the up-to-1,300cc sports car class. Tom Dickson of Perth now had a new 1,100cc car and celebrated this with a wonderful first outing at Crimond on the same day, winning three races including one for unlimited-capacity cars. His achievement was made all the more remarkable by the fact that he had only collected the bits to build his new car on the weekend prior to the race, and had worked flat-out through the week to construct the car in time. Tom's old Eleven was driven at the same meeting by Andy Walker who followed the previous owner home in second place in the up-to-1,500cc race.

August Bank Holiday Monday was a very active one with the BRSCC holding a championship meeting at Brands Hatch and the BARC staging their meeting at the Crystal Palace. In Kent, heat 1 of the 1,100cc race was won by Cliff Allison in the team car, and in heat 2 Graham Hill, driving Dr. Manton's new car, was first with Peter Ashdown second and Ivor Bueb third. The result in the final was well mixed—Cliff winning with Peter second and Ivor Bueb third. Colin Chapman won the up-to-1,500cc sports car race after Archie Scott-Brown in the very fast "flat-four" Elva-AJB had dropped out. Bill Frost finished third behind Graham Hill, who was now driving the new Willment 1,500cc sports car. Keith Hall and Alan Stacey had gone to "the Palace" and bored the spectators by finishing first and third in both the second heat and final of the 1,100cc race and also in the sports car scratch event.

Mallory Park held their meeting on the day after the Bank Holiday and Tom Dickson won the up-to-1,500cc sports car race and the first semi-final unlimited event. A fortnight later Lotuses were at the Mallory circuit again in strength and Malcolm Graham in his new Eleven came second in the "S" scratch race. At this event John Campbell-Jones proved that he was not only a great asset in the development shop at Hornsey,

Edward Lewis was loaned one of the works 11s several times during 1957 for hill-climbing, while awaiting delivery of his own car. Here he is climbing Rest-and-be-Thankful.

but could also handle an Eleven on the track when he won the 1,200cc scratch race in a 1957 Eleven.

In Denmark on August 17th and 18th a gala race meeting was held at Roskilde. Cliff Allison in the 1,500cc team car was star of the meeting, winning the event for racing sports cars up to 1,500cc with fellow team member Alan Stacey third. The boys had to work hard for their laurels as on each of the two days all competitors took part in two 6-lap heats and a 16-lap final, results being decided on a points basis. At the end of the first day Alan led with 42 points, Cliff was second with 39, Peter Ashdown was fourth and Bill Frost sixth. The second day's racing enabled Cliff to overtake Alan, after which all the competitors adjourned to a magnificent dinner in the famous Tivoli gardens in Copenhagen. A week later Cliff had a big slice of luck at Spa, where, with two laps to go in the 1,500cc race he was five seconds behind the race leader, de Tomaso, in the new desmondromic-valve OSCA and pushing him hard. Then the OSCA blew up most expensively under the terrific pressure, and a very surprised Cliff won the race, a lap ahead of a de Beaufort's Porsche.

Snetterton was very wet, cold and windy on September 1st, but this did not prevent Ivor Bueb from winning both the up-to-1,100cc and up-to-2,700cc sports car races. At Charterhall, however, the weather was bright and sunny, where Tom Dickson added wins to both the 1,200cc and 2,000cc sports car races.

For a change Bill Frost tried a sprint on September 7th, and at the Brighton Speed Trials won the 1,101-1,500cc class, also finishing second in the Brighton and Hove M.C's handicap class. On the same day another new Eleven was figuring in the results at the "Sunbac" meeting at Silverstone. M.G. Dickens was the owner of this car which was fitted with the new FWE 1,220cc Coventry Climax engine. This power unit was a successor to the engine tried by Mike Hawthorn a year earlier, and was designed for the American market with an eye on the 1,300cc international Grand Touring class. The new car won the under-1,500cc 6-lap sports car race.

Team Lotus entered in strength for the *Daily Express* Trophy meeting of the BRDC at Silverstone on September 14th—three cars were in the up-to-1,100cc section and two in the 1,500cc race. For this race the entry was made up of 21 Lotuses out of a total 35 cars. Ron Flockhart in John Coombs' car won the event with the 1,100s of Keith Hall, Ivor Bueb and Alan Stacey in second, third and fourth places, and Team Lotus, 1,500cc car finished fifth, driven by Henry Taylor to give an all-Lotus result. Brian Naylor added to the crop of successes by the new car when he won the under–2,700cc section of the unlimited sports car race.

A week later at Mallory Park Gordon Jones recorded his first wins in his 1957 model, winning both the up-to-1,500cc race and heat 1 of the Formula Libre event, with Malcolm Graham second in both cases. Goodwood a week later saw the new cars in fine fettle—the 1,100cc race result being 1, Stacey; 2, Hall; 3, Ashdown, with a new

Below: Lotus 11s became as prolific on hills as in circuit races. This is J.S.E. Leighton winning his class at Brunton.
Bottom: A new Lotus is always a good story for the Press.

class record going to Alan Stacey, in company with Innes Ireland, at 88.71 mph. The unlimited sports car race saw some very fast driving by Roy Salvadori in John Coombs' 1,500cc car and by Brian Naylor in his 2 litre. Unfortunately the latter was to crash, without serious personal injury, at Woodcote Corner and the former to spin at Lavant Corner. In spite of the "gilhooley" Roy won the 2 litre class and set a new record lap at 90 mph! Bill Frost took second place after a steady drive in the 2 litre section. Bill's consistent performance with the new car throughout the season, in both top-line international and Club events, earned him the John Coombs Lotus Trophy at the first Club Lotus annual dinner and dance at the Casino Hotel on Taggs Island on February 7th, 1958.

Peter Ashdown wound up the season for the new car with a heat win at Brands Hatch on October 6th and second FTD a week later at Stapleford hill climb, where he only gave best to the ERA of W.F. Moss.

It had been a very busy season, but the tireless Team Lotus mechanics were quite willing to tackle a pre-Earls Court record attempt at Monza. Two engines were taken to the high-speed-track—the Le Mans 750cc Climax and an 1,100cc unit. Both these engines were supercharged, and unfortunately suffered piston failures before the record attempts had really started. However this did enable Cliff Allison to get back in good time for the Motor Show, and the second driver Jabby Crombac was able to return to his desk in Paris before he was seriously missed!

At about this time the engine shop lost two members, Graham Hill and John Campbell-Jones leaving to go into other occupations in the motor trade, and their places were taken by Steve Sanville and Keith Duckworth. Although Keith was primarily concerned with perfecting the five-speed garbox, these two were in fact filling the post of development engineer, although this in no way usurped Mike Costin and his able assistant Bill Griffiths who continued their most important research under racing conditions in charge of Team Lotus. The output of the assembly shop and the number of employees engaged on production had warranted another change in administration. This resulted in Nobby Clarke taking on more "admin" duties as works manager and being helped in his task by Roy Badcock as foreman.

The Lotus stand at the motor show was again a focal point for all sporting enthusiasts, and two versions of the 1958 cars—a Le Mans and a Sports—were on view. The satisfaction and success of the 1957 car was acknowledged by the fact that the models for the new year were practically identical to their predecessors. During the show the Esso Petroleum Company gave a cocktail party in London to which many of the Lotus drivers, mechanics and helpers were invited. Colin Chapman was presented with a fine oil painting of the 750cc car at Le Man's and the two drivers Cliff Allison and Keith Hall received wrist watches for their part in the magnificent "Index" win. Colin had risen from an Asian 'flu sickbed with a temperature of over a 100 to attend the presentation, made a very good speech and then shot straight back to bed, and had to stay there for another ten days! During the last few months of the season there had been much building activity at 7, Tottenham Lane, and in early November a new office block was ready. Built on the strip of land in front of the repair and racing shops, the new building presented a showroom surmounted by an illuminated "LOTUS" to the passing world. On the ground floor behind the showroom was an office for Colin Bennett and his secretary, facing out on to the road. Beside this room for the first time Lotus had "the usual offices" for both sexes! On the floor above, a well-lit drawing-office ran over the showroom, and behind this were the boss's office, overlooking the adjacent yard, and small offices for Ron Clover of "Accounts" and John Standen of "Purchasing". Mr. Chapman Senior was now spending more time in the Lotus offices, as a director of the company, and perhaps was glad that he had originally allowed Colin to use his yard, for the new offices were extremely handy. A further improvement to the amenities was the raising of one end of the roof over the stores in the main assembly shop. Now it was possible to employ normal-sized people as storekeepers! At last it looked as if Lotus had found time to turn round and build themselves a certain degree of comfort in which to pursue their fast-moving life of production and development.

14.

Celebration in the Sarthe

ARITHMETIC PROGRESSIONS ARE difficult things to master, but it appeared that some such rule was governing the number of Lotus cars appearing at the Le Mans race. First, there had been the lone Mark 9, then the three Elevens and in 1957 no less than five cars were accepted, one of which was to be a reserve.

An intending competitor in the 24-hour race has to start form-filling as early as February for a race to be held at the end of June. At that early date the initial entries are made and then follows a succession of requests for information such as type of fuel to be used, RAC certificates of verified engine capacity, nomination of first, second and reserve drivers, etc, etc. During this paper-work a little astute "rearrangement" was effected by the boys at Hornsey. The original Lotus entry was of four cars. Three came from Team Lotus—a 1,500cc car, a 750cc car and an 1,100cc, one being qualified for the Biennial Cup. The fourth car was privately owned by John Green and to be driven by Bob Walshaw and John Dalton—Bob had been disqualified for allegedly refuelling a lap early during the closing stages of the 1956 race. Of these four the organisers put the 750cc car on the reserve list, no doubt a move to protect French interests in the Index of Performance. This number was swelled to five when the two Frenchmen, Hechard and Masson, decided they would like to drive a Lotus in the race instead of the DB Panhard which they had provisionally entered. The works readily agreed to build them an 1,100cc car. However, in order to make sure the 750 became a runner they nominated this car as its Biennial Cup entry, and swapped places on the reserve list with the Lotus 1100.

The driver position therefore finally resolved itself into the private owners with their two 1100s, Cliff and Keith in the 750 (which now became the Biennial Cup car) Mac Fraser and fellow-American Jay Chamberlain in the 1500 and Peter Ashdown and Alan Stacey in the reserve 1100. Colin nominated himself, together with Graham Hill, as reserve driver on all five cars.

The cars for the race were to follow the basic specification of the current model but a great deal of thought had been given to making the full-width windscreen aerodynamically more efficient. The solution was very clever. The back of the body of the car was raised to the height of the top of the tail fins so allowing the windscreen to be curved over into a line which gracefully flowed to the very back of the car. This had the effect of reducing the frontal height of the headfairing and turning the car virtually into a very low saloon with a plastic canopy, openings being left for the driver's head and access to the passenger compartment. The problem of covering the space over the passenger seat head also received a lot of consideration. Here two conflicting requirements had to be met. First, the regulations demanded a removable, flexible, cover whilst, secondly, aerodynamics required a flat hard surface for uninterrupted air flow. The answer was ingenious—a pneumatic cover in the shape of a thin rectangular bag which would hang down into the cockpit and when inflated would give a hard, flat, top surface. Unfortunately, the short time available to build the cars did not allow for the perfection of this idea and as a compromise plain covers of "two-way-stretch" material were fitted.

The troubles with the back axle of the F2 car had kept Team Lotus very busy right up to Whitsun and so only a week remained after the holiday in which to complete assembly and preparation of the five special cars. Round-the-clock shift work was the only answer. The car for the Frenchmen was rushed through first and it left on a trailer behind M. Hechard's Renault Fregate on the Sunday before the race, Peter Ashdown and Alan Stacey hitching a ride with him to Mayet. When Colin left the works in the early hours of Monday, the Dalton/Walshaw car had been collected (still with much work to be completed) and was rushing for the midnight boat from Dover, but the mechanics still toiled on the three team cars, their goal being the Dover/Dunkirk boat at midday.

Colin had realised that he would be more valuable as team manager and so had sacrificed his desire to drive. Perhaps he thought that conditions might resemble those of the previous year, in which case why not leave the driving to others! All the accommodation and transport arrangements had been handled by myself, and Monday morning saw me, together with Colin, Hazel and Alfred Woolf, in a Silver City Bristol Freighter droning across the Channel and hoping that the lashings on Colin's Ford Consul held fast. Alfred Woolf was travelling with the team as interpreter—a task which was to keep him very busy during the following week. The trip from Le Touquet to Le Mans was quickly achieved, the Ford simply gobbling up the miles. For a great part of the way Colin slept on the back seat—catching up with the many hours lost during the past week. Lunch was taken at Grubers, the famous meeting place for all those connected with the 24-hour race. This restaurant in the central square of Le Mans has now become a furniture repository, a fate which should occur to some other restaurants we know!

Leaving the remains of a most unpalatable repast the occupants of the Consul were soon humming down the Mulsanne straight en route for the hostelry which knows all about good food—the Auberge de St. Nicholas.

Time passed very quickly in preparing a rather ancient garage to receive the team cars—whitewash was required for yet another glass roof, and fluorescent tubes were purchased for the inevitable nocturnal toils. Three-fifteen pm on the Tuesday was the Team Lotus deadline at scrutineering, and everyone had their fingers crossed for a telegram had arrived from Mike Costin saying—"Hope to be on midnight boat—will make scrutineering a.s.a.p." And it can be costly in fines if your cars are late at "verification".

As M. Hechard was staying at Mayet and was receiving the valuable assistance of Jabby Crombac, this car had been virtually completed in the hope that if the French car was accepted then the rest might sail through "verification" on the assurance that "they're all the same old boy!" At 3 p.m. the "show" car began its journey down to the scrutineers' table and was quickly joined by John Dalton who drove his car into the large fenced enclosure, with his mechanic in the passenger seat—a true sports car! The minutes ticked by and the Lotus contingent just hoped that the transporter would at least make it by 6 p.m. when the day's scrutineering ceased. Rapid calculations showed that if the boat arrived on time it would be good going for the team cars to be in Le Mans by 5 p.m. At 3.13 p.m. a most incredible thing happened—the crowd in the road leading to the gates of the scrutineering arena parted and there on the horizon was the transporter, whereupon a tremendous cheer went up! Four sleepwalkers emerged from the converted bus and willing hands unloaded the cars. It had been a fantastic ride across France, and all Mike could give as a reason for their remarkably quick journey was the fact that the brakes of the transporter no longer worked! The resources of a true racing mechanic are amazing. These boys, who now looked dead on their feet, had been unable to catch the midday boat so they had driven into the square of Dover, unloaded cars and welding bottles, and, much to the surprise of the inhabitants, had continued to prepare their charges.

It was a wonderful sight to see the five identical green cars in the scrutineering shed. Identical that is with one exception—the 750 had magnesium wheels instead of spoked ones. A great deal of detail work was still required on each car—this was

When it all feels worthwhile! From left to right: Bill Griffiths, Frank and Mike Costin, 'Index' winners Cliff Allison and Keith Hall, with Fred Studdard between them, M. Mica, Colin Chapman and Graham Hill.

all listed, as no item must be missed. One official thought he was being cheated, and brought a smile to Jabby Crombac's face as he explained that he wished to see one hood and one set of supports for each car, not one hood which was passed down the line! The flimsy hoods were produced–the product of a most ridiculous international regulation. All went well until the 1,500cc car reached the end of the line and they wished to check the silencing, for the new twin overhead camshaft engine had never been run and would not start despite a whining starter motor. In a flash Mike realised that it was not fuel in the tank but paraffin left there by the panel-beater who had tested the tank–such had been the rush at Hornsey. Quick draining and fresh fuel brought the engine to life and Colin kept the rev-counter at a steady 2,500 revs. The noise was deafening, but the official was satisfied, which was curious, for when one looked under the side of the car it was easy to see two plain pipes leading straight from the exhaust ports! The rest of the exhaust system had not yet been designed, let alone made and fitted. Apparently, for a car to be insufficiently silenced it had to be possible for the official to hear individual engine beats. No doubt this was why Colin kept the revs up!

At last the first hurdle was over and the cars, with the exception of the 750, were reloaded and the Team returned to Mayet. Peter Ashdown drove the little car proudly sporting the Biennial Cup roundel back on the road. It looked most purposeful with its high back and sloping nose. As the Ford Consul overtook the projectile on the Mulsanne straight the occupants of the larger car had heart failure as the Lotus appeared to be driverless. It was only as you drew ahead of the car that you could see the top of Peter's head as he sat back and down out of the airstream. M. Mica had a fine meal waiting and then the weary mechanics crawled into bed while the "staff" unloaded the transporter.

On the Wednesday the team was complete. Mac arrived to join Jay Chamberlain, who had been at Mayet since Sunday following his long journey from California. Cliff and Keith arrived in the former's Vauxhall Victor, bringing with them mechanic Phil Butler and "signaller" John Lawry.

The party was completed by Eleven-owner Jack Richards, who had come over with his friends Alan Smith and Bob Blanchard to help in whatever way they could. This party, travelling in Jack's very swift Lancia Aurelia, had with them the sixth member of the team of mechanics—Graham Hill. The two comparatively "fresh" mechanics were in the thick of preparation all through Wednesday, as were Mike, Bill Griffiths, Fred Studdard and Dave Warwick, who appeared to be remarkably wide-awake after one night's recuperation from the ravages of the past days.

The four Lotuses made a wonderful sight in line-ahead formation on the road to the circuit for the first practice session. In each case the number one drivers were at the wheel and Graham Hill took the French car along. Jay Chamberlain followed the procession in Mac's Ford Zephyr and was so enamoured with the scene ahead of him that he spent most of his time behind his movie camera, leaving the steering to his passenger—not an easy job as Jay's foot was intent on keeping up with the "dicers".

At the circuit, tanks were drained, the official fuel was put in each car, tank capacities were checked, and without more ado the three cars were on the track. Practice at Le Mans only occupies the evenings of two days, so no time must be lost in making the best use of the available training.

The Wednesday session for both the 750cc car and the 1100, which was still a reserve, were highly satisfactory. Cliff Allison and Keith Hall were soon at home and without any trouble were lapping in the low five-minutes-twenties. Peter Ashdown and Alan Stacey took things gently to start with as both of them were new to the Sarthe circuit. However, Peter soon turned in a 5 min 1 sec lap and Alan replied with two 5 min 3 sec laps. Jay Chamberlain also tried this car and equalled Peter's fastest lap. There were several snags with the twin-cam 1,500cc car and the drivers did not have much time on the circuit with it. Mac Fraser recorded the fastest lap of the session with 4 min 35 sec. As practice had started at 6 p.m. all the drivers were able to learn the course by daylight but they were soon confronted with the difficult task of estimating whether the headlights behind

118

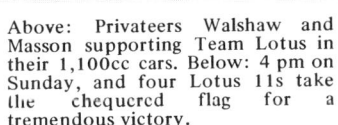

Above: Privateers Walshaw and Masson supporting Team Lotus in their 1,100cc cars. Below: 4 pm on Sunday, and four Lotus 11s take the chequered flag for a tremendous victory.

were from such as a 4½-litre Maserati travelling at 170 mph or a 750cc Panhard which would stay behind. Graham Hill tried the Frenchman's car and put in some very rapid laps at under 5 min, his best being 4 min 56 sec.

Team Lotus therefore were able to return to Mayet after the midnight termination of training in fairly confident mood, with fastest practice times in both the 750cc and the 1,100cc classes. There was much work to do on the 1,500cc car and some very fast practice times by the 1,500cc Porsches of Maglioli/Barth and Herrmann/Von Frankenberg to beat. From the early hours of Thursday the mechanics toiled on the twin-cam car in preparation for the evening's practice. It had been decided not to run the other two team cars again and Alan and Peter were full of glee on hearing that their reserve was to be a runner.

After carburettor settings on the 1,500cc car had been adjusted it really began to motor on the second evening of practice and Mac circulated in 4 min 28 sec. Jay was still learning the circuit, but put in several laps around the 4 min 35 sec mark. Then just before the light began to fail the team manager donned his blue helmet so as to see for himself how the twin-cam worked. Colin's knowledge of the circuit, gained from competing in the previous two years, showed immediately—his first flying lap was 4 min 37 sec, then 33 sec, then 32–28 and finally 4 min 26 sec. A new 1,500cc lap record—something for Porsche to think about. It was a happy 1,100cc and 1,500cc classes. But jubilation was dashed when just before midnight Mac Fraser stopped at Mulsanne with an engine showing unmistakable signs of a dropped valve—the twin-cam bogy had struck again.

Desperately Colin Chapman tried to think of ways and means of replacing the damaged engine, but time was too short and so it was decided to concentrate on the other two cars. Poor Peter and Alan had to stand down in favour of Mac and Jay as drivers of the 1100—after all Jay had come 8,000 miles to compete at this race!

At 4 p.m. on the Saturday everything was set fair—the weather could not have been better and in the Lotus pit excitement was high! This had not, however, affected the mechanics who had set up a model of efficiency in their pit—everything in its correct place, looking just like a well-ordered motor accessory shop. From flag fall the Lotus progress was nearly monotonous, the team 750cc and 1,100cc cars taking the lead in their classes, a lead they were never to relinquish. The unfortunate Roger Masson ran out of fuel on the Mulsanne straight and pushed the car four miles back to his pit, dropping exhausted on arrival.

Routine pit stops for fuel and driver changes came and went like clockwork and the two Team Lotus cars drew further and further away from the opposition. First the DB Panhards and then the Stanguellinis tried to match the speed of the 750 but one by one they crashed or went out with mechanical failure so hot was the pace. As night came and the lights blazed round the circuit the four little green cars from Hornsey went on their way without a falter. The Dalton/Walshaw car did have an adventure at Tertre Rouge, and lost some oil through the dipstick hole in the early hours, but all was well and its duel with the 1,100cc Cooper was resumed.

Dawn at Le Mans creeps up on you. Suddenly you realise that the passing cars are no longer a blaze of light and a glimpse of a number but now have a more definite shape. With light came the treacherous mist, but still the four cars tore round. The 750 was miles ahead on "Index" and the 1,100cc team car was now ninth in general classification. Porsche had taken up the challenge on "Index" but the Maglioli/Barth experimental car crashed at Tertre Rouge and then the Herrmann/Von Frankenberg car went out with ignition failure. With the German challenge present the 1100 was speeded up and began lapping consistently at 105 mph. The 750 was never speeded up—the only signals going out were for less speed in case the very experimental engine was asked to do too much. Throughout the race the lap times of this car did not stray far from 5 min 20 sec to 5 min 30 sec, except in the last few hours when it was slowed still further as it then held a gigantic 16-lap lead!

With an hour to go the last Porsche of Storez and Crawford ended a desperate bid for the Index of Performance with a broken crankshaft. The terrors of the last few laps seemed to have been minimised for the Lotus pit personnel by the clockwork regularity of the cars; it did not seem possible that anything could go wrong with these cars which had run to order for nearly 24 hours. And nothing did go wrong. Just after 4 p.m. the four cars crossed the line together to receive their share of the applause for another Jaguar victory and a British win in the Index of Performance.

After the flowers, the photographs and the thronging crowd it was good to escape to the smaller-scale celebrations in the accessory bars above the pits. Here, over champagne, the full realisation of the achievement dawned. The marque had won the Index, the Biennial Cup, both the 750 and 1,100cc classes and had also finished second and fourth in the latter, the two team cars achieving their results without a spanner being used on them—just a wheel hammer to change a rear wheel on the 1,100cc car. For once Colin let his hair down and consumed glass after glass of champagne—even Mike was lapping up the golden liquid. Rather more by luck than good road driving the complete team reached Mayet that night—Hazel having to be quite firm with Colin after his boisterous exit from the paddock.

The indefatigable M. Mica put on a splendid celebration dinner that evening—truly a remarkable achievement after having supplied the team with food and drink throughout the 24 hours. Unfortunately, the cuisine was not fully appreciated by the tired diners—in fact some heads were nodding over their plates!

On the Monday the papers were full of the race, and breakfast was a mad scramble to try and translate the reports, an interesting fact being that the 1,100cc car had been timed over the measured kilometre on the Mulsanne straight at 206.4 kph (128 mph) as against 183.8 kph (114 mph) by the 750. Esso were on the spot early with their congratulations and Reg Tanner dropped in for breakfast! The cars were checked and loaded, and in the afternoon the mechanics left for Rouen in preparation for the meeting there a fortnight later. Inquiries in Le Mans about payment of prize money brought the realisation that the team would have to attend the Fiftieth Anniversary Dinner of L'Automobile Club de L'Ouest. Nobody had bothered to request tickets for this function, little thinking that their attendance might be most important. In an effort to look the part, suits were donned, where possible, and Colin's Ford Consul and Mac's Ford Zephyr carrying a dozen people in all shot off for the Chateau de Cheverny. Unfortunately, there was a long distance to cover, and it was well after the official "17 heures 30, Reception des Invites" that the two cars forced their way through gesticulating gendarmes, roared up the gravel drive to a magnificent mansion, and spilled figures who proceeded to run across the immaculate lawns towards the group of elegantly dressed people in front of the impressive building. A little breathless, Lotus collected armfuls of trophies and also a few inquiring glances from those in evening dress. There followed a cocktail party held in one of the hunting rooms adjoining the Hounds' Kennels. Walls, pillars and ceiling were a mass of stags' antlers. From the conviviality of free drinks I was dragged by Colin Chapman, who had two cheques for over 6,000,000 francs burning holes in his pocket. Following a chat with Stirling Moss, who had advised him to buy a yacht at Cannes, Colin had decided to cash his cheques and pay the drivers their shares there and then. Thoughtfully a mobile bank was to hand, manned by two gentlemen fingering sten guns. Soon a mound of French notes was piled on the counter and one by one the four drivers were found and given their "wad". This watering process left a thick parcel containing £3,500 in francs. Colin won the toss, and the bundle belonged to me for the evening—how cheerless the grounds of the Chateau looked once one had left the protection of the two sten guns!

At 20 heures 15—"Diner de Gala" was announced, and the assembly moved into the floodlit Chateau to the accompaniment of a group of red-coated horn players. Apparently a feature of the architecture of the time of the Chateau was to erect a thin building which would provide a magnificent fascia to the world. In fact one could enter the front archway and pass into the gardens beyond, hardly noticing the interior at all! It was on the lawns of these gardens under a wood-walled marquee that the dinner took place. A table for Team Lotus did not present a difficulty—the first one without name cards was commandeered! As luck would have it, it was adjacent to that occupied by fashion models distributing the gifts after the meal! Champagne flowed like water—no sooner did you drain a glass than a white-gloved hand poured more from a napkin-covered bottle.

The dinner was followed by a most impressive display of ballet on a stage set in the middle of a tree-lined lake. The dancers were lit by a myriad of coloured lights, intensifying and dying with the music. The spectacle was breathaking as the dancers whirled and turned, their flowing garments catching the lights and in the case of the fire dance, looking terrifyingly real. As if all this was not enough, entertainment was then rounded off by a marvellous firework display. As the rockets showered their colours from the sky the twin turrets of the Chateau were floodlit and from their balconies came the strains of the golden horns of the huntsmen.

Until midnight the bright flashes and sharp cracks of fireworks filled the air—at times the whole lawns and driveway of the Chateau were as light as day. No doubt as he watched all this Colin was thinking of that other magnificent show enacted the day before on the track at Le Mans by his cars, drivers and mechanics.

Sunday morning pit stop for the Hechard/Masson 11. Ian Smith and Vanwall's David Yorke lap score as Colin Chapman gives instructions via interpreter Jabby Crombac on the pit counter.

15.

Better late than never

ALTHOUGH COLIN CHAPMAN and Mike Costin had intended to improve the specification of the Mark 6 at the end of 1954 it was not until the Earls Court show at the end of 1957 that the Seven made itself known. This three-year time lapse had been occasioned solely by the pressing need to attend to other projects, and the new car only appeared in 1957 because of two strong influencing factors—the first was business, the second a promise.

At the 1956 Motor Show the number of inquiries for the old Mark 6 had been enormous, this interest being backed up by the lucrative secondhand business which was being done in the "square-cut" car. There was a definite demand for this type of car, so with an eye to increasing sales Lotus decided to build a limited quantity of "up-to-date Mark 6s". The other reason for the Seven involved Edward Lewis, who had already owned a Mark 6 and a Mark 9. At the end of 1956 Edward had built up a second Mark 6 with a de Dion rear axle and powered by an 1,100cc Climax engine. He planned to use this car extensively during the coming season for hill climbs and sprint events. Colin saw this car during the winter while he was considering the form that the Seven would take and, following a discussion, agreed that Lotus would sell Lewis' car for him and provide him with a very special car based on the 1957 Eleven. The sale went through quickly and the car became the property of an overseas enthusiast but the new "special car" did not materialise so quickly. Poor Edward Lewis was forced to borrow the works cars for his competition motoring throughout nearly the whole season—an imposition which he bore very good-heartedly. For the Brighton Speed Trials in September, however, he did have his new mount.

The idea behind the Climax-engined prototype Seven was that the increased power would give the whole car a thorough testing before it was finally decided what form the standard production model would take.

Lewis was soon successful with his new car. After a rather dicey beginning at Brighton, where excessive acceleration nearly ended him in the sea, he won the 1,100cc class at Prescott a week later with the excellent time of 47.85 seconds.

Just in time for announcement at the motor show the Ford-engined version of the Seven was completed and the standard specification agreed. The space frame was very similar to the 1957 Eleven, being a multi-tubular unit comprising 1 in and ¾ in square and round tubing of 18 gauge steel. The propeller shaft tunnel and floor were both stressed members forming an integral part of the frame. The rear engine mounting was carried by the tunnel and at the front two rubber mountings supported the power unit.

The F2 wishbone suspension was used at the front and at the rear a proprietary live axle was suspended on combined coil spring and damper units, the axle being located by twin parallel trailing arms with a diagonal member to provide lateral stabilisation.

Hydraulically operated, two leading shoe cast-iron drum brakes were fitted—those at the front being 9 in diameter by 1¾ in and at the rear 8 in diameter by 1¼ in. A combined master cylinder and hydraulic fluid reservoir served both

Left: Jack Richards' 7, perhaps the most immaculate of them all. Below: The tubular frame of the 7 was reinforced by stressed panels to form a very rigid 'box'. Bottom: Little more than knee-high to globe-trotter, the car measured only 27½ inches to the top of the scuttle.

Left: Formula 2–type front suspension and a lower, wider radiator cowl were immediately identifiable differences from the Mark 6. Below left: Lotus carried through a continuous programme of improvements on the 7, but private owners also produced some interesting results. Here is a car with formula-type suspension all round, disc brakes and special wheels and tyres.

front and rear brakes, and a horizontally mounted hand brake operated the rear brakes through a mechanical linkage. Burman worm-and-nut steering gear was fitted with a universally jointed steering column.

The trusty Ford 100E 1,172cc side-valve engine was fitted and transmitted its 40 bhp via a single-dry-plate clutch to the Ford three-speed gearbox. Standard ratios were: 1st 3.664 to 1, 2nd 2.007 to 1, top 1 to 1, reverse 4.79 to 1, but close-ratio gears of 2.34 to 1, 1.33 to 1 and 1 to 1 were available as an optional extra. The final drive was a hypoid unit with a standard ratio of 4.875 to 1, but optional ratios of 5.375, 5.125, 4.22, 3.89 and 3.73 to 1 could be fitted. Final transmission to the road was taken through bolt-on 15 in wheels fitted with 5.20 by 15 tyres. A provision for a spare wheel was made at the tail of the car and with the same size tyres on all four corners this item would be more useful than in the case of the Mark 6, which invariably had much larger rear tyres.

A tall, but extra-light, fin-and-tube radiator with integral header tank was fitted, sloping backwards as on the F2 car. That other essential liquid—fuel—was contained in a light-alloy rear tank of 7-gallon capacity, and was pumped via an AC engine-mounted pump. In an effort to keep down costs AC also provided the instruments, comprising a 3 in speedometer, oil pressure gauge, water temperature gauge and ammeter. For the "lead boot" boys a tachometer could be purchased at extra cost!

The bodywork closely resembled that of the earlier Mark 6, but the nose tapered rather more and at last there was a little more room behind the seats for small luggage! Unlike the Mark 6 there were no removable panels on each side of the engine bay, enabling the complete sides of the car to be fully stressed by attaching the aluminium panels to the frame. Another change from the Mark 6 was the scuttle, which was flat instead of sporting an "instrument bulge". This meant a narrow dash panel—but the essential dials were all easily visible. The upholstered dash panel was located by Dzus fasteners which enabled quick removal for access to the back of the instruments. This quick release system was also employed on the nose cowling in order to provide ready access to the front suspension and radiator system. A full-width windscreen with specially cast aluminium stays was fitted, being of sufficient height to locate a practical hood. For racing purposes the screen could be replaced by a small Perspex driving screen—another optional extra. Overall, the Seven was an extremely low and compact vehicle, measuring only 27½ in from the ground to the top of the scuttle—just the thing to trip over on a dark night outside a pub! Overall length was only 10 ft 3 in and width 4 ft 5 in but in the interests of good roadholding the distances between tyre contact points were generous—wheelbase 7 ft 4 in and front and rear track 3 ft 11 in. The low build of the car did not make it very suitable for the roughest of going, ground clearance being only 5 in. Without fuel but otherwise complete in every way the Seven was very light, weighing only 725 lb.

It was announced at the outset that no departure from the standard specification would be considered for sale. However, Jack Richards purchased the second prototype chassis, with the de Dion rear-end, disc brakes and Climax engine, for use in hill-climbs. Jack's Seven was one of the most beautifully finished sports-racing cars ever to be seen—every possible part on the engine was chromium plated, even down to the dipstick. The other prototype Seven was sold to Paul Fletcher, and the car eventually passed into the hands of the Chequered Flag racing team, who fitted it out with magnesium alloy wheels and a 1,500cc single-cam Climax engine—possibly the fastest Seven ever seen in competition.

So exciting was the performance of the Climax-engined Sevens, and so numerous the inquiries, that Lotus decided after all to market an addition to the range, despite their earlier statement. It was called the Super Seven, and it had an identical chassis to the standard car, with no de Dion axle, disc brakes and so on, but the Coventry-Climax 1100cc engine was specified, and wire wheels enhanced the lines of the little car.

One of the best-known Super Sevens was the first—7 TMT. While it was still a Lotus demonstration car, Graham Hill entered it for the 1958 Boxing Day Brands Hatch meeting. With the engine in 75 bhp Stage 1 tune, and shod with Firestone tyres, Graham managed to win the 1,100cc sports car race against some of the fastest 1100 sports-racing cars in the country—Elevens, Elvas and a Lola! The car had the optional B-type BMC gearbox with Lotus close-ratio gears, in place of the standard A30 unit.

1959 was the hey day of the 1,172cc Ford-engined Seven, which made up the greater part of the field in all 1172 Formula races, and many new drivers competed for the first time in these cars. But the BMC A-type engine was obviously a "natural" for the Seven, being amenable to extreme tuning, besides being a very pleasant (and economical) engine in standard form and having the excellent four-speed BMC gearbox. Accordingly, on October 1st, 1959, a new model called the Seven "A" made its appearance, powered by the BMC 950cc unit; the Ford-engined model was designated the Seven "F", and the Climax-engined version the Seven "C". At the same time Lotus Components Ltd., the firm concerned with the production of this car, widened its field of activities by appointing a network of area distributors and sub-agents, to be known as Lotus Centres, throughout the British Isles.

The overall excellence of the Seven as it stood at this time was shown by the fact that it had sold so well for so long with but detail modifications. The Seven had been basically an adapted Eleven chassis, and during the early part of 1960 much work had been going on at Cheshunt on a new chassis—the Seven Series Two. This was finally announced in June, 1960.

The space frame had been completely redesigned and simplified, though remaining similar in conception. Front suspension remained the same, but the rear suspension was modified, the rear axle, now a Standard unit, being located by twin parallel trailing arms as before, with a new triangulated "A" bracket with its apex picking up beneath the differential casing. The steering column was more nearly horizontal, eliminating a universal joint which had given some trouble on the earlier version. The wheels were now 13 in in diameter, as opposed to the previous 15 in. Glass-fibre was used for the first time on a Seven, the reshaped nose cowl being of this material, as well as the four wings.

The price of the new car remained the same, at £587 for the 100E Ford-engined model and £611 for the BMC "A" version. The Climax engine was not suitable for the Series Two, so the Seven "C" left the range. For the first time, the hood, spare wheel and windscreen wiper were included in the above prices, representing a saving of more than £35.

But a much greater price cut than this was to come. The new year, 1961, was heralded in by the second BRSCC Racing Car Show, and at the Show, as well as the sensational new Lotus Twenty, was a beautifully finished, dark green Series Two Seven—and the price tag? £339 plus engine! Most people though it was a mistake. £100 off! But there was no mistake, and the new price made the Seven easily the best value for money of any small sports car, bar none.

The popular 105E new Ford Anglia engine was listed for the first time, and as Lotus Components were offering 105E engine/gearbox units for £100 to go with the Series Two, that made the total price, absolutely complete, £499—at last, a Lotus for less than £500!

In days when sports cars were becoming more and more luxurious, and closed GT cars so popular, it was refreshing to consider the number of these comparatively stark sporting cars sold for road use in Britain, in the States and elsewhere, proving that even in the '60s a good market existed for a car whose roadability and good manners brought the fun back into motoring—and blow the discomfort!

16.

Joining the Elite

NO DOUBT WHEN working alone on his first creation, to be known later as the Mark 1, Colin day-dreamed in the little lock-up behind Hazel's home. Even his wildest dream, however, would not have shown the descendant of the car on which he worked as a shining model slowly rotating on a floodlit turntable at the international motor show at Earls Court–and being acclaimed on all sides as the star of the show. For star it was, only ten years after Colin had towed that ancient 1930 Austin 7 fabric saloon back to Muswell Hill.

The Elite coupe hit the headlines with a bang–the surprise of the 1957 Show. The secret of this beautifully proportioned, all-glass-fibre Grand Touring coupe had been well kept, and it was in fact quite a surprise to many Lotus employees themselves that the new car was actually completed in time for it to take its pride of place at the Show with the other two Lotus exhibits.

Since the days when he had first started production of the Mark 6 Colin had nursed a secret hope that one day Lotus would build a lightweight coupe of general appeal to the motorist who took a delight in his motoring. Over the years the interest and inquiries for a Grand Touring car of this nature increased, and following ten days in front of the public at Earls Court in 1956 Colin decided that the time had come to have a crack at French, German and Italian products in this market.

In accordance with the Lotus tradition built up over the years the chief requirements of the proposed car were a rigid chassis and low all-up weight. Recent developments in glass-fibres and various resins had attracted Colin's interest and he decided to see if it would be possible to construct a complete body/chassis unit of these substances. He went to great lengths to glean as much information as possible about the subject. He took a specialised course, examined countless samples and listened to innumerable representatives. All this research convinced him that his idea was a possibility and when preliminary stress calculations showed very satisfactory figures of strength and lightness it was decided to take the plunge.

The first person to hear of the proposed coupe was a friend of Colin's–Peter Kirwan-Taylor–and he greeted the idea with great enthusiasm. An accountant by profession, Peter had a natural ability for body-styling and spent a great part of his spare time engaged in designing graceful lines for various vehicles. His skill had been tried earlier on a Lotus when he constructed a streamlined body for his Mark 6–the result was unusual but perhaps not wholly successful. Immediately he heard of the new project he was round at Gothic Cottage and soon covering Colin's drawing board with suggested shapes. Together, these two built up the silhouette they required. Colin saw that the requirements of rigidity could be met and Peter evolved a flowing line to cover the necessary chassis construction and other essentials of the car. It is interesting to note that the early design thought up by Colin and Peter did not alter greatly in spite of all the subsequent opinions given by various experts. The majority of these opinions came from the styling department of the Ford Motor Company. Also from Ford's came John Frayling. Initially, John advised Colin on the technicalities of producing the moulds for the various body sections. Then, as plans matured still further, he left Ford's and joined Lotus to work full-time on the production of the first prototype. Frank Costin was, of course, brought in on the design stage and he vetted the proposed shape, making sure that Peter's beauty-of-line was also aerodynamically efficient.

Throughout the planning stage responsibility for the structure was, naturally, Colin's. Bit by bit the construction resolved itself, major items being settled on the drawing board and more minor difficulties being overcome as production proceeded. Space at 7, Tottenham Lane was scarce already so it was quite impossible to consider attempting to mould, trim and assemble a glass-fibre construction there. Also, it was most desirable to keep the project a secret in order to prevent a stream of inquiries about the car and to keep the advanced principles being employed from prying eyes. Lotus were lucky in being able to take over a small assembly shop in the course of construction at Edmonton. At the end of a cul-de-sac and behind plain doors the secret project was safe. John Frayling took charge of this special department of Lotus Engineering Company Ltd., and his main responsibility was the sculptural work on the moulds for the various units. With such a lot of accurate hand work to be undertaken progress was understandably slow, and Colin was not able to give as much of his time to the project as he would have liked owing to his occupation with the normal production at Hornsey and Team Lotus activities. At the inception of his idea of the coupe at the end of 1956 he had thought in terms of three cars of this type for Le Mans in 1957. As that season progressed, however, it became very clear that it would need a great effort to have one prototype car ready for the October motor show.

With the scale models in existence Colin and Hazel amused themselves trying to think of a good name for the new car and for a time Lynx was favoured. Finally, however, it was decided to use a name alliterating with "Eleven" and this led to the choice of ELITE. Perhaps a future edition of this car and its successor, the Elan, may be called the "Elusive"!

The formation of the chassis-body unit of the

Left: Elite trunk shape was compact but practical. Centre and bottom left: The prototype takes shape. Below: A well laid-out dashboard. Bottom: Star of the Show at Earls Court.

Elites in action. Below: Keith Greene. Centre: J. P. Williams. Bottom: Peter Lumsden (on his way to winning his class in the 1960 Tourist Trophy at Goodwood).

Elite was unique and of great technical interest—the first car in the world to rely so completely on glass-fibre for construction. In view of this a detailed description makes intriguing study.

Polyester and epoxide resins were the main materials used in the various mouldings making up the different sections of the structure. These were joined together by an epoxide resin adhesive which made a pure bond between the joints and eliminated the necessity of riveting. In production it was planned to make the greatest possible use of epoxide resin mouldings, both in stressed panels and where there was to be bonding. Dependent on the loads to be carried the bond was either glass-fibre mat or woven glass cloth and the mould thickness of the various panels also varied between 0.06 in and 0.20 in according to the loads to be taken.

The structure of the car was made up basically of eight box scetions. At the rear a triangular box provided attachment points for the final drive unit and suspension items. From this, four boxes travelled forward as stressed sections, the main one being a deep propeller-shaft tunnel. Below each door opening box sections connected the rear wing valances with the scuttle, and the fourth box section was provided by the roof. This latter unit took its origin from the sandwich techniques used in the aircraft industry and had twin thin skins of woven glass filled by polyurethene—a substance akin to a rigid foam rubber. At the very front of the roof there was a small box section into which was bonded the only major steel reinforcement in the car—a steel tube which passed down ahead of the door openings so tying together the stress-carrying members of the roof, scuttle and door sills. The tubes projected slightly beneath the car to provide jacking points.

Ahead of the scuttle line, rectangular box sections, incorporating moulded-in fuel tanks, ran forward into the front wing valances and connected up with a boxed cross-member. This construction gave a box fore and aft joined by similar structures meeting at the main stress point—the tubular hoop. The front box section provided anchorage points for the front suspension and also an air tunnel to the ducted radiator. The floor, being an important load-carrying structure, was kept as one complete entity, with only small flanged openings beneath the engine and final drive units.

The moulds to produce this intricate layout were meticulously made and a satisfactory exterior finish was obtained. As the prototype car was in fact a "die" with which to perfect the moulds the exterior finish required a little smoothing on completion and had to be paint-sprayed. For production it was planned to also impregnate the glass-fibre with a colour as well as paint spraying for a final finish.

From a practical usage point of view the construction of the Elite offered outstanding advantages. Glass-fibre can withstand much heavier blows than would a similar thickness of aluminium and has the great advantage that once moulded its shape cannot be altered—on impact it will give, but will immediately regain its original form. If impact be heavy enough to cause a fracture then it is a relatively easy job to cut out the affected section and graft in new glass-fibre. One outstanding advantage of this material is that it is fatigue-free and so has an unlimited life. This was to become an excellent sales line for motor traders when selling a secondhand Elite!

An example of the resilient properties of glass-fibre was seen one day outside the filling station owned at that time by John Coombs on the Guildford by-pass. Whilst reversing her Austin A 30 a woman driver backed into the side of a glass-fibre bodied Jensen and drove away leaving an appreciable dent in the stationary car. A mechanic went over to examine the damage and was amazed to see the dent suddenly pop out, leaving a smooth unmarked panel!

Special study was made of the attachment points for such vital items as suspension units, engine, gearbox and final drive mountings, and steering, for if possible it was desirable to fix these to metal. A straight bond of metal to glass-fibre was not desired, for weakness would occur at the bond. The answer was found by welding the attachment points to perforated steel plates which were bonded in over a relatively wide area to the epoxide resin moulds. This might appear to be contrary to Lotus practice in that it was adding weight, but it was found to be the only satisfactory answer to the bonding problem. In any case the chassis-body unit without the plates would have been far too light and would have brought very tough problems in the roadholding department!

Great attention was paid during the design stage to the driving position and cockpit layout of the proposed car. Colin borrowed as many different sports cars as he could wheedle out of people and drove them in order to discover any faults in their interior layout. He wanted to keep the overall size of the coupe small but also provide generous leg, head and entrance space for the occupants. This he and Peter Kirwan-Taylor achieved very cleverly. The novel construction of the car helped them greatly for two reasons. First, the petrol tanks could be moulded into the front wings, so allowing the seat backs to be immediately ahead of the rear axle; this also, incidentally, provided a space for a large luggage compartment behind the axle. Secondly, with the light construction the doors could be large, as could their openings, for they were bounded on all sides by a rigid box section of either wing valance, sill or sandwich roof. The large doors were kept light and strong by recess moulding the inside, to form an arm rest, and by constructing them in a double skin section.

Airflow also received much painstaking consideration. A ducted radiator system was provided and also a draught-free air conditioning system for the car's interior. The latter was provided by a controllable inlet at the base of the windscreen and exit slots in the roof section above the rear window. The lines of the car were superb, being extremely graceful but also full of purpose. The compact vehicle had an overall length of 12 ft and width of 4 ft 10 in. Windows were large and gave excellent visibility. For a car of only 3 ft 10 in overall height the headroom and ease of entry through the large doors was exceptional. In order to maintain a deep luggage compartment and impart power to the lines of the car the back was squared off. Some people criticised this part of the styling when the car was first introduced but a little consideration showed another practical point—neat location of the rear number plate.

The F2 car provided the suspension system for

the Elite—the wishbone front and strut rear being used. The question of load change was an important one with the new car and so the strut system with its slight camber angle change with different loads was most suitable. This meant that handling changes were reduced to a minimum between a light-load car with just a driver aboard and the other extreme of two occupants, full tanks, loaded boot and perhaps two spare wheels. In order to accommodate such variations in load the wheel deflections were increased from the 6 in on the F2 car to 7 in. Another factor aiding the roadholding and steering of the new car was the special, nylon-thread, high performance tyres produced by the Firestone Company especially for the Elite. Colin Chapman was very pleased with the co-operation he received from this company who were most keen to produce a special tyre to suit the 11 cwt of the Elite. Both Dunlop and Michelin also showed great interest in the lightweight car and produced versions of their tyres to suit this new field of motoring.

Brakes were also very "Formula 2", being Girling 9½ in diameter discs, mounted outboard at the front and inboard, each side of the final-drive unit, at the rear. Detachable pads were fitted and the handbrake operated separate mechanical calipers at the rear. In order to aid brake cooling, knock-on 15 in wire wheels were fitted front and rear carrying the special 4.90 by 15 in tyres. Steering was by lightweight rack-and-pinion.

The power unit chosen for the car was a new one. In order to get nearer to the top limit of the 1,300cc Grand Touring class the 1,100cc FWA Coventry Climax engine was enlarged to 1,216cc. The new engine was designated FWE and whilst it retained the 2.625-in stroke of the 1100 it used the 3.0 in bore of the FWB type 1½ litre engine. With an 8.5 to 1 compression ratio and a single 1½ in horizontal SU carburettor this unit developed 75 bhp at 6,100 rpm. A B-type BMC gearbox was used in conjunction with an 8 in diameter Borg and Beck clutch and drove a hypoid final-drive unit via a short propeller shaft. In fact this shaft did not exist in the prototype which was rushed to Earls Court, as there was insufficient time to fabricate one, and also the haste did not allow a full water system to be fitted. These two omissions led to Colin effecting a very quick "sale" on press day! Denis Jenkinson of *Motor Sport*, who had for long favoured the air-cooled rear-engined Porsche for his continental travels complimented Colin on the new car and added "if it didn't have a prop shaft and hadn't got any water I'd buy it"—just the customer that Colin was waiting for!

The team that had designed the Elite fully realised that the car was to be sold to a rather different market than that for the existing Lotus sports-racing cars. Because of this they built in creature comforts such as fully adjustable aero-type seats, full trimming, map pockets, provision for a heater and radio and all the requirements of road driving such as a full complement of lights, twin horns and direction flashers. However, they did not allow the luxury to go too far as the "latest from Hornsey" had to acquit itself well in competition with such rivals as Alfa Romeo and Porsche. Hence the functional steering wheel and instrument panel, and the mounting space for two spare wheels behind the passenger seats.

For some months before the new car was announced Colin and his father had spent a considerable amount of time trying to obtain some land on which to build a new factory for the production of the new car. Facilities at Hornsey and Edmonton were no longer adequate, and a site in North London, preferably within easy reach of Barnet, was the only answer. Colin did not want to buy existing premises but to put his basic training to good use and build just the type of factory he required. The ban on further industrial development near the centre of London proved to be the stumbling block and finally Lotus were forced, as a standby, to take an option on land at Cheshunt—hardly ideal but better than nothing.

With the gleaming prototype installed in the new showroom at 7, Tottenham Lane, two further glass-fibre cars were put in hand at Edmonton for test work early in the New Year. As the new Lotus factory could not possibly be ready until 1959 at the very earliest, the boys at Edmonton had the task of perfecting their moulds so that they could be handed over to outside firms who would have to be used in order to obtain a volume production of the new car.

The first Elite ever to run under its own steam on the road was a left-hand-drive model destined for the Geneva motor show on March 22nd. Unfinished and untrimmed, this car was fitted at the start with an 1,100cc motor, no FWE engines being immediately available. The little car was so nearly "right" in all respects on its first trial at Brands Hatch, that the future looked extremely rosy indeed for the new GT.

However, it was obvious that a tremendous amount of development was needed before production cars could be offered for general sale in a competitive market. Accordingly, a limited number of pre-production Elites were assembled for selected private owners, who by their racing and road work could indicate the many minor and major faults that were bound to crop up. The first private owner was Ian Walker, who had a fabulously successful racing season in EL 5; in its first two races, on consecutive days, Ian romped away with the up-to-1,600cc class, a habit to which the pair became thoroughly addicted, culminating in an easy class win in the *Autosport* Championship, having won outright most of the qualifying events and many other GT races as well.

Originally the Elite was conceived as a structure in glass-fibre-reinforced plastic with metal bonded in at certain attachment points, but in the production model, as shown at the 1958 motor show, the metal bonding at the mounting points for the final drive unit and rear suspension assembly was eliminated, in its place being thicker-section plastic in which rubber bushes were inserted. The only alterations to the mechanical layout after a year's development involved moving the engine mountings an inch to the rear and raising the power unit half an inch to increase ground clearance and provide more room for the silencer. The cooling system was provided with an electrically operated thermostatically controlled fan, fitted within the radiator ducting.

Two Elites shared the Lotus stand with a 1959 Formula car at the 1958 Motor Show, which was outstandingly successful in terms of interested customers and inquiries from literally all over the world. One of the Elites was sold to Chris Barber, jazz-band leader and Lotus addict, who proceeded to use the car regularly on his long Continental

One design finished, another one started. The Lotus drawing office at Hornsey was immediately above the compact showroom which had to suffice until the company moved to Cheshunt.

The two most famous racing Elites. Below: Graham Warner's 'LOV 1', which was raced under the Chequered Flag banner. Bottom: Les Leston's 'DAD 10'. The rivalry between these cars and drivers added so much excitement to GT racing at the beginning of the Sixties.

and British journeys, with the odd race for good measure.

Barber was to become one of the most consistent entrants of Lotus cars, his successful Elite giving way to an Elan, which also became a prolific race-winner.

Many more Elites went racing in 1959, one of the most prominent belonging to Ian Scott-Watson, the car being driven under the Border Reivers emblem by Jim Clark, in his second full season's racing. The Reivers' first Elite was a white one, raced on Boxing Day, 1958, and replaced by the green car which had been a works-sponsored entry at Le Mans in 1959. In this, in addition to countless other successes, Jim eclipsed the opposition in the Snetterton final of the *Autosport* Series Production Sports Car Championship; it was probably the most successful Elite that season.

Peter Lumsden had considerable success on the Continent in his Elite. Co-driving with Peter Riley, the 1100 Kms race at the Nurburgring saw a 1300 GT class win from sixteen Alfa-Romeos—the car being kept down to predetermined lap times. In the rain the Elite was gaining thirty-two seconds a lap from the nearest Alfa! Le Mans resulted in yet another class win—this time the 1,500cc class—eighth place in general classification, fifth on Index, and second in the new fuel consumption category. It was given out over the loudspeakers that theirs was the only car competing which had not had a spanner laid on it during the race!

Up to September, 1959, manufacture of the glass-fibre chassis/body units had been sub-contracted, while the installation of all the various components which go to make up a complete car were carried out at the Lotus works. But at that time, with a view to considerably increasing Elite output, Lotus Cars placed a contract for the quantity production of integral chassis/body units with Bristol Aircraft Ltd. The contract was one of the largest ever awarded to a plastics manufacturer by a British car firm, and called originally for an output from Bristol of fifteen bodies per week, but early in 1960 Lotus asked for production to be stepped up to twenty a week by July.

In view of the decline in interest in big sports-racing cars during 1960, and the fact that there was no new Lotus eminently suitable for this class anyway, it was decided to run Elites only at Le Mans. But one of these cars might well have carried off first prize outright, so great was its potential. This was an Elite, outwardly indistinguishable from a standard model but for the 6.00 by 15 rear tyres in conjunction with 5.00 by 15 front tyres; but the bonnet housed an FPF 1,960cc Coventry Climax twin-overhead-camshaft engine. To cater for the 180 bhp of this power unit, double front wishbones, with separate anti-roll bar, were used to cope with increased braking loads from very high speeds. The diameter of the front brake discs was increased to 10½ in, the rear suspension was standard in layout, but stiffer springs and adjustable shock absorbers were used all round. Transmission was by a front-mounted ZF four-speed all-synchromesh gearbox (as used in the 1958 2½ litres Fifteen), drive to the wheels being via a ZF differential unit with 3.2 to 1 cwp. The fuel tanks were modified to accept twenty-nine gallons, and special racing seats and Lucas windscreen wiper were fitted.

Great hopes were attached to this machine for, in order to comply with the 1960 Appendix C regulations, open sports-racing cars would have to carry high windscreens in any case; a coupe of this potential should compare very well. Drivers selected for Le Mans were Innes Ireland and Alan Stacey, but tragically Alan met his death at Spa, and efforts were made to find another driver. Jonathan Sieff seemed likely, but a nasty crash in the Taylor and Crawley Elite (from which he had a miraculous escape) put him out of the running. This left only John Whitmore, but as he had only completed one or two laps during official practice, it was reluctantly decided to withdraw the car.

However, four 1,216cc Elites started. Two of these retired, but the French-entered car of Robert Masson and Claude Laurent went exceedingly steadily and, after a trouble-free run, won the 1,300cc class, was 14th overall and came second in the Thermal Efficiency Index; this new Index was won, however, by Elite number 41, driven by Tony Marsh and John Wagstaff, their car coming second to the French entry in the 1,300cc class. The win in the Efficiency Index was a fine tribute to the Elite, taking into account, as it does, fuel consumption, weight of car, and distance covered during the race.

The most successful Elite raced in Great Britain during the 1960 season was undoubtedly that of Graham Warner, LOV 1. Entered under the auspices of the Chequered Flag, Graham's fantastic record that year was twelve first places, three seconds and a third, with three GT class lap records; only one mechanical failure had been experienced throughout the year, and one non-start due to a puncture on the line. Warner retained the car for 1961, its third season.

Giving some idea of the performance of highly tuned Elites of this era, some road test figures taken with the Chequered Flag Elite will be of interest: maximum speed 130.4 mph (over 8,000 rpm with the 4.9 Brands Hatch cwp); standing ¼ mile in 15.1 seconds; 0-60 mph, 6.6 seconds; 0-80 mph, 13.8 seconds; 0-100 mph, 17.2 seconds. These amazing figures for this closed coupe are better than the acceleration times of works Lotus sports-racing cars of a year or two earlier!

At the motor show in 1960, a new Special Equipment Lotus Elite was exhibited for the first time. The standard Elite was now offically Series Two, with a slightly modified trailing link component of the strut-type rear suspension. The engine of the Special Equipment model was the FWE Coventry-Climax 1,216cc unit, but with two 1½ in horizontal SU carburettors and a tuned four-branch exhaust system the power was raised from the 75 bhp of the standard unit to 83 bhp in this model. The four-speed, all-synchromesh gearbox contained ratios of 2.53: 1 in first, 1.71: 1 in second, 1.23: 1 in third and 1: 1 in top; final drive ratio was 4.22: 1. With the Michelin "X" tyres fitted as standard to this car, this gave a road speed of 16.15 mph per 1000 rpm in top gear. A special heavy-duty 12 volt, 57 amp-hour battery was installed, and headlights were the Lucas F700 type. A heater and de-misting unit completed the equipment.

So the Elite had really grown up, from the rather immature, rough-shod youngster of 1957 to an exceedingly highly developed and ultra-desirable Grand Touring car, all set for even higher production figures and greater success in 1961.

17.

The championship trail

LUCKY STARS HAD shone brightly over Team Lotus during 1957, and hopes were high for equally good fortune in the 1958 season. At any rate, they were not short of driver talent: Cliff Allison, Keith Hall and Graham Hill were to drive the Formula cars, and Peter Ashdown and Alan Stacey would drive in sports car events. For the first time, Lotus were to race Formula 1 cars in grand prix events. But before thoughts had been seriously turned towards Formula racing there was the announcement, early in 1958, of the Lotus Fifteen—the new sports car.

This car had been designed with an eye on the 24-hour classic at Le Mans, and with the 2.2 litre Climax engine its *theoretical* maximum speed was about 205 mph! The main mechanical change from previous sports Lotuses was at the rear, where Formula 2-type strut rear suspension had been installed, and the five-speed gearbox/final drive unit was also as first used on the Formula 2 car. A new body had been designed by Frank Costin, and the frontal area of the Fifteen, despite its bigger engine, was in fact less than that of the Eleven. An extremely low bonnet line was obtained by canting the engine to the right, using specially made curved manifolding for the Webers.

The frame, again typically Lotus, was built up of 1 in and ¾ in 18- and 20-gauge round and square tubes, the propeller shaft tunnel and floor being stressed and integral parts of the frame. The front suspension had the wishbone layout of the Formula 2 and the Series 2 Eleven, and brakes with 9½ in discs all round were mounted outboard at the front, inboard at the rear, the latter deriving extra cooling by means of an underbody air scoop.

The spare wheel was mounted upright in the head fairing, beside capacious tanks for fuel, engine and gearbox oil. Magnesium bolt-on wheels, as used on the works cars, could be supplied to private owners with 5.50 x 15 Dunlop racing tyres.

The cockpit had more leg room than the Eleven, largely because of the rear-mounted gearbox. A full range of instruments confronted the driver, whose left hand would fall naturally on the positive-stop gear lever, which had to be pulled back for first gear and changing down, and forwards for changing up; reverse was selected by a separate knob behind the passenger seat. While the 1½ litre FPF twin-cam Climax engine was standard, 2 and 2.2 litre-powered examples were also offered.

Three new Fifteens had been entered for the British Empire Trophy—Pierre Berchem's 1½ litre prototype car to be driven by Roy Salvadori, and 2 litre works cars for Graham Hill and Cliff Allison. On Friday, the official practice day, one of the works 2 litres went fantastically well, Graham putting up fastest 2 litre time, taking 3.4 seconds off the offical sports car lap record in the process, while Cliff was only 1.4 seconds slower. Meanwhile, back at Hornsey, the second works car was still in the process of assembly!

At dawn on the Saturday, Mike Costin set off in the brand-new Fifteen to drive it up to Oulton for the race that afternoon. Twice during that hectic journey the rear end was dismantled, the first time to clear a blocked gearbox oil filter, and the second to strip the gearbox in order to braze-up a snapped selector pawl. Mike made it with fifteen minutes to spare, numbers were slapped on, fuel and oil added, and after one warming-up lap Graham took the car to the front of the grid!

Three Lotus Fifteens, all with registration numbers 001 MH, catapulted into the leading places. Heat one was on, but Graham, who took the lead, soon shot into the pits to have a loose sparking plug replaced. Only a meteoric drive could ensure him a place in the final now, and although he managed the fantastic lap time of 1 min 50.8 sec, well under the sports car lap record, it was to no avail.

Cliff Allison went on to win the heat, so qualifying for the final, and in this, his pursuit of Stirling Moss was memorable, Moss having to push the 3.9 litre DBR2 Aston Martin to a lap time equalling Hill's effort earlier on in order to elude the Lotus. Cliff's oil pressure vanished, however, before the race ended and he had to give up.

And so, two weeks later, to the first World Championship Grand Prix in which Lotus competed—at Monte Carlo, on May 8th. For this important step, it was decided to rely on the two faithful 2 litre Formula 2–based cars, and not to attempt to fit the 2.2 litre engine, which had been flown out to Monaco.

For once, the cars had arrived at the circuit in good time, and by the start of practice on Thursday they looked very spruce, with newly painted chassis, long-distance fuel tanks and guessed-at rear ratios. Graham was out first, but had trouble with locking brakes, and Cliff only managed a few laps before overheating called a halt for the head to be removed. "Reserving his best efforts for the morrow", a local paper said. The next day, after test runs with the assistance of the local police on the main road to Nice, Graham had more brake-locking trouble, and at the station hairpin he ran right over the kerb and stuffed the front of the Lotus between the straw bales. The driver was not amused, however, when a French newspaper reported that Hill was dissatisfied with the power output, and "had decided to feed the horses".

Both cars qualified, in thirteenth and fifteenth places out of the sixteen allotted. One advantage of the low grid placing was that the Lotuses were well out of the shunting match which took place at the start, and Cliff pulled up a couple of places before coming in on the 35th lap for water, the engine being nearly as hot as the driver. After pressing on again he suddenly found himself with no brakes and survived a dramatic spin, after which he slowed the car by pumping furiously at the brake to get the calipers to the discs. By using one gear higher than normal over the lap, Allison only called for water once more, and finished sixth (and last), ten laps behind the winner, Trintignant (Cooper).

Graham Hill was less well off. As he said, he "started last and remained last for several laps, but received lots of information from the pits". But on the 71st lap, the tail of the car thumped the deck when a drive shaft failed, and Graham finished the lap on foot, to the sympathetic applause of the crowd.

And so on to Zandvoort, for the Dutch Grand Prix, only a week later. The cars were not returned to England but went straight to Holland, and the brand-new 2.2 litre Climax engine was fitted to the car which Cliff was to drive. At first both Lotuses were hopelessly under-geared, but after alterations to the final-drive ratios all was well, and both cars beat the old circuit record in practice, although this was only good enough for the fifth row of the grid. Graham discovered the ultimate cornering speed—and proved the little car's strength—by spinning off backwards very rapidly into a four-foot deep gulley. Undamaged, the Lotus was hauled back by twenty Dutchmen and a long rope.

Cliff started the race steadily and rose to seventh place when he overtook Collins' Ferrari, and to sixth when Lewis-Evans (Vanwall) retired; and there the Lotus finished, out of the eleven which completed the race. Graham had sweated into the pits, on the 22nd lap—pushing the Lotus after one of the ignition contacts had broken off, and he gave up for good on the 40th lap, with serious overheating.

The Belgian Grand Prix which followed came so close to giving Team Lotus its first GP win. Cliff revelled in the ultra-high-speed cornering required at Spa, and gradually worked his way up to fourth place, behind Brooks (Vanwall), Hawthorn (Ferrari) and Lewis-Evans (Vanwall), while on the twelfth lap a con-rod in Hill's 2 litre engine appeared in the daylight. As Brooks rounded La Source for the last time, his gearbox tightened up—he would never have been able to do another lap in order to win. Next through to the chequered flag was Hawthorn, accompanied by a large and impressive cloud of white smoke; a piston had broken. The top right-hand wishbone on Lewis-Evans' Vanwall broke on the last lap, and he only just managed to finish. Then, storming through in fourth place came the first car to be still going well—Allison's 2.2 litre Lotus! The duration of the race had been 1 hour 37 min 6.3 seconds, whereas the F.I.A. minimum duration regulation for grandes epreuves specified two hours. If only... but nothing could be done about the rule-bending by the organisers.

No less than four works Lotuses and two private entries turned up at Sarthe for the 1958 G.P. d'Endurance at Le Mans, and all six were built especially for the race. A 2 litre Fifteen was the number-one car, drivers Cliff Allison and Graham Hill having an eye on an outright win, as well as the 2 litre class. Despite efforts by both Coventry Climax and Lotus Engineering, the canted engine with curved inlet manifolds had never really worked properly, and in the Le Mans car the engine was set 17 degrees to the other side, this giving a virtually straight inlet tract. However, the greater height of the engine in this position necessitated a bulge on the bonnet, which made more difference to the air flow than had been realised. A 1½ litre Fifteen, to be driven by Jay Chamberlain and Pete Lovely, had the same engine arrangement. The works 1100 Eleven was equipped with Stage 3 engine, and MGA gearbox with close-ratio gears for drivers Innes Ireland and Michael Taylor (in his phenomenal first season's racing). The other 1100 was entered by Car Exchange and driven by Bill Frost and Bob Hicks.

Two 750cc Elevens appeared, in an attempt to emulate the Index-winning performance of 1957. The Team Lotus car (Alan Stacey and Tom Dickson) was practised with a brand-new single-cam FWM Climax engine, enlarged from 650cc to 742cc for the race. This broke in practice, however, and the 1957 adapted 1100cc unit was fitted instead, but the French-entered car

Below: Variations on a theme. The sports car 15 and the single-seater 16 had many similarities. Bottom: No mistaking the Frank Costin touch in the 16's Vanwall-like body. Right and below right: Graham Hill out-sprints Roy Salvadori to their 15s at Goodwood but Roy's car is quicker off the mark.

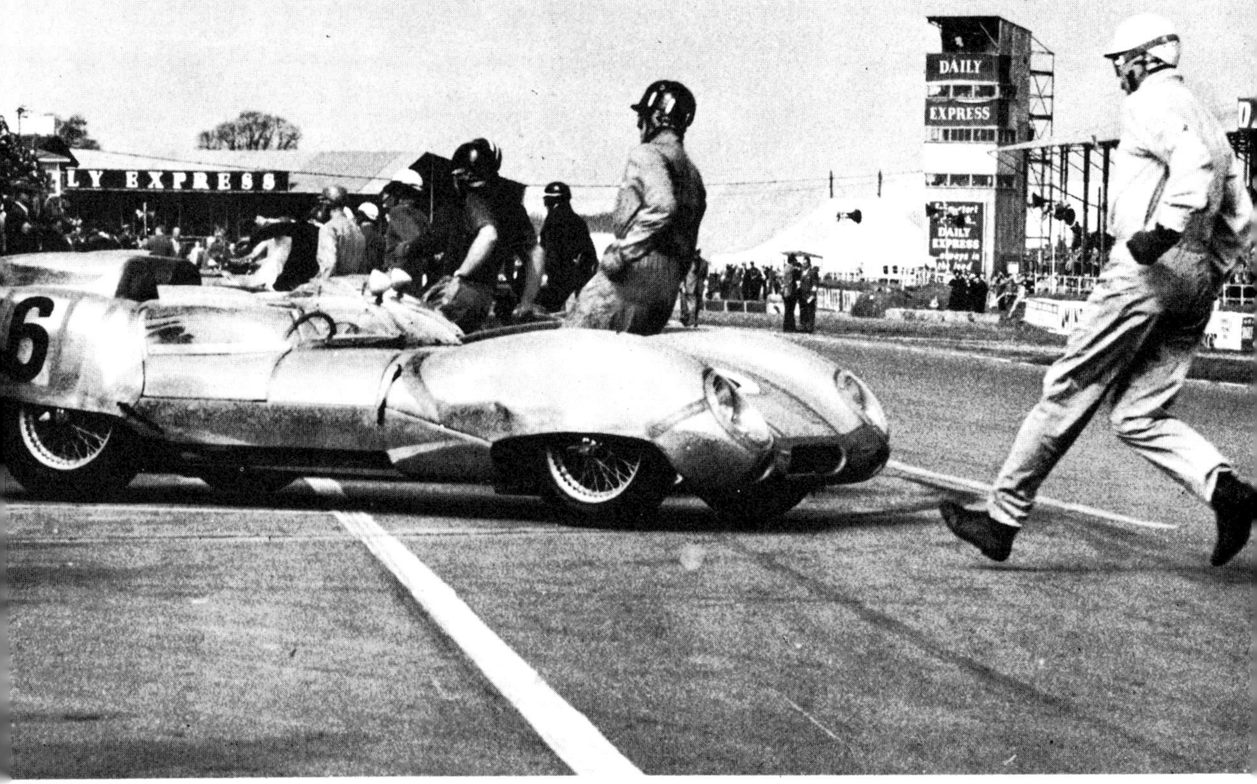
LY EXPRESS
DAILY
EXPRESS
6

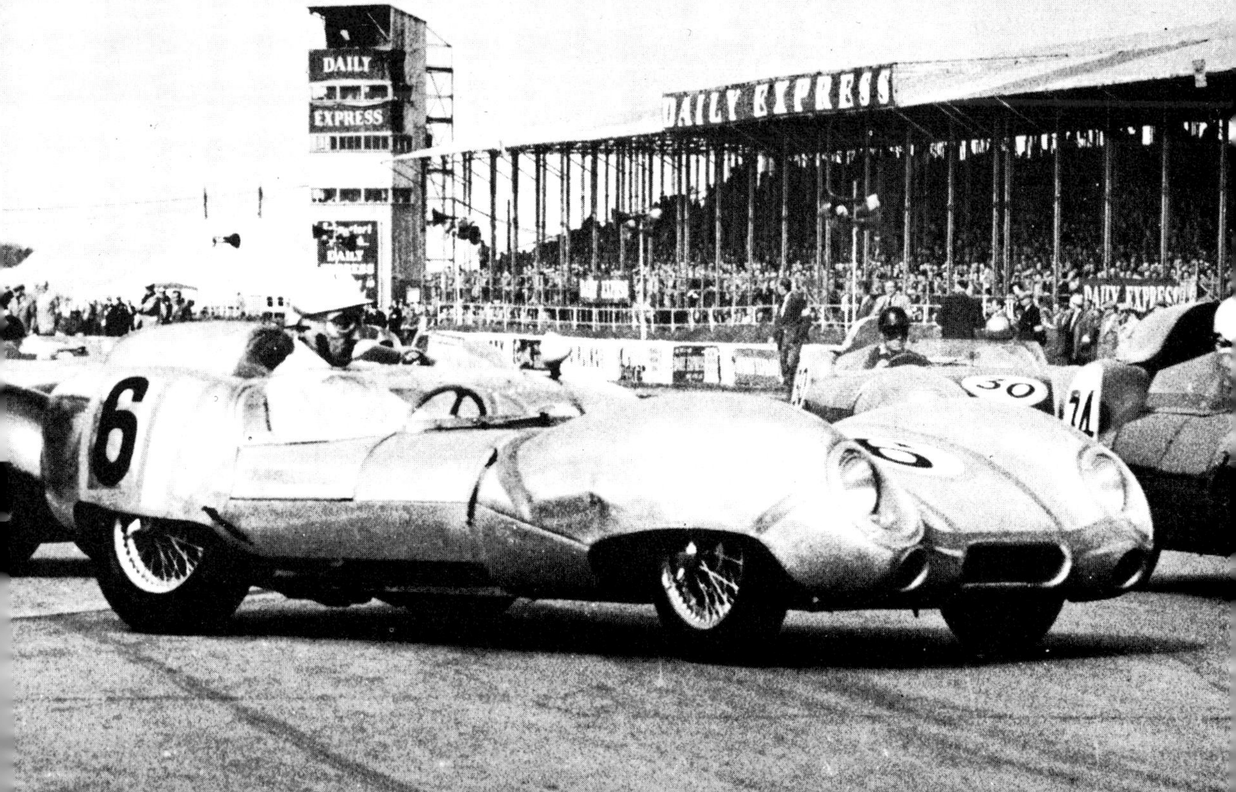
DAILY
EXPRESS
DAILY EXPRESS
6
30

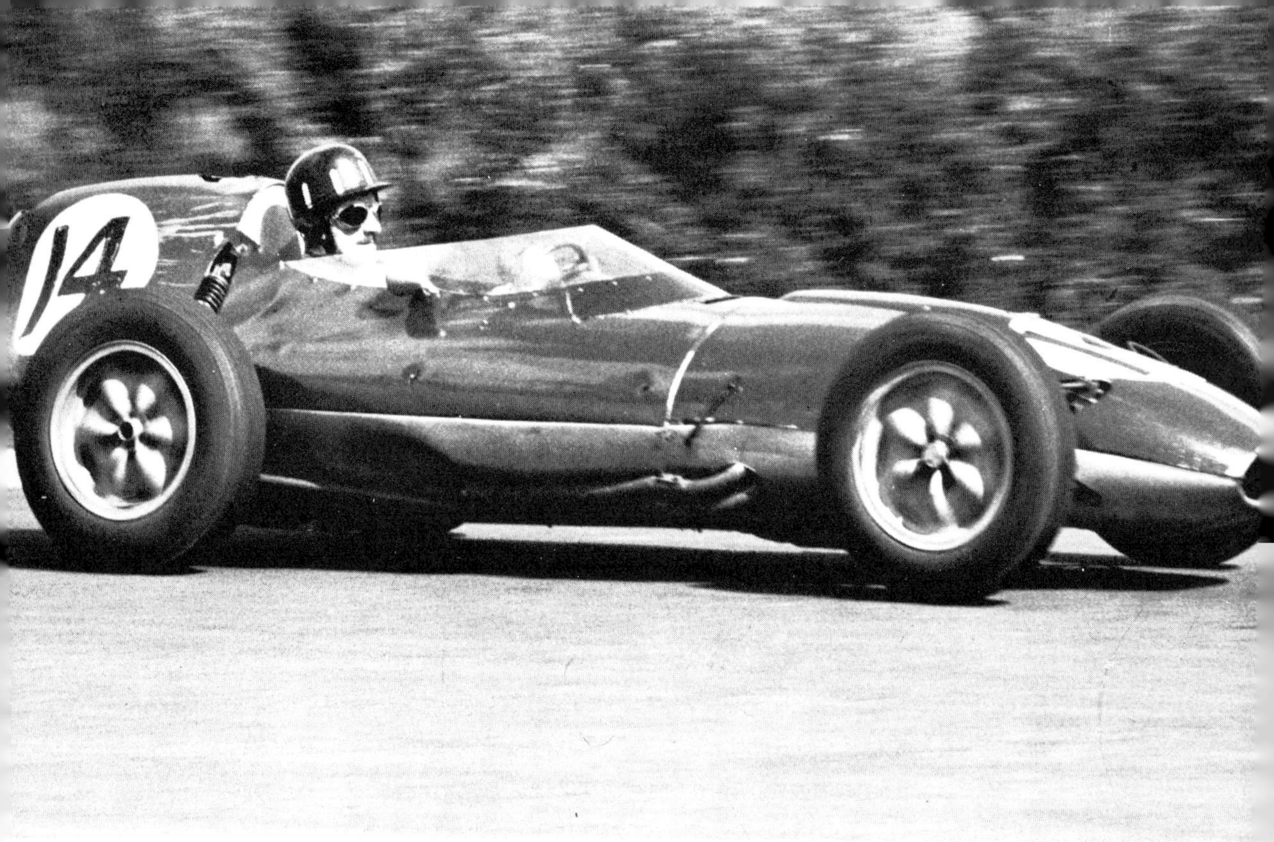
14

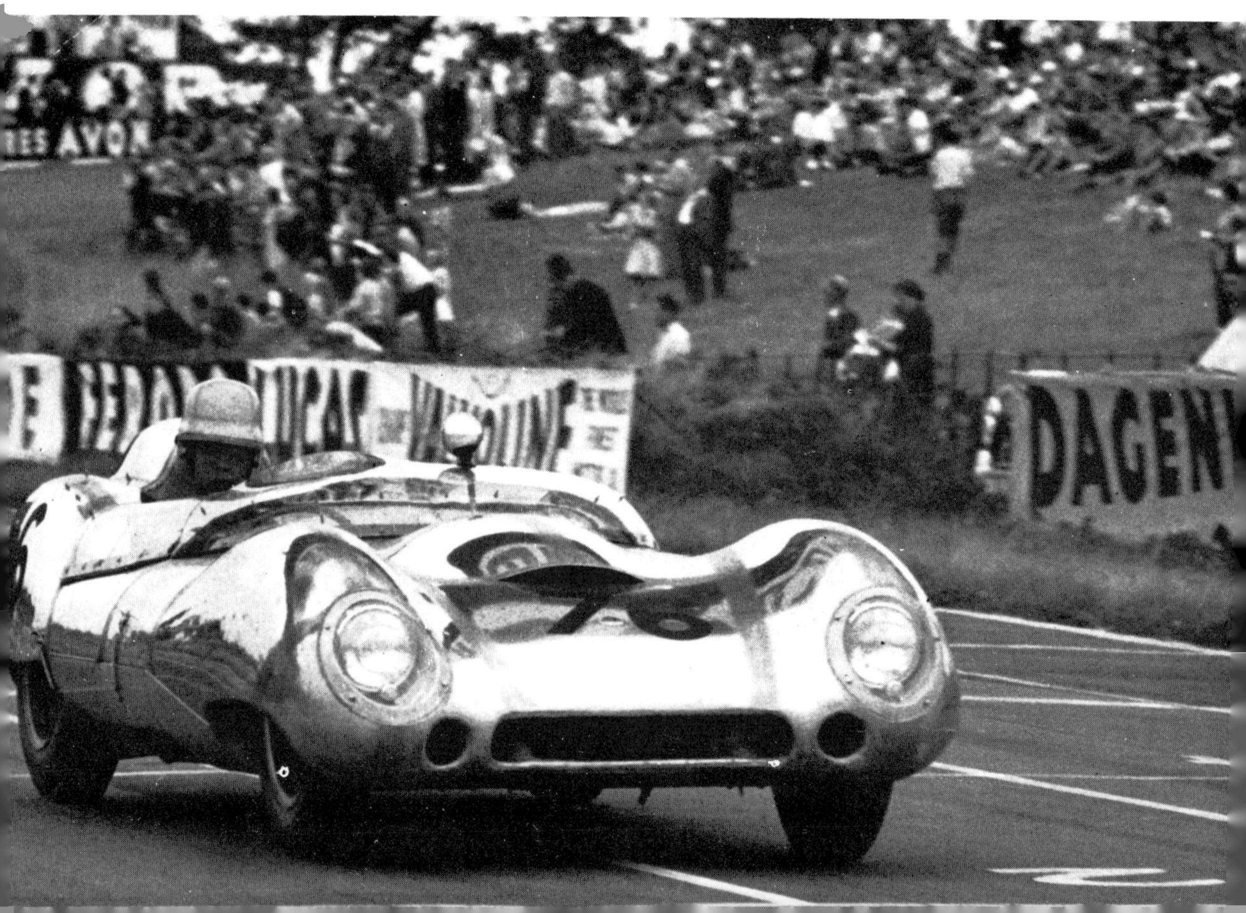

Left: A relaxed Graham Hill in an exhaust-scarred Lotus 16. Below left: Tommy Dickson, from Scotland, in his rapid 15. Below: The 15 unveiled to reveal its generous radiator flanked by cooling ducts, the large fuel tank behind the inboard rear brakes, and the roomy cockpit with 'push-pull' gear shift.

of Roger Masson and Andre Hechard retained its FWM 742cc engine. The 750s had live rear axles to reduce transmission power loss, drum rear brakes and magnesium wheels, while the Fifteens, whose tyres would have to be changed, were equipped with knock-on wheels.

The 2 litre car was very fast in practice, being quicker than all the Ferraris, but would it last? Unfortunately not. After only three laps, Cliff was in with gasket trouble, and the car was pushed away. Hill had still never driven at Le Mans. The 1½ litre Fifteen was a persistent caller at the Team Lotus pit with misfiring, which was eventually traced to faulty ignition, but this Lotus was eliminated when Chamberlain crashed heavily in avoiding a slower car.

Meanwhile, Bob Hicks had spun on the curve on the Mulsanne straight, and the gendarmerie stopped him driving off again from the infield. The problem was settled when a soild Alfa-Romeo wrote off the stationary Lotus by running into its back. The French 750 was involved in a multiple crash at White House. The works 1100 had only one headlight by the time a wet night fell—the result of an off-course excursion by Mike Taylor—but Innes flogged manfully on. On Sunday morning, when it was the only 1100 car still running, the distributor drive broke. Tom Dickson had driven the works 750 into a sandbank backwards, and set out to dig it out, first with a headlamp cover, then with a shovel which was miraculously lying nearby—surprise, surprise! The only Lotus still running at 4 o'clock on Sunday, the 750, ended up 20th—and last—in the Le Mans of 1958.

Best regarded as the 1959 car undergoing rapid development on the track, the new Formula car—the Sixteen—was completed and announced in time for the Grand Prix de l'ACF, at Reims, where it appeared in 2 litre form for Hill to drive, along with a 1½ litre-engined model for the Formula 2 race. Cliff Allison stuck to the faithful "old banger" 1957 car with the 2.2 litre unit.

The chassis of the Sixteen was basically the same as that of the 1957 Formula cars, but the same amount of metal was spread over a greater area, and the suspension was identical, except that longer radius arms were used in the Chapman strut-type layout. The extremely beautiful body was Frank Costin's latest effort—almost inevitably somewhat similar to the Vanwall, considering Frank's association with the latter car. Wheelbase was 7 ft 4 in, track 3 ft 11 in, overall length 11 ft 8 in, and overall height only 2 ft 11 in.

The rear-mounted five-speed gearbox/final drive unit incorporated a new casing with the gears of the original five-speed box, having its own sump and with the first gear train acting as an oil pump. However, this did not prove entirely satisfactory, and two further systems were tried later, one using an external pump, and the other being self-lubricating, with circulation aided by splash from the crown wheel. Gear selection was by a new positive-stop mechanism.

Hill's 2 litre car at Reims had the engine "on its side", with the propeller shaft passing to the left of the driver. In the 1½ litre car, the engine of which was tilted 17 deg. to the left, the transmission was taken under the driver's left leg to the gearbox, which was offset 4 deg., thus creating awkward angles throughout the transmission. A third layout used was the "upright" engine offset 10½ deg. to the right, bringing the gearbox back into alignment with the drive shafts; the driving position and pedals were all angled to the right, and the exhaust system was temporarily set outside the bodywork in this version.

The 2.2 "old banger", glad to be back home, went quite splendidly in practice for the Silverstone British Grand Prix on July 19th, carrying Cliff Allison to fifth fastest time in practice—second row of the grid. Graham Hill had the Reims 1500cc car with a 2 litre "upright" engine, and Alan Stacey was given his first-ever grand prix drive in the first Sixteen with "sideways" 2 litre unit. Both new cars were a lot slower than the 1957 model in practice.

On the 18th lap, Graham Hill's backside, in close proximity to the gearbox in this version, became so warm, and the oil pressure so low, that he called it a day. Cliff's oil pressure also vanished, and Alan retired with overheating. Even allowing for experimentation, Team Lotus were having a very bad time.

Cliff, Graham and Pete Lovely were in works 1½ litre Fifteens in the big sports car race, and Salvadori was driving John Coombs' beautifully turned out white 2 litre Fifteen. The latter car finished second overall to Moss's Lister-Jaguar, winning the 2 litre class, Cliff was third, and first in the 1½ litre section, and Alan continued a remarkable season in his Eleven by finishing fifth overall and easily taking the 1100 class.

Outwardly identical with the "upright" engine Fifteen, a Series 2 Fifteen was announced about this time. The simplified transmission of the new car was designed for export to countries where Lotus spares might not be immediately available—in fact, the first car was shipped to Pete Lovely in America. A BMC "B"-type four-speed and reverse gearbox was coupled direct to the Climax engine, with ratios of 1 : 1, 1.25 : 1, 1.67 : 1 and 2.5 : 1, and a variety of BMC final drive ratios was available, installed in a chassis-mounted Lotus casing. Otherwise, the car was no different to the "standard" Fifteen.

By the time of the Grosser Preis von Deutschland, all hopes of using the horizontal engine layout had been abandoned, and both 1958 cars sent had the upright arrangement. Cliff Allsion, driving the only Formula 1 entry, had a 2 litre engine (the 2.2 had been badly damaged at Silverstone) and Graham Hill was driving in the Formula 2 section with a 1½ litre car. Ivor Bueb had brought his 1957-type Formula 2 Lotus. Cliff got down to 9 min 39 sec on his first visit to the Nurburgring, justifying many hours of practice in his Austin A35 the week before, but Graham's 1½ litre engine tightened up as he was going into a corner, and he spun. After limping the car back to the pits, it was found that the water-pump drive had sheared. So he took Allison's 2 litre car out for some more practice, and lost it on a downhill section, badly crumpling the nose and supports. With the help of the Esso mechanics this was straightened out, and luckily the new large-size radiator appeared not to have been damaged.

Before the Grand Prix, Cliff took out a works 1½ litre Fifteen for a 6-lap sports car race, and driving brilliantly, he held third place behind Behra (Prosche) and Bonnier (Borgward) until a rear radius-arm mounting broke after brushing the verge. David Piper's 1100 finished ninth after

Left: Graham Hill racing to second place in the 1959 Kentish 100 race at Brands Hatch. Below: Graham had given the 16 its British debut at Silverstone the previous year, two weeks after its first-ever public appearance in the French GP.

losing over a minute at the start when the engine refused to start.

Allison, despite his excellent practice lap, started from the back of the grid through having completed insufficient laps during the training session, but his first lap was sensational, and he was soon in fourth place behind Hawthorn and Collins in Ferraris, and Brooks (Vanwall) although to be fair there had been a lot of retirements among the leaders early in the race! Brooks then

Left: The epic duel between Graham Hill in the 15 and Jack Brabham in the Cooper Monaco preceding the 1959 British GP at Aintree, which Hill won. Below left: The offset engine of the early 16. Below: The neat spare wheel location on the 15.

passed the Ferraris, which were both soon eliminated by Collins' tragic crash and Hawthorn's subsequent retirement. Great excitement—was Cliff to be second? But by the greatest misfortune the radiator must have been damaged after all in Graham's shunt in practice; it split, and Cliff had to come in for a temporary repair, which dropped him to last.

Graham's 1½ litre had never gone well, and he was glad enough to retire when an oil pipe broke. It was later found that some piston rings had broken up. Once again, Lotus had come very close to a place on the GP map but had just failed to make it. If only Graham had not been forced to practise in Cliff's car . . .

The Grande Premio de Portugal was held on the road circuit at Oporto, and all at Lotus hoped that this might bring a change in luck, as the little cars should be well suited to the course. But once again luck was not with Cliff. Coming out of the roundabout on to the Avenida de Boavista during practise, he hit gravel, the nose struck a straw bale, and the Lotus whipped round, flinging itself on to the nearby walls and ending up wrecked. Allison, unhurt. The Lotus had been a 2 litre with the gearbox "on the bonk", i.e., set at an angle to the centre line, and with the exhaust system within the bodywork. Cliff, undaunted, took up the offer of the Centro-Sud 250 F Maserati, and started from the fourth row of the grid, with Graham beside him in the other Lotus.

Cliff was not too happy in the Maser, which made him appreciate to the full the lightness and ease of handling of the Hornsey car, and he retired on lap 16 rather than hold up the fast boys, and wear out the car in the process. Hill's car had the 2.2 engine in line with the gearbox, and an outside exhaust, and at half distance he was just winning a private battle with Salvadori's works 2 litre Cooper when the Lotus lost all front-end adhesion and mounted the bales; Graham was able to lift the car down on to the road, but not to restart.

The Portugal accident left Team Lotus a car short for the Italian Grand Prix at Monza on September 7th, so the 1957 "old banger" was resurrected for Allison to drive. A 2 litre engine had been fitted, but a rod came through the crankcase when a big-end bolt let go during practice, and so the only spare engine, a 1½ litre, was fitted instead. Graham's Sixteen had the 2.2 litre, as at Portugal, and the scuttle had been modified slightly to give him more room. Both cars had cooling holes and slots cut wherever possible—it was very hot indeed at Monza!

The Lotuses still tended to overheat, but Graham did well enough to start from the fourth row, with Cliff behind him. Hill was in the second main group in the race when a persistent misfire forced him to slow, and eventually to come in to see what was wrong. The insulation on a plug lead had burnt through causing it to short on the cylinder head, but once sorted, the Lotus went on as well as ever. Cliff came in to find out why he was becoming covered in oil, but all seemed to be well, and he pressed on steadily to finish seventh and last, nine laps behind winner Brooks. Graham did one lap better, and ended up sixth—his first points score in a championship race in eight tries. Both drivers were cooked to a turn at the finish, and Colin produced some most welcome iced lollies.

The same two cars (Cliff's now with the 2.2 engine again) were taken to North Africa, for the Grand Prix du Maroc, to be held on the Ain-Diab circuit at Casablanca. All eyes throughout this race were to be focussed on Moss' titanic but vain struggle to wrest the World Championship from Mike Hawthorn. Cliff spun on oil in practice, and hit the straw bales, needing a new radius arm and half-shaft, but Graham had gone well, and settled for the fourth row on the grid. In the early stages Cliff was still getting to know the circuit, and the car was not handling too well, but Graham was going well until on the tenth lap he stopped for water, despite the new, *big* versions of radiator, oil cooler and air intake. Three more times he had to come in, and on the last, as Jim Endruweit undid the filler cap, a fountain of boiling water shot in the air, this being promptly directed at the luckless Graham by the bonnet lid which Jim had rapidly lowered. These stops, and one for a plug change, dropped Graham to last, but at least he was still going. Cliff plugged on steadily throughout, with the side body panels removed, and ended up tenth overall in the "old banger"

And so ended the 1958 grand prix season—Lotus' first season in the class, and a very instructive one, if not exactly the most successful. The F.I.A. announced its decision to downgrade the 2½ litre formula to one of 1300–1500cc with a 500 kg minimum weight limit, to take effect in 1961. Colin expressed his views. "Just ridiculous", he said; "the reduction of capacity to 1½ litre for what is the highest grade of racing is in itself a retrograde step, while the imposition of a weight limit will not only put a brake on design but will have the effect of reducing safety for it will allow more people to race less highly developed cars". Chapman never really thought that the 1½ litre formula would ever actually come into being. But then, nor did a lot of other people.

Throughout the English 1958 racing season, Elevens had still been going very strongly indeed. By far the most successful driver in 1100 events was Alan Stacey, who made his G.P. debut the same year—his record of wins and reliability was fantastic, owing as much to Mr. Basson's meticulous assembly and maintenance as to Alan's superlative driving. In his first season's racing, Mike Taylor and his Eleven won the Brooklands Memorial Trophy from Keith Greene in a similar car, and also carried off the Club Lotus Lotuseer cup for the most outstanding performance by a driver in his first year of Lotus driving. To Innes Ireland went the John Coombs Trophy for the most meritorious performance by a non-works driver.

During December Cliff Allison went over to Modena to try the Ferrari Formula 1 car and the 3 litre Testa Rossa sports car. Favourably impressed by the cars (as Enzo Ferrari was with him), Cliff signed a contract to drive Ferraris in Formula 1, 2 and sports car races during 1959. So, with good wishes from all at Hornsey, Cliff at long last left Team Lotus for Italy.

The end of the 1958 season. Graham had done some phenomenally fast laps in 1959 Lotuses at Brands Hatch, and the new factory at Cheshunt was going up fast. There was good reason, therefore, to hope for better times in the upcoming season.

18.

A matter of handling

A COMPLETELY NEW SPORTS car for 1959 was the Seventeen, a new 1100cc or 750cc machine, which was a logical development of the very successful Eleven, but lighter, smaller, and with potentially better roadholding.

The spaceframe was built up of $\frac{5}{8}$ in and ¾ in square and round 20-gauge tubes, with the floor and propshaft as usual acting as stressed members. The front suspension was for the first time of strut type, with each wheel located by a wide-based lower wishbone and Armstrong coil spring/damper unit, mounted almost upright; this gave very little camber change on bump. At the rear, the strut suspension was similar to that on the Formula cars. Brakes were Girling 9½ in disc type, outboard at front and inboard at rear, and steering by a new lightweight rack-and-pinion gear. Cast magnesium wheels were fitted as standard, and the power unit was either the 1100cc FWA Stage 3 Climax engine, or the FWM 742cc unit. Transmission was via a hydraulically operated clutch and short propeller shaft to the chassis-mounted differential unit.

The Seventeen was clothed in an extremely pretty new body designed by Len Terry and the Lotus drawing office staff. Every inch a Lotus, it was nevertheless sufficiently distinctive to stand out in 1100 races—the Seventeen was 3 in shorter than an Eleven, 4½ in narrower, 3½ in lower at the scuttle and 7½ in lower overall. The turning circle was reduced by 6 ft, partly because of the 3 ft 6 in front track, the wheelbase was 6 ft 10 in, and the rear track 3 ft 9 in. Weight, less fuel, was 750 lb.

The other sports car unveiled at the beginning of the year was the development of the Fifteen, officially designated Series 3. In this, the chassis frame had been stiffened, and the top wishbone of the front suspension reversed, so that the anti-roll bar was now behind the wheel centres; this permitted the fitting of a large radiator and oil cooler. At the same time the front track was reduced by 1 in.

Cooling troubles had been one of the main bug-bears of the 1958 season. Due to the location of the water pump, and the low bonnet line required, a conventional header tank could not be made large enough to effectively separate the bubbles, which entered the eye of the impeller and caused cavitation. The new system incorporated double swirl and overflow pots, and removed bubbles by a centrifuge, allowing the water expelled by thermal expansion to be returned again on cooling. In other words, the cooling system would always remain air-free.

The standard power arrangement was to be the 2 litre unit, mounted with the 17 deg. tilt to the left, transmitting through a four-speed BMC B-type gearbox to a chassis-mounted differential, as on the Series 2 Fifteen. The greater torque of the 2 litre obviated the need for the more complicated five-speed box which, however, could still be supplied in improved form if required.

Before settling down to the serious business of grand prix racing, Team Lotus had entered for a number of non-championship races in Britain. Only one 2½ litre Climax engine was forthcoming, so only Graham Hill had a drive in the Formula 1 races at the BARC Goodwood Easter Monday meeting and the BARC Aintree 200. At

Goodwood, Graham retired with no brakes, and at Aintree he was plagued by so many things going wrong that he just got nowwhere—and not very fast, either. A 1½ litre engine had been fitted for the Formula 2 British Empire Trophy, and Graham went well to start with, rising to fifth place before an undiagnosed engine vibration put him out on the 15th lap. Bruce Halford went well in John Fisher's 1958 motor show car, holding second spot for a long time until all the gears disappeared.

Pete Lovely drove a second 1959 Formula car at the BRDC International Trophy meeting at Silverstone, with Graham in the original 2½ litre. Innes Ireland was in a works Formula 2 car, but Stacey's similar machine non-started. Innes was the first finisher, in tenth place, and Lovely was 14th and last, after coming in for more engine oil. Hill's brake pipe burst.

The first Continental event was the Gran Premio Siracusa for Formula 2 cars, on April 25th. Hill, Halford and Piper all had gear-selection difficulties in practice, but Halford was very fast and started from the second row of the grid. Bruce, however, never completed a fast race lap, and after being delayed by more selector difficulties, he retired when an oil pipe tore out of the engine casting. Graham was out on the 37th lap with a collapsed hub race, and Piper hobbled home 8th with the front of the chassis separate from the remainder.

Would fortunes be better at the first championship grand prix, at Monaco, on May 10th? Two Team Lotus entries were sent, for Graham Hill and Pete Lovely to drive. By this time, the general layout of the 1959 Sixteen had been more or less finalised. A number of important modifications had been made, despite the similar external appearance. A new frame with the layout of the tubes drastically altered incorporated what was to become a Lotus feature—a combined tube and drilled sheet metal scuttle hoop. The front suspension was the new "reversed type", with anti-roll bar to the rear and kinked to clear the engine. The rear suspension now incorporated a wide-based lower wishbone to take transverse and longitudinal loads, in place of the trailing arm. The "upright" engine layout was used—17½ deg. tilt to the left and offset 10½ deg. to the nearside and the engine was fed through either 50 mm or 58 mm Weber carburettors. The cooling system incorporated the double swirl and overflow pots which replaced a conventional header tank. The propeller shafts passed obliquely under the driver's left leg, to the improved five-speed gearbox/differential unit, the selector mechanism of which had been revised.

The Lotus transporter broke down on the way from England, and there was thus a desperate rush to qualify as the works cars had arrived only just in time for the last practice session. Unused to Webers, the mechanics were having trouble with the carburettors, and both cars were spitting and banging their way out of the hairpin. Graham nevertheless just managed to qualify, as did Bruce Halford in the Fisher Formula 2 car. But Bruce was out almost immediately, involved in a crash through no fault of his own which also eliminated both the other Formula 2 cars, and Graham never went really well, and on lap 22 leapt out of the car to extinguish an oil fire, after which he was unable to re-start.

Meanwhile, back home all was not well with the Seventeen. At Goodwood on Easter Monday the handling was atrocious, but Alan Stacey made some suggestions which might improve matters for Aintree on April 18th. In the wet the car seemed OK, but on a dry road, the oversteer—vicious and unpredictable—seemed as bad as ever. Despite this, Alan came from the back of the grid to lead, until second gear disappeared. Testing at Silverstone determined a lot of modifications—the ride level was lowered, and stiffer front and rear springs fitted. This produced a nearer approximation to neutral steer than with any other Lotus, meaning there was less understeer! Up to the Whit Monday Crystal Palace meeting the motor had definitely been down on power, but this was sorted in time for the race. Practice time was under the 1100cc circuit record, but before Alan had covered 25 yards in the race, the crankshaft broke.

For the Dutch Grand Prix at Zandvoort, Team Lotus had collected themselves for a determined effort to recoup some of their slipping reputation. To further this aim, the whole outfit arrived a day early, Graham lapping very fast and steadily from

The 17 was the smallest aerodynamic sports Lotus to date. Left: The cockpit was the epitome of simplicity. Below: Outward-hinging bodywork gave better-than-ever accessibility. Bottom: Smaller than the 11, the car could also be identified by the horizontal line running between front and rear wheel openings. Designed to combat the Lola 1100, initially it was beset with handling problems.

Right: The Alan Stacey/Tom Dickson 742cc 11, which was to be the only Lotus to survive the 1958 Le Mans 24 Hours. Below: Graham Hill giving the works Lotus 17 an airing at Brands Hatch.

the start of practice. His team-mate was to be Innes Ireland, getting his first and well-deserved drive in a grande epreuve. Innes had already worn his Zephyr into the ground—the Zandvoort track—the day before, and was soon very much at home with the considerably more powerful 2½ litre. The newcomer lapped in a creditable 1 min 38.3 sec, but Graham did even better, with an invigorating 1 min 36.7 sec to land himself in the second row.

Both Lotuses were well up in the field from the start, in the mob struggling for fourth place. As the field spread into bunches, Graham and Moss (Cooper) found themselves held up by Behra's Ferrari through the fast, winding sections, but unable to pass the bigger car on the straight, but at last Moss managed to pass, Graham shortly following him through. Then a puff of smoke appeared at Graham's elbow, and thinking of the fire at Monaco, he stopped by the track and waited for the car to blaze. But nothing happened so he carried on, but his front brakes were no longer with him, causing the Lotus to snake viciously as he braked with the rears only.

Innes, meanwhile, had been slowly coming through the field, despite some trouble with a locking offside front brake and considerable understeer at the hairpin, which had not shown itself in practice. Then Shelby's Aston seized, dropping oil, and Ireland hit the slick, but managed to drop only two wheels off the track. Innes was also held up by Behra, but passed the Frenchman by following the leading pair, Moss and Bonnier, as they went through. Fourth place! Colin did a war dance on the pit counter. Innes was closing fast on third man Gregory when the offside front tyre ran bald, so the Scot eased up, and that was how he finished. Fourth in his first grand prix, and Graham was not disgraced, taking seventh place. Zandvoort was a fine and much-needed fillip for the Hornsey team. Everyone was delighted.

But the sports cars did not do so well in the Le Mans 24-hour GP d'Endurance. Strong bids for an outright win were provided by the 2½ litre Fifteen, to be driven by Graham Hill and Derek Jolly from Australia and a 2 litre Fifteen to be shared by Innes Ireland and Alan Stacey. Two Seventeens were running, owned by John Fisher and Michael Taylor and entered by Team Lotus, both with 742cc FWM Climax engines. The Fifteens were of 1959 reversed-wishbone type, with the new five-speed gearbox. This was similar to that used on the single-seater, but with the gear trains on top of each other and in line with the final drive, instead of horizontally offset as on the Formula cars.

The 2½ litre car went well in seventh place until it started jumping out of fourth gear, then Derek Jolly over-revved because of this, and cooked the engine. A front wishbone collapsed on the 2 litre, which caused a considerable delay, and after the mechanics had got the car going again, a rod blew a hole in the crankcase.

The Stacey/Keith Greene Seventeen seemed well set for the Index, being the fastest 750 ever to have appeared at Le Mans, and when the Osca retired, the Lotus led, but distributor trouble caused overheating, and as water could not be taken on within 30 laps, the car was abandoned. A similar bother had afflicted the Taylor/Sieff Seventeen from the start, and it retired early.

Jim Clark and John Whitmore in the Border Reivers Elite were delayed by starter motor trouble, and the Vidilles/Malle Elite had more distributor trouble which caused overheating, the red-hot exhaust pipe setting the wiring on fire; the Elite was gutted while the optimistic Frenchman, who had been told that glass-fibre would not burn, stood by watching in vain for the fire to put itself out. The one Lotus triumph was the victory of Peter Lumsden's Elite, co-driven by Peter Riley, in the 1500cc class, after an absolutely trouble-free run.

Carburation trouble dogged Team Lotus when they went to Reims for the French Grand Prix on July 5th. For the first time the 2½ litre cars were fitted with 58 mm Weber carburettors, whereas up till then 50 mm had been used. Graham's car was fitted with a cold air box over the intakes, with a long trunk feeding this with air from the nose, but there was no time to fit this to Innes' car, which had the air box only. But neither car got going in practice, and both were on the fifth row at the start. The story of the race, as far as Lotus were concerned, was simple; Hill was out on the eighth lap when a stone went through his radiator, and Ireland retired six laps later with a seized front wheel bearing.

Team Lotus were by now short of 2½ litre Climax engines, supplies of which were difficult. So only two Formula 1 cars could be entered for the British Grand Prix at Aintree, leaving the other engine for a Fifteen for Graham to drive in the preceding sports car race; this turned out to be one of the finest drives of his life.

Hill took an immediate lead, but Brabham in the 2 litre Cooper closed on him, starting an extremely fierce duel. As rain began falling hard Graham's gear lever came loose, but this disadvantage merely stirred Hill to greater heights, and the Lotus drew away again to win. Stacey had been a long way back, but Brabham spun on the last lap and let Alan in his 2 litre car through to second place and a class win. Graham graciously handed Colin the gear lever before climbing out of the car.

Graham was definitely driving the number 1 2½ litre Sixteen in the Grand Prix, but Innes was still very sore as a result of leaving the road at Rouen, and after practising the other car decided that he could not race it, whereupon it was handed to Alan Stacey. Graham settled down eighth in the race, but spun in a big way at Tatts corner, scattering marshals and photographers wide and letting Salvadori's Aston Martin catch him. Hill started his second dice of the day as these two began to mix it, to the detriment of the bodywork of both Lotus and Aston. But the Lotus' clutch began to slip, and Graham dropped back as he nursed the ailing car to the finish. Alan had had trouble, too, finishing eighth; Graham was ninth—a lap behind.

Disappointing Lotus showings made the A.v.D. very reluctant to accept entries from the team for the German Grand Prix, to be held on the horrible Avus circuit in West Berlin, but two Formula 1 Sixteens were in fact taken, although they were down on maximum speed on this circuit of flat-out blinds, and Innes' car suffered a chassis breakage after a very short time from pounding on the banking. Both were eliminated early in the first heat of the race, Innes on lap 8 when his crownwheel and pinion gave up the struggle, and

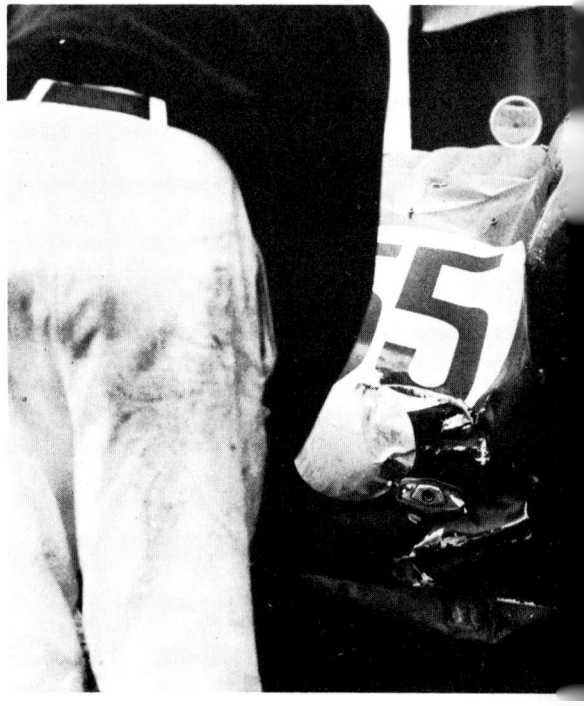

The scars of Le Mans. Lotus met with little luck in their attempts to repeat their 1957 success the following year. Left and below left: The sole survivor out of six entries, the Stacey/Dickson 11 visited a sandbank backwards in the course of its race into 20th and last place, poor Dickson having to dig it out with the aid of a headlamp cover and shovel.

Graham three laps later by a broken selector spring in the gearbox. The spring was repaired before the start of the second heat, but the organisers refused to allow Hill to start.

Lotus luck and reputation were both low. Luckily there was a 15-lap Grand Touring car race in which most of the fastest Alfa Romeo Sprint Veloces on the Continent were entered, and David Buxton who had brought his Elite over, proceeded to beat them all and set up fastest lap in the 1300cc class as well. After Lumsden and Riley's success in the Nurburgring 1000, followed by Buxton's splendid effort, one felt that maybe Lotus stock in Germany was not quite so low after all.

There was no time for a proper practice session at Lisbon, where the Portuguese Grand Prix was held on the Monsanto circuit. The transporter broke down again during the long trek across Spain, and by the time the cars arrived there was only just enough time for Hill and Ireland to qualify, and as Graham had trouble with a brake master cylinder and Innes' gear selector mechanism was playing up, that alone took a bit of doing. Innes was soon out of the race when gear selection became impossible. Graham, however, was driving well in eighth place, but spun on the sixth lap as the course left the dual carriageway. Up the bank he went, then down again, and into the path of Phil Hill's Ferrari—both cars suffered sorely.

A week later Graham again hit top form, back home at Brands Hatch for the Kentish "100" Trophy Formula 2 race. Starting well, but losing many places through having to take to the grass in avoiding the spinning Chris Bristow, he carved his way back up through the field to second place at the end of the first part of the race, which was won by Brabham. Graham started the second part badly, but was soon in second spot again, and in closing on Brabham, he equalled the latter's new lap record. Graham closed to within a couple of seconds, and the overall aggregate results gave him second place to the Australian.

Hill had a busy day. The big sports car race saw him take the 2½ litre Fifteen through to a win from David Piper's 2 litre Fifteen, and Alan Stacey was a comfortable third. Graham's third race was in the redesigned Seventeen, now with wishbone front suspension, but the little car (handling much better than formerly) still could not deal with the Lolas.

It appeared that tyre changes would be a prominent feature of the RAC Tourist Trophy race at Goodwood, so wire wheels were fitted to the works 2 litre Fifteen and to Piper's similar machine. Graham was third overall in the works car after an hour's racing, but soon afterwards the ignition timing started slipping, and as this got worse, the car had to be retimed. David Piper's nearside front tyre burst at Madgwick, the resulting crash landing David in hospital, and the only Lotus to finish was the Greene/Marsh Seventeen, in 11th place overall.

The last European grande epreuve of 1959 was the Italian Grand Prix at Monza, on September 5th. Graham's car had been badly bent at Lisbon, but it was cannibalised to make a runner out of the earlier Sixteen which Hill had driven at Zandvoort. The race, however, hardly even started for Lotus, Graham being out with clutch trouble on lap two and Innes retiring on lap 15 with no brakes. After this, some journalists were predicting that Lotus would enter no more grand prix races, or in any case would never be accepted. Looking back over the supremely invigorating 1960 season, it is hard to realise how low the morale of Lotus had become. There is no doubt that many firms, lacking the resilience and optimism of the Lotus organisation, and of Colin Chapman in particular, would have thrown up grand prix racing as a bad job after two such disastrous seasons. But Lotus optimism and industry was to be rewarded during the 1960 season of G.P. racing.

Meanwhile one grand prix remained to wind up the 1959 series—but the European teams had to travel a long way to compete—to Sebring in fact, for the first Grand Prix of the United States. By December 12th, the date of the race, Graham Hill had signed to drive with BRM for the 1960 season, the circumstances of his parting unfortunately leading to a certain amount of friction which, much to everyone's relief, was settled out of court. Innes was the new number one, and Alan Stacey accompanied him to the States.

After a lap Innes was fifth, but Stacey was out with a useless clutch. Ireland was really racing, and he climbed to fourth, where he and Allison in the Ferrari mixed it until the latter retired. But Brooks came through from behind in the other Ferrari, displacing Innes, who nevertheless did exceedingly creditably to end up fifth.

This was to be the last time a works Sixteen was to form the spearhead of the Team Lotus attack, but even Chapman did not fully realise this then. The Eighteen was on its way, conceived as a Formula Junior car only about three weeks before the U.S. Grand Prix.

In June, 1959, Lotus made their big move to the new factory at Cheshunt in Hertfordshire. At last, space! Some reorganisation of the administrative side occurred with the move. Lotus Cars Ltd., concerned with the Elite, was to be run by Colin Chapman as director and general manager, with Graham Lewis as production manager and Len Laverock as works manager. Lotus Components Ltd. was formed to deal with the Seven in particular, and other models in general. The new factory was officially opened on Wednesday, October 14th by Godfrey Lagden, M.P., at a ceremony attended by over 200 guests, including representatives of all companies associated with Lotus, and many prominent racing drivers and motoring journalists.

Two similar buildings separated by a central roadway comprised the manufacturing part of the factory, and a separate block, facing on to Delamare Road, housed the administrative part of the organisation. To the right of the contemporary-styled entrance hall was a showroom, capable of taking three or four cars.

A great feature of the space behind the factory (besides being useful as a car park, old tyre dump and surplus store), was that it offered room for expansion—and it looked as through they were going to need it!

19.

Simplicity breeds success

AS WELL AS being one of the most advanced, and most interesting grand prix cars ever built, the 1959 Formula 1 Lotus was, it must be admitted, one of the least successful. In view of the way the firm was expanding, and its numerous other commitments, Colin had decided that for the 1960 season a basic, simple and easily maintained design was called for, rather than a technically superior but more complicated one. With simplicity in mind, the essentials were to minimise power losses, reduce frontal area to an absolute minimum, and to keep the centre of gravity right down. The obvious answer ("what *is* John Cooper going to say?" said Colin) was to put the engine behind the driver, whose size would then dictate frontal area. The only disadvantage appeared to be the low polar moment of inertia, indicating a greater potential tendency to spin than with the old front-engined design.

The first rear-engined car to appear had been the prototype aluminium-bodied Formula Junior car, which had raced on Boxing Day at the B.R.S.C.C. Brands Hatch meeting, having been developed from the drawing board stage in five weeks, just in time for practice. Early in the new year, while the Junior was down at Goodwood undergoing further development, the Formula 1 version of the car had been built with a view to sending it to the Argentine for the first grand prix of 1960, on February 7th.

Although so different from the 1959 Sixteen, the overall conception of the new car was still typically Lotus, including the space frame, made up mainly of 18- and 16-gauge ¾ in and 1 in mild steel tubes, but no 20-gauge, hitherto often seen in Lotus designs. Basically, the chassis comprised three sections. The forward section, fully triangulated and in itself a complete structure, carried mountings for the front suspension, pedals, brake and clutch master cylinders and rack and pinion. Forward of this braced section was a separate, lighter frame carrying the water and oil radiators, and oil tanks.

The rear extent of the front chassis bay was marked by a Lotus feature, the fabricated sheet and tube scuttle frame which eliminated the need for cross bracing. This formed a convenient place to mount instruments, steering column, gear lever, switches and handbrake.

The mid-part of the chassis, braced on three sides only but drawing torsional rigidity from the structures around it, connected the scuttle hoop with the engine bulkhead and rear chassis bay. At the bottom this comprised two straight tubes converging at the lower rear suspension pick-ups, a top frame braced by a Y-shaped diagonal (detachable to permit easy engine removal), and a fabricated steel sheet/tube frame. In effect triangular, this rear frame was in fact nearer a circle in shape, to permit accommodation of the inboard rear brake discs.

The front suspension was the design developed in nearly all previous Lotus models since the 1957 Eleven, with the latest modification of a separate anti-roll bar, positioned slightly below and to the rear of the wheel centre line, picking up through ball joints on the king-posts. The tubular top wishbone was fitted with a threaded ball joint attachment at its outer end to permit easy adjustment of camber angle, and the lower wishbones took the lower mounting of the composite spring/damper units. The rigidity of the whole front suspension set-up prevented any of the front-wheel judder on braking which had sometimes occurred in 1959.

The rack and pinion unit was mounted on the chassis just ahead of the wheel centre line, connected by a straight steering column to the 14 in alloy and leather wheel.

There was insufficient height at the rear to instal the familiar strut suspension, so Chapman designed an entirely new "double transverse link" arrangement, whereby the transverse links were formed by the lower tubular transverse links, and the unsplined drive shafts. The transverse links were located at the inner ends (by threaded joints to adjust camber) near the centre line of the chassis on the underside of the rear frame unit, the outer ends being attached to the bottom of the deep hub casting. Parallel radius arms ran from the engine bulkhead, the upper to just above the drive shaft, and the lower to the bottom of the hub casting. A separate anti-roll bar was mounted near the top of the fabricated rear frame, connected to the forward lower hub-casting pick-up point by an upright link. Combined coil spring and damper units were also used at the rear.

Each hub casting housed two deep-row ball races of sealed type (as opposed to the taper-roller bearings used in the 1959 cars).

The bolt-on cast magnesium front wheels, carrying 5.00 x 15 Dunlop R5 racing tyres, were the same as used the year before, but the cast rear wheels were redesigned to give a better standard section rim and complement the overall suspension design. 6.50 x 15 tyres were used at the rear.

The outboard front brakes were 10½ in Girling discs. The 9½ in Girling disc rear brakes were mounted inboard, and one of the reasons for the trip to the Argentine was to see if the heat would prove too much for them in this position—no trouble was experienced. Provision, however, was made for mounting the rear brakes outboard, with the calipers ahead of or behind the hubs.

The body shape, as explained, was designed basically to obtain minimum frontal area. The square chassis dictated a square body. The increased drag coefficient, it was reasoned, would be cancelled out by the reduction in frontal area over the efficient, elliptical, front-engined cars. All body panels were quickly removable, and located by Dzus fasteners.

A 22-gallon fuel tank was located over the driver's legs, with a further 9½-gallon tank to the right of, and behind, the seat. The idea was to run on the front tank until the best handling was obtained, then switch over to the smaller tank for the rest of the race. Water and oil pipes ran from radiators to engine outside the body, thus affording additonal cooling. The tail of the car was completely open, and was designed with a taper so that the swirling air would enter the rear opening, cool the gearbox and rear brakes, and leave via openings in the undertray. In spite of the high temperatures in the Argentine, gearbox temperatures were remarkably low.

The engine chosen was, of course the latest 2,495cc four-cylinder 3.7 in x 3.54 in Coventry Climax FPF unit, developing about 237 bhp at the beginning of the year. The tachometer drive was taken from the front of the exhaust camshaft and the fuel pump drive from the rear of the inlet camshaft. The Lotus five-speed gearbox/final drive unit was bolted directly to the engine, and was basically the type as developed in the 1959 Fifteen which ran at Le Mans, but even more compact. The drive was taken via a twin-plate Borg and Beck clutch with sintered copper linings, underneath the differential unit to the gear train, where it was transmitted vertically, and so to the hypoid bevel final drive gears. Each pair of gears was in constant mesh, with selection by a selector sleeve splined to the inlet shaft and provided with external dogs engaging on internal dogs on the desired gear. The selector mechanism was made more robust, and a migratory system was used, as opposed to the original positive—stop mechanism. The unit had its own lubrication system.

First and second gears were fixed, but seven pairs of gears were available for third, fourth and fifth, giving a total of fourteen alternative ratios; with the final drive at 4.1 : 1, fourth and fifth were usually overdrive ratios on fast circuits. Ratios could be changed in minutes, being only a matter of undoing nine nuts securing the rear cover and sliding out the gears.

Wheelbase was 7 ft 6 in, with 49 in front track and 47½ in rear track. Dry weight was approximately 770 lb, but at the start of a race in addition to 180 lb of driver, about 270 lb of fuel, 50 lb of oil and 20 lb of water would be carried! Approximately 56 per cent of the load was carried on the rear wheels, at normal ride level.

Three cars were to go out to the Argentine, the new rear-engined car for Innes Ireland, who was to be first-string Formula driver for 1960, and 1959 front-engined cars for Alan Stacey and local boy Rodriguez Larreta. The 1959 cars were sent off by boat which, however, was late leaving England through engine trouble, and then had to "heave to" in the Bay of Biscay because of bad weather, losing two days in the process. The new car was to go over by plane, and the day before its scheduled flight was still a mass of bits and pieces; by prodigious non-stop working Colin and the mechanics managed to complete the car, give it a 100-yard test run outside the factory and pack it into crates in time to load on to the plane. The personnel of Team Lotus were to have travelled by a Comet belonging to Aerolineas Argentinas, but as the flying crews decided to strike the day before the flight there was no alternative but to go by another, very obscure airline which only just managed to cross the Atlantic, arriving late on Monday, February 1st. Exhausted by the journey and by the hair-raising driving in Buenos Aires (Innes spending some hours in gaol for a traffic offence!) the boys were hoping for a good night's rest; but the local Fidel Castro gang threw a loud and disrupting bomb at the front door of the shop opposite the hotel, which rather spoilt *that* idea.

The next day they went to the circuit to see if the rear-engined car had arrived, and were told it would be there at two o'clock. At six o'clock Colin, Innes, Alan and the mechanics commandeered a lorry and went down to the docks, where they found the car. They promptly loaded it on to the lorry, complete with Customs official, and to the accompaniment of loud protestings from all officials drove off back to the garage. There the Customs man completed his paperwork, and the car was made ready.

The first official practice period was the next day, Wednesday, and Ireland soon evolved the new technique needed to drive the car, despite brake trouble, an inaccurate rev. counter, and an inexplicable vibration which set in at over 130 mph down the straight; his time of 1 min 47 sec was the third best of the day. That evening the wheels were balanced and changed round, and numerous other adjustments made, but on Thursday the shaking persisted, until Colin called Innes in on seeing the rear wheel nearest the pits jumping up and down in a horrifying manner; it transpired, after a complete change of rear wheels, that there was a minute dent in the wheel which had not been noticed. Carburettor trouble, and getting used to the handling, resulted in no very fast times that day.

Friday, and the two 1959 cars had still not arrived, and neither had the works Coopers. The new car was going well now, although Ireland was still unused to rear-engined handling, and recorded a time of 1 min 38.5 sec. The times on Saturday were counting for grid positions, and Innes was out early, putting in a time of 1 min 39 sec. After some adjustments, 1 min 38.5 sec was the result, and everybody else then started trying hard to beat this time. But only Moss succeeded, and on its first race the new Lotus was in second place on the grid! The old cars arrived just in time for the other two Lotus drivers to practise, Stacey managing 1 min 43 sec to put himself on the third row, and Larreta, driving his first Formula 1 car, doing very well to record 1 min 45 sec.

When the starter appeared and immediately dropped the flag, the little Lotus leapt into the lead, and was two seconds ahead of Bonnier's BRM on the second lap. Coming out of the hairpin on the third lap the gears disengaged—the car went sideways on to the grass, and Ireland had to pause to sort out a gear, rejoining in sixth place. The opportunity then arose to sit behind Brabham and learn a bit about driving rear-engined racing cars; the lesson was put to good use, and Innes soon passed Jack and worked up to second place, though well behind Bonnier. It had become necessary to take the whole lap in top gear, as the gearbox was jumping out of all other gears and the selectors were beginning to feel the strain. But, just as second place seemed secure, Ireland hit an oil patch which he had not seen through the low

Top: Innes Ireland holding off Brabham's Cooper to win the 1960 International Trophy race at Silverstone with the Lotus 18. Above: Stirling Moss scored the first world championship race win for a Lotus at Monaco two weeks later.

sun being in his eyes, spun, and banged the kerb hard, breaking a steering arm bolt. Half a lap later most of the nearside front hub passed over Innes' head, tearing a hole in the brake disc on the way, and resulting in an extremely wobbly front wheel but a still drivable car—just! Although the Lotus' lap speeds were drastically reduced, Bonnier had slowed with valve-spring trouble, and for a brief moment Ireland was again in the lead, but soon McLaren roared through, followed by Allison's Ferrari and Moss' Cooper. At this point there was another bang in the hub, and Innes slowed even more, reasoning that the wheel might stay put for the remaining three laps although by now apparently held on by grease and luck alone. Sixth place was the result, and the extremely encouraging debut of the new Formula car resulted in jubilant telegrams being sent back to England with little delay.

But Team Lotus moved on to Cordoba, for the Formule Libre non-championship Grand Prix of Buenos Aires City, the field for the race being virtually the same as for the Argentine GP the preceding weekend. Innes put in sixth fastest qualifying time, but the 1960 car had to be repaired before the race after hitting a kerb. Larreta's car was plagued by ignition trouble. At the start, both Ireland and Larreta broke their transmissions, neither completing a lap. Stacey, in sixth position, was forced to retire with sunstroke, and Innes, who took over his 1959 car, was out on the 67th lap of the 75.

The Grand Premio Siracusa on March 19th was limited to Formula 2 cars, and two Lotuses were entered, the new rear-engined car for Ireland, and a 1959 car for Stacey. There was only just time to remove the 2½-litre engines after returning from Argentina and instal the 1½-litre Climax units, and the cars looked a trifle tired and travel-stained on arrival. During the first practice session Stacey's car, on SU's, was having carburettor trouble and missing at high revs, but Ireland soon settled down to some fast times. Before the next session the two upper ratios were raised by one tooth each (the change taking only 5 min 45 sec!), and Innes knocked nearly a second off his time, settling for 1 min 58.1 sec, second on the grid to Moss (Porsche) with 1 min 57.6 sec. On fast corners it was

Innes Ireland winning the Glover Trophy race at the 1960 Goodwood Easter Monday meeting, where he beat Stirling Moss in both the F1 and F2 events.

noticeable that the Lotus was cornerning very steadily, on neutral-steer with apparently something in hand, while the Porsche looked decidedly "twitchy."

Ireland leapt straight into the lead from the start, but was soon overhauled by von Trips (Ferrari) and Moss, the latter then pulling away from a very hard dice between Brabham (Cooper) von Trips and Ireland, Innes losing the advantage he was gaining on corners and on braking by having some difficulty changing gear. Brabham then retired, and Innes was settling down to third place when on the 25th lap the Lotus went on to three cylinders and was passed by Trintignant. Moss dropped a valve, and Innes pulled into the pits for a brief stop, then doing two more laps before a plug change restored full vigour to the little car. But von Trips was by then securely in the lead, followed by Trintignant, but Stacey's car was overheating badly, and retired with a blown gasket on lap 40. On the next lap Innes passed Paul Frere (Cooper) into fourth place, having pulled up at the rate of 4 seconds a lap, but the flying Lotus could not catch Gendebien (Cooper); and so they finished.

April 2nd, at Oulton Park, was a triumphant day for Lotus, heralding to the public in Britain their return at last to the forefront of motor racing. In the Formula 2 race for the Oulton Park Trophy, Innes Ireland in the lone team car led from the second lap onwards, and after an absolutely trouble-free run—lapping at around 1 min 49 sec—won at 91.11 mph by 16 seconds from Surtees' Cooper. Innes knocked over five seconds off the previous Formula 2 lap record, and left it at 1 min 48 sec. With Clark's victory in the Formula Junior event (with a new Formula Junior lap record), Dickson's win in the sports car race (new sports car lap record), and Summers leading in the GT cars (with a new class record also) it was a wonderful outing for the cars from Cheshunt.

Very soon afterwards, it was announced that Stirling Moss had decided to drive a new rear-engined Formula 1 Lotus in the 1960 World Championship Grand Prix races, starting with the Monaco Grand Prix. Of this, more later.

Three works cars were taken to Brussels for the Formula 2 race there on May 10th, with high hopes after the Oulton Park victory; the original prototype, and two new cars with glass-fibre bodies, one of which had the new pressure die-cast (and cheaper!) Weber 45DCOE carburettors. Jimmy Clark, in the prototype, was easily fastest of the Lotuses in practice, and fifth fastest overall. In the race Ireland drove the original, while Clark took one of the new cars ; perhaps too new, as on the fourth lap a rod appeared through the side and that was that. Alan Stacey was dicing with Bianchi when the Belgian missed a gear in his Cooper at a hairpin, and thumped the Lotus, whose off-side front suspension was wrecked. Innes was going steadily meanwhile, but was having gear selection bothers, and only managed seventh place in the first heat.

Between the heats the gear ratios were lowered in Innes' car and Stacey's suspension was repaired with parts from Clark's machine. Lotus fortunes did not improve, however, and Ireland retired with more gear trouble after a nasty spin, while Stacey gave up with no fuel, due to a leaking carburettor.

For the Easter Monday Goodwood meeting, Team Lotus sprang to the fore again in a well-publicised exhibition of reliability and speed. Ireland had a phenomenally good day, and the "popular dailies" of the following morning hailed this "new star" this "up-and-coming new boy!" In the Formula 2 Lotus, Innes passed Stirling Moss' Walker Porsche between Madgwick and Fordwater, and then proceeded to hold off the German car, whose driver was trying exceedingly hard, to win by 6.4 seconds.

After this triumph, Ireland was in a Formula 1 car for the big race, in which Moss was driving the Walker Cooper-Climax. It took Innes five laps to gain the lead, and from there on he dominated this fine race, the other competitors being forgotten by all who watched the fantastic efforts made by Moss to catch and pass the cool, determined Scot. Hardly ever was the gap between them more than a second. The Lotus put in the first over-100 mph lap ever at Goodwood, and Moss replied at 102 mph, but did not pass. And so, by 2.8 seconds and at 100.39 mph, the Lotus took the chequered flag after one of the most titanic duels ever seen at the Sussex circuit.

However, the Formula 2 Aintree 200 saw the

eclipse of all the British cars entered by Moss in the Porsche of Rob Walker. Ireland made a good start, but spun on lap three when in second place, while Stacey held on to a precarious fifth position. Clark discovered that he had brakes only on his rear wheels, too late to avoid a spin at Melling. Brabham and Salvadori were away in front, but Innes was coming through very fast and reached fourth place when a tyre punctured. Back in the pits, he called in Clark, then in 20th place, and took over his team-mate's car, managing to raise it to 9th by the end of the race. Alan Stacey was dicing splendidly with the leading group, but gear selection trouble forced him to come in and take over Innes' original car, which by this time had a new wheel fitted. The Porsches of Moss, Bonnier and Hill swept into the leading three places on the 25th lap, holding their positions to the end. So Lotus' fluctuating fortune was low again.

Drivers in the Formula 1 cars for the B.R.D.C. International Trophy race, so often a guide to the following season's grand prix racing, were Ireland, Stacey and John Surtees, the latter taking over the car originally destined for Jim Clark. Mike Taylor, as a private entrant, was driving the original Argentine car. Moss, in a 1959 Walker Cooper pulled away into the lead, but by lap 15 it was becoming apparent that Ireland, still not fully recovered from a recent tonsillectomy, was steadily overhauling Stirling and pulling away from Brabham in the very latest 1960 Formula 1 Cooper, which was carrying too much fuel. Breaking the lap record in the process, Innes passed Moss, and for eight laps these two passed and repassed each other—until one of Moss' wishbones broke, and he was out. After this Brabham started to hang it out a little more, and began to close the 6-second gap. The Lotus was misfiring, but after a superbly-judged and driven race Ireland led in the world champion by 1.6 seconds—but, in Innes' words, "It certainly was a bit twitchy, mate!"

Alan Stacey had driven his usual exceedingly steady race and was fourth, but Surtees retired early when losing oil, and Michael Taylor had misfiring trouble. Innes Ireland's average speed of 108.82 mph was the highest speed recorded in a race in Great Britain since Brooklands; that he set a new lap record (at 1 min 34.2 sec, 111.86 mph) almost goes without saying.

Four days later, on May 15th, Rob Walker was delivered a brand-new Formula 1 Lotus chassis, and the same afternoon Moss tried the car for the first time, at Goodwood. The body, to be finished in Walker blue, was not ready, so the chassis was clothed with the front part only of one of the works cars' bodies. In this form, Moss turned in the fastest unofficial lap ever recorded at Goodwood at 1 min 23.7 sec.

The Walker Lotus was virtually identical with the team cars, but a Colotti five-speed gearbox was destined to be fitted in time for the Monaco G.P., which meant that the disc brakes would have to be mounted outboard, and to allow for this the rear radius rods were increased in diameter. In fact, the Colotti box was found to be so tall that it would have to be canted over, and there was not time to do this redesigning before Monaco. The camber angle of the front wheels was set up to give slight oversteer.

This was the car that was to give Lotus their first long-awaited Grand Prix victory, in Moss' hands, at Monte Carlo. Driving well within his own limits he set fastest practice time at 1 min 36.3 sec, with Brabham and Brooks next to him. Ireland qualified just in time, making the third row of the grid, and Stacey and Surtees, both at Monaco for the first time, qualified the other two works cars.

Bonnier's BRM took the lead from the start, and on lap five Moss slipped by Brabham into second place. Stirling then sat behind the Swede until lap 17, when the fighting group behind him began to close up; he then passed Bonnier and immediately pulled away. In the rain, the surface was terribly slippery, and troubled by wheelspin Moss was passed by Brabham, who led until spinning at St. Devote. So Stirling led by 14 seconds at half-distance, when the rain stopped.

The works cars were not doing so well. A bolt head had dropped off the crown wheel and jammed the gear selection mechanism in Surtees' car, and Stacey retired after walloping a kerb; his throttle had stuck open due to broken engine bearers allowing the Climax unit to tilt forwards. Ireland's car was misfiring badly, and eventually

Above: Alan Stacey's 18 narrowly leading Stirling Moss's Porsche in the 1960 Aintree 200 for Formula 2 cars. Below: John Surtees getting the feel of his Formula 1 Lotus at Brands Hatch.

stopped altogether at the bottom of the hill before the Casino. The heroic Scot then proceeded to push the Lotus all the way back to the pits (needing medical attention on arrival), where it was found that the magneto earthing wire had rubbed through and was shorting on the rev-counter drive.

On lap 60 Bonnier re-took the lead as Moss shot into the pits on three cylinders. A plug lead was replaced, and Moss set off in plenty of time to catch the BRM. With 35 laps to go the Walker pit signalled to their driver that there were but 5, whereupon for two laps he rocketed round until reassured by a correct pit signal. But he nevertheless soon carved off the BRM's lead, and the Lotus went on to win by nearly two minutes from McLaren (Cooper) and Phil Hill (Ferrari). Ireland's car was pushed over into an official seventh place, although only four cars would have passed any technical inspection at the finish.

Although International rules stated that there should be a minimum of a fortnight between major races, just one week after Monaco the Dutch Grand Prix was held at Zandvoort, meaning a lot of very hard work by the mechanics. Lotus decided to work on the cars in Monte Carlo rather than bring them all the way back, and during the week the chassis on Ireland's car was straightened, having been bent on hitting a kerb. New engine bearings were fitted to Stacey's car and the gearbox rebuilt for the car Surtees drove. As at Monaco, the qualification system was in force. Surtees had gone off to the Isle of Man to ride motor cycles, so Jim Clark was given his first drive in a world championship race.

Practising went well for the Lotuses, despite Clark's bottom-gear pinion breaking in an unofficial session, and Moss put in the fastest time at 1 min 33.2 sec, to Brabham's 1 min 33.4 sec and Ireland's 1 min 33.9 sec. Stacey was on the third row, Clark on the fourth.

Brabham, Moss, Ireland, Stacey—that was the order after one lap, and so it was on the 16th with Moss on the Cooper's tail, then Ireland and Stacey duelling between themselves some way behind. But, on the next lap, trouble—Brabham's Cooper flung up a lump of rock which smashed the Walker Lotus' offside front wheel rim and deflated the

After the complexities of the 16, the Lotus 18 was a relatively simple car on which to work. Note the detachable top section of the rear chassis diaphragm to facilitate engine and transmission removal.

tyre. The pit stop to change the wheel took nearly two minutes, as first the jack would not go under the tilted car, then the hub and roller races had to be dismantled to remove the wheel. Moss rejoined the race 12th, but started a typical race against odds and the clock, setting a new lap record at 1 min 34.4 sec on lap 39. Clark, meanwhile, had been harrying Graham Hill's BRM, and in fact passed it into fourth place behind Brabham and his team-mates before being forced to retire on lap 43 with transmission failure. The same fate overtook Stacey 15 laps later, and Moss went hell-for-leather after Graham Hill in a fantastic but vain effort to snatch third place from the BRM, finishing a second behind. Moss' very last lap took 1 min 33.8 sec (99.98 mph)—another record.

Speeds had been measured over a flying kilometre during the race. Brabham had recorded 234 kph, while Ireland, Moss and Stacey had all recorded 237 kph, fastest of all. Next best was Clark at 231 kph, then the Ferraris at 228 kph. It was obvious then, that super-efficient body shapes were going to play a very small part in design from here on.

In England, hot saloon cars are brought to meetings on trailers. In Belgium, you drive your grand prix car to the circuit, at least, that is what the works Lotus and Cooper teams did, from their base at Stavelot to the paddock at Spa, for the Grand Prix of Belgium. Before practice, Moss had said that he was perfectly happy with his car, not in the least worried about the high speeds that would be reached, but a little concerned about what would happen if anything broke. At three o'clock on the afternoon of June 18th, he found out. At 130 mph, in the right-handed Burnenville corner, the left rear wheel attachment flange broke off the axle shaft and the car slid wildly on the hub casting, though not overturning until hitting a bank and throwing Moss out. Stirling landed on hands and knees, breaking his nose, sustaining transverse cracks in both legs just above the knee, and crushing a couple of vertebrae. Ironically, it seems likely that the fatigue fracture causing the crash was probably because the component had been made *heavier*!

Unfortunately, just at the same time, Mike Taylor, in the Taylor and Crawley Formula 1 Lotus, had broken his steering column at La Carriere, going straight on into a wood, writing off the car and sustaining injuries which were to keep him out of racing for the rest of the year. The steering column of this, the prototype car, was not the same, incidentally, as was fitted to all subsequent Lotuses.

Of the Team Lotus cars, Innes Ireland managed third row of the grid, having had to contend with a slipping clutch in practice, Clark was just behind him and Stacey was on the back row, the latter two making their debut at this very fast and difficult circuit.

Jim stalled on the grid, and Bianchi, who was just behind with his Cooper, also stalled in avoiding him and the Team Lotus mechanics at the start. After two laps Brabham led, with Ireland down his exhaust, followed by Phil Hill, Bonnier, Gendebien, Graham Hill and McLaren. Hill's Ferrari passed Ireland, and drew away with Brabham. Innes had to stop on the sixth lap with chronic clutch slip, but went away again after the limit stop for the hydraulic actuating mechanism had been removed. Pulling up through the field, he took Jim in tow, and these two dropped Stacey. But after two more pit stops and a violent spin at Blanchimont, Ireland called it a day. Clark was in on lap 14 with blocked jets, so Stacey was the first Lotus, lying 10th—not too good. Mechanical failures in other cars raised Alan's position to sixth, still driving steadily yet very fast; just what was wanted. Then on lap 25 the terrible news came through; he had crashed, badly. It seems certain, from signs on and around the scene of the accident, that he was struck in the face by a bird, probably stunning him. The car went out of control, hit a bank and went end-over-end, flinging Stacey out. He was killed instantly.

Brabham had the race wrapped up, but just as it seemed Graham Hill would be second the BRM blew up, and he was replaced by McLaren. Jim Clark was fifth out of the six finishers, two laps behind.

Alan Stacey was only 26. The story of his motor racing career—his life— has already been told in this book. Faithful to Lotus throughout, he had developed into one of the steadiest and most reliable drivers in grand prix racing; yet his drive at

Zandvoort had shown that he could be as fast as the best. He was one of the most intelligent drivers in motor racing, and his death was a terrible loss to Lotus, and to motor racing. With Chris Bristow also being killed in a Cooper, a few minutes before Stacey, the 1960 Belgian Grand Prix was a terribly sad race.

It was Team MacLotus for the French Grand Prix at Reims on July 3rd, and Colin sported a Tam o' Shanter for the occasion—Scotsman Ron Flockhart had joined Ireland and Clark in the works cars. Flockhart was having his first-ever drive in a rear-engined Lotus, and his car was a brand-new one, with the engine tilted over to the right so that the carburettors were entirely under the "bonnet". Moss' car at Spa had sported a long snorkel tube from the nose of the car to the Webers, and this device was tried on Innes' car at Reims, while in addition nose cowlings of a revised, narrower shape were fitted for this fast circuit.

At an early stage in practice "bogey" time was set at around 2 min 20 sec, Moss' lap record in a BRM standing at 2 min 22.8 sec. Ireland settled straight in and managed 2 min 18.5 sec, to put him on the second row of the grid, while Jim Clark did 2 min 20.3 sec and Flockhart 2 min 23.4 sec, although because of a mix-up over the numbers Flockhart was credited with 2 min 19.5 sec, and set on the third row. David Piper, in the 1959 front-engined car, broke the valve gear in his Climax engine, wrecking the cylinder head and being unable to start through not having a spare.

The start was utterly chaotic, with many shuntings after the starter had dropped his flag, two seconds after the 30 seconds-to-go signal; Graham Hill, on the front row, had not even put the BRM into gear. All the Lotuses got through safely and, behind the leading trio of Brabham, von Trips and Phil Hill, Ireland soon settled down to a side-by-side duel with Bonnier (BRM), while Gendebien kept the Yeoman Credit Cooper close behind. When McLaren joined these three, the result was an intensely struggling foursome. Bonnier packed it in with engine trouble, and on lap 34 Innes called at the pits with a very wobbly left front wheel, the anti-roll bar having detached itself when a proprietory made ball joint decided that it did not approve of grand prix racing. Four laps later, after a quick repair, Innes was away again.

Jim Clark was running very steadily in fifth place, but Flockhart was getting faster and faster as he became used to the car, and he just failed by a wheel to pass Clark, who maintained his fifth place. Ireland finished seventh after having been several times in second spot after the Ferraris had dropped out and left Brabham, the winner, on his own.

The fortunes of Team Lotus in 1960, however, always seemed to be better back on home ground, and at the British Grand Prix they atoned for the disappointing showing in France. John Surtees, making a brilliant entry into car racing after doing all that was possible on two wheels, took the wheel of one of the team cars, with Innes Ireland as number one in a similar machine with the long air intake to the carburettors running from the nose of the car. Jimmy Clark was given the very latest version, with canted engine, which Flockhart had driven at Reims. Practice speeds of the Lotuses were down on their May times, and Ireland could only manage the second row of the grid, with 1 min 36.2 sec. Surtees and Clark were behind him, while private entrant Piper was at the rear.

Soon settling down in the leading group, Ireland was third, Surtees and Clark fifth and sixth, with the works Coopers duelling with Bonnier's BRM for first place. Then Ireland went after the leader, Brabham, these two pulling away from the pack, and by the thirteenth lap Surtees and Clark had pulled up to third and fourth places, changing places six laps later. The feature of the British Grand Prix that year was the fantastic drive of Graham Hill, who, after a bad start, carved through the entire field into the lead. After 32 laps Hill began to press Ireland, and soon passed him. By the 56th lap, Graham led, and Innes was having hub trouble. Two laps later, Clark's near-side front wheel collapsed, and the unlucky Scot lost his place and about seven laps, too, while suspension parts were replaced. Surtees, however, was still going strongly in third place, having passed Innes who, though worried about a rear hub, was maintaining fourth spot. Graham Hill spun after a wonderful drive, with but six laps to go, and Brabham won by 51 seconds from the immaculate Surtees, who led in team leader Ireland. Jimmy finished, just, but was last.

A highlight of the British Grand Prix meeting is often the saloon car race, but no-one could have foreseen the fantastic dice that was to ensue between Jack Sears' 3.8 Jaguar and Colin Chapman, making a most welcome return to the track in John Coombs' similar model. At times about two inches less than two inches apart, the two intrepid drivers used every ounce of the power and all the track and much of the grass; they were virtually side-by-side for the last six of the twelve laps, Colin just managing to take a quite impossible line inside Jack at Woodcote and thunder over the line first. What a way to conduct one's only race in a year! He must have liked the car, as soon afterwards a Mk 2 3.8 Jaguar became part of the Chapman household.

In many people's opinion one of the best circuits in Europe, Solitude, near Stuttgart, was used for the first time for a car race on July 24th, 1960, the Formula 2 race attracting full works entries from Ferrari, Porsche and Lotus, and a single works Cooper, giving a most exciting foretaste of the 1961 1½-litre Formula 1. Jim Clark and Trevor Taylor were driving in the supporting Formula Junior event, and drove two of the Team Lotus 1½-litre cars in company with Innes Ireland.

Jimmy had the benefit of practice in the Formula Junior car as well, but nevertheless his fastest lap of all in practice at 4 min 23.6 sec was exceedingly creditable, beating as it did von Trips in the new rear-engined Ferrari and Hans Herrmann in a works Porsche. From the start all the Porsches displayed tremendous acceleration, jumping into the leading positions, but in the first few laps Clark, driving one of his finest races ever, rose from 9th to 1st place, then breaking the lap record at 4 min 8 sec and pulling away to a lead of 12½ seconds. But all was not well—the water temperature was rising due to a blown head gasket, and on the tenth lap he shot into the pits for water, rejoining the race in tenth place. Herrmann was now leading, Ireland scrapping with Phil Hill (Ferrari) for sixth place but still in the leading group, so close was the race. Trevor Taylor retired when a cam follower broke and Von Trips won by 4 seconds from Herrmann and the other three Porsches, with Ireland in sixth position.

Immediately following the Solitude event, the 1960 German Grand Prix was also run as a qualifying round of the Formula 2 Constructors Championship. Held on the South Circuit at the Nurburgring, the race will be remembered for being one of the most miserably wet affairs on record. The first 9 entries were selected by the A.v.D., comprising works drivers and a few other favourites—Innes Ireland being included in these drivers guaranteed a start. Jim Clark was told he would have to qualify, so in protest Colin sent him off back home to practice at Brands Hatch. Dan Gurney was having his first drive in a Lotus, the car being a new 1½-litre model owned by Mrs. Louise Bryden-Brown and managed by David Phipps. Dan was in fact faster than the works entry in practice, Innes having trouble with a locking front brake.

A new Dunlop racing tyre appeared in practice, the "SP" variation for wet weather, and a set was fitted to most cars, including the Team Lotus entry, but not to Gurney's car. The American, on R5's, was not happy in the race on the flooded track, and settled down behind Ireland in eighth place. The fog came down, and in the murk Bonnier could just be discerned winning, with the Lotuses in the same positions a lap behind.

The 50-lap Silver City Trophy race on August Bank Holiday at Brands Hatch was for Formula 1 machines, and works entries Clark and Ireland were at the front of the grid, Surtees behind them in the third Team Lotus car, and David Piper on the fifth row. Brabham shot straight into the lead, but for eight laps was thoroughly harried by Jim Clark, but then the Lotus dropped back and eventually retired with gearbox trouble. Surtees was an early visitor at the pits with clutch slip, but recovered well despite a misfiring engine to make sixth place at the end. Innes, on SP tyres in the dry, was in real trouble, and after never really going well called it a day. So the Team Lotus challenge faded with Clark's demise, somewhat redeemed by the Scot's fastest lap at 1 min 40.6 sec, equal to Brabham's best of the race. Graham

Hill just failed to catch Brabham, who continued his winning ways.

Jack Brabham also won the Grand Prix of Portugal, this meaning a lot more to him as in so doing he clinched the world championship for the second year running. For this event Stirling Moss was back in the grand prix fray, in the Rob Walker Lotus, which had been completely rebuilt. The front suspension had been modified by Alf Francis to obviate a fault that had twice given trouble to the team cars; instead of coupling the front anti-roll bar to the top wishbone pivots by eye-bolts, it was now connected to the lower wishbones by short links. Ireland, Surtees and Clark comprised the works team.

Surtees had a lot of trouble in practice, as the crown wheel was slowly breaking up and pieces from it were jamming the selector mechanism; this was not discovered until the crown wheel and pinion disintegrated. While Ireland was playing about with gear ratios and fore-and-aft braking ratios, Clark tried a new line to avoid the tramlines, but this made the corner too sharp, and Jim hit the kerb and smashed through the straw bales, bending the car considerably but himself not at all. By the end of the final practice session Surtees had shaken everybody and made BTD, at 2 min 25.6 sec, to Gurney's time in the BRM of 2 min 25.63 sec and Brabham's 2 min 26.05 sec.

As the flag fell, most of the front row were already at the first corner, accompanied by Graham Hill who had started the trouble by creeping up among them. The Lotus mechanics had spent the night working on Clark's car, which was bent more or less straight again with the aid of exhortations from Colin, blocks of wood and blow torches. As its handling was a trifle unpredictable, Clark was given instructions not to push it too hard early on; and so at the end of the first lap he was tenth, with Moss second behind Gurney, and Surtees close behind. Innes Ireland came in with fuel trouble. Surtees passed Moss, who stuck to his tail, these two passing Gurney who was bothered by oil leaks. Innes had the fuel system modified to feed only from the scuttle tank and joined the race about seven laps down.

On lap 19 Moss left Surtees on his own when the Walker Lotus went on to three cylinders, not cured by two pit stops to check for loose plug leads and change all the plugs. Surtees was now 10 seconds ahead of Brabham, who had resigned himself to second place, while Clark was going extremely well and had slowly made his way up to fourth place. Fuel, however, was leaking from a split in Surtees' front tank, and slopping over his feet and the pedals and a slip off the brake pedal put John off the road and into the straw bales! This damaged the radiator, which soon split, and as a result Brabham was holding a secure lead, McLaren safely behind him, and this is how they finished, with Jimmy justifying the Team Lotus mechanics' hard work by his third place. Moss spun on the 51st lap, and was disqualified for running against the direction of the race to restart the motor, while Innes was sixth, out of the seven finishers.

Clark had driven beautifully, and it was also Jimmy's day at Brands on August 27th, when he won the 1½-litre Kentish "100" Trophy. Innes was penalised one minute for jumping the start, and John Surtees collided with Geoff Duke, in Reg Parnell's Lotus, eliminating them both. There was a tremendous battle between Clark, Ireland and Dan Gurney in Lotuses and Bonnier and Hill in Porsches, Gurney just failing to catch Jim by two-fifths of a second.

The Italian Grand Prix, Grand Prix of Europe 1960, was to be run on the combined road and banked circuit. Rightly or wrongly, Lotus, Cooper and BRM boycotted the race, as they felt that the bankings were so hard on the chassis and tyres that the race would be needlessly dangerous. So, the Cheshunt firm went unrepresented. The British teams bore the brunt of considerable criticism, and reports in Continental papers stated that constructors considered that their cars were simply not strong enough, which was not the case. In their efforts to get the race run on the road circuit alone, however, it was justifiably felt at home and abroad that less "strong-arm" and more diplomatic tactics might have been used.

Tony Vandervell was one of the many to see the potential of the Lotus Eighteen chassis, and had ordered one in which to install one of his own 280 bhp Vanwall four-cylinder engines. The first appearance of this interesting and hairy beast was

Innes Ireland leads Alan Stacey in the 1960 Dutch GP.

at the Snetterton International meeting on September 17th, where it demonstrated enormous speed in practice but stretched its valves and non-started in the Formula 1 Lombank Trophy race.

Clark, Surtees, Ireland was the second lap order, then Innes lapped at 1 min 32.8 sec to put up a new lap record and pass Surtees, who dropped to fifth and later retired with a very rough engine. Lap 13 was unlucky for Jimmy, as he forgot he was driving a Formula 1 car and, taking his Formula Junior braking point, shot up the escape road at the Esses. But his second place to Ireland was secure, and this is how they finished.

Some of the best Formula 1 racing of 1960 in Britain was to be seen at Oulton Park, on the occasion of the final race of the year. Clark and Ireland pulled into an early lead from the world champion and Stirling Moss (Lotus), who had started badly. Surtees was out early with fuel pump failure, then Clark was eliminated when Naylor, who was being lapped, failed to see Jimmy and pulled in front of him, a collision resulting. Ireland was thus in first place alone, but dropped behind Brabham and Moss after going straight on at Cascades. But he recovered well, and driving as well as ever he has done, he shot past these two to regain the lead. Alas, the gearbox could not keep up with Innes, who was forced to retire, the thrilling race going eventually to Moss in the Walker Lotus, from Brabham's works Cooper.

The 6th Grand Prix of Modena for Formula 2 cars saw no Team Lotus entries, but Moss appeared in Reg Parnell's Lotus, and Tony Marsh brought his own. Scuderia Centro-Sud had bought a Lotus chassis and installed a Maserati engine, but as this power unit was longer than the Climax, poor Ian Burgess was decidedly cramped.

Moss broke the lap record early in the race, but also his valve gear, and although the Lotus-Maserati looked promising, it retired from the race.

The last world championship 2½-litre Grand Prix of 1960, and of the old Formula, was at the Riverside International Raceway in California, on November 20th. Stirling Moss, in the Walker Lotus, ran away to a clear win, giving the Cheshunt firm its second world championship Grand Prix victory. Team Lotus were represented as usual by Ireland, Clark and Surtees, these three lining up on the second and third rows of the grid. Stirling, on top form, was in pole position. Brabham, however, led away, but Moss was not far behind, with Innes fourth. Clark and Surtees were soon in close company—too close, as on lap four they touched, John requiring a front wheel change and Jim subsequently retiring.

American Jim Hall was driving his privately entered Lotus in his first Formula 1 event and, going really well, worked up to sixth place by 20 laps, by which time Moss led Bonnier, Ireland and McLaren. Lap 60, and Bonnier's engine sounded terrible—Innes passed him to take second place, and Hall was then fifth. Stirling won from Innes by 38 seconds, and Jim Hall had the terrible misfortune to break his transmission on the very last lap, dropping to seventh place before coasting over the line.

So ended the 1960 season of grande epreuves. Lotus had won two of them and Stirling Moss, the driver on both occasions, was third in the world championship placings behind Brabham and McLaren. Innes Ireland was fourth, Clark eighth equal and Surtees eleventh equal.

Soon afterwards Colin announced his Formula 1 plans for 1961; Ireland and Clark would form the two-car team, with Trevor Taylor as first reserve driver. Stanley Chapman, for so long the staunch and hard-worked team manager, decided to retire at the end of 1960, to live in Devon with time at last to fish, shoot, and be away from the hectic racing circus! Andrew Ferguson, late of Coopers was to replace him as team manager for 1961, and in fact to remain with Lotus for nine years.

20.

And one for Junior

COLIN CHAPMAN HAD had no intention of producing a Formula Junior Lotus until the number of enquiries at the Motor Show in October, 1959, and the enthusiasm for the Formula shown by the other constructors convinced him that the project would be worthwhile. In any case a new, simple and easily maintained design for Formula 1 and 2 was called for; and fortunately the chassis with very few minor alterations would be suitable for Formula Junior.

The prototype Junior was finished only just in time for official practice at Brands Hatch for the B.R.S.C.C. Boxing Day meeting, arriving completely untried and in its natural aluminium finish. Its unveiling caused a considerable stir—one weekly journal expressed the hope that "the extremely ugly, tank-like body" would only be temporary. The body was indeed unusual, for those accustomed to the erstwhile sleek Lotus line, but it fulfilled the double need of clothing a chassis wide enough to hold a driver while presenting a minimum frontal area to the wind. All panels were removable, and maintenance was obviously going to be an easy task.

Besides the shape, the major topic of conversation round the car was the fact that it had the power unit behind the driver, the first Lotus ever with this arrangement. This was for a number of reasons. The Formula imposed a weight limit, and there would therefore be nothing to be gained by advanced detail design and lightweight construction. Engine power output would be somewhat restricted by the limited tuning allowed by the regulations. So essentials would be the minimum possible frontal area, a low centre of gravity, and only small transmission power losses. The only satisfactory way to fulfil these requirements was a rear-engined, rear-drive machine, with the engine in unit with the transmission.

The chassis and suspension of the 1960 Formula Junior Lotus was identical to that on the Formula 1 car, described fully in the preceding chapter. Standard pattern Lotus 15-in magnesium alloy wheels were used with bolt-on hubs, the tyres being 4.50 at the front and 5.00 at the rear. All four brakes were mounted outboard, being 9 in x 1¾ in Lockheed with finned Alfin drums.

The Ford 105E 997cc four-cylinder engine as fitted to the Anglia was tuned by Keith Duckworth of Cosworth Engineering, and was guaranteed to be delivering at least 75 bhp on delivery. But camshaft trouble on Christmas morning with the engine destined for the prototype meant that a standard unit had to be fitted, equipped only with twin carburettors and a special exhaust manifold.

The power unit was bolted directly to the transmission via a special Lotus bell-housing, and the Renault gearbox, mounted behind the final-drive line, was inverted to allow the pinions to revolve in their normal direction. Four or five speeds were offered; the former as used in the Renault Gordini and Floride, the latter the Redele box. In practice, the five-speed box was used with first gear blanked off, thus giving closer ratios than the four-speed gearbox which, however, was more reliable.

On Boxing Day the car was not fitted with the

Two accelerating Lotus FJ stars.
Above: Peter Arundell leaving the hairpin at Mallory Park.
Below: Trevor Taylor leaving the chicane at Goodwood.

Below: The prototype FJ Lotus 18, unpainted and without roll-over bar, made its debut at the 1959 Boxing Day meeting at Brands Hatch. Right: Henry Taylor drove an inspired race in the wet to win the 1960 British Empire Trophy race at Silverstone.

Right: Peter Arundell on pole position for a 13-car FJ race at Mallory Park. Centre: A typically relaxed Jim Clark winning the first FJ race of the 1960 season at Goodwood, in which John Surtees made his motor racing debut. Below: Changing Junior — by taking his clothes off and tipping him on his side!

roll-bar stipulated by the regulations. To the many who protested, Colin pointed out that no minimum height for such an attachment was mentioned, and that on the Lotus the frame hoop behind the driver fulfilled the function. But this was far lower than the driver's head, pointed out the critics. Chapman then asked to be shown a roll-bar on a Junior which was higher than the driver's head; all protests were withdrawn! In fact after this meeting the Lotus Juniors were fitted with a roll hoop higher than the heads of most who drove the cars.

The 10-lap race drew an entry consisting of four Coopers, three Geminis, six Elvas, a Lola and the Lotus. In practice, the flywheel disintegrated in Graham Warner's Gemini, smashing the bell-housing and causing the car to spin into the banking in front of the main grandstand. Graham then offered the Ford engine to the Lotus equipe, and Colin Chapman and Mike Costin set about removing the standard engine and fitting the replacement. The crankshaft of the Gemini engine, however, had been damaged and had to be replaced by the standard one. Work on the car was much easier with a new rear-engined design, and the refitting was just completed in time for the race.

Alan Stacey was entered to drive the new Lotus, and started from the fourth row of the grid. The correct springs had failed to arrive in time for the race, and those fitted were much too soft. From the start, Stacey made up to seventh place then spun at Druids, clouting the bank backwards. After this, Alan took it more easily, as he could hear grating noises on full bump, making him think that the suspension had been damaged in the spin. Nevertheless, he climbed back to his seventh place, where he finished, and his best lap time was only 0.6 sec slower than the fastest lap of the race, by Chris Threlfall's Elva. Afterwards it was found that the sump on the Gemini engine was deeper that that on the Lotus and had been contacting the track and creating the untoward noise!

The next public appearance of the Formula Junior Lotus was at the B.R.S.C.C.'s first annual Racing Car Show, where a new car appeared clothed in a green glass-fibre body, improving the appearance somewhat, although presumably some were disappointed that the overall body shape was unchanged! The statutory roll protection hoop had now been fitted, to comply with the spirit of the regulations. Otherwise, the specification was unchanged since its initial outing (testing session) at Brands. Orders for some twelve or so chassis were taken at the show.

Early tests were extremely encouraging, and a few alterations to the suspension set-up were devised, including harder springs at front and rear, and the addition of a rear anti-roll bar, mounted on the frame at the top suspension pick-ups and coupled to the lower wishbones by ball-jointed uprights.

To drive Formula Junior cars entered under Team Lotus, Colin signed on three of the most outstanding young drivers in the country; Jim Clark, Trevor Taylor and Peter Arundell. These three had an almost unbelievably successful 1960 season.

Trevor won the BARC Formula Junior Championship race from Jim and Mike McKee in Jim Russell's privately entered Lotus, the works cars sharing a new Goodwood Formula Junior lap record. The *Motor Racing* National Championship for 1960 was shared between Clark and Taylor, and Clark also won the John Davy Trophy for FJ races at Brands Hatch.

Every FJ race in Britain of any prominence at all was won by a Lotus, with usually the works entries pulling off the prizes, but Henry Taylor winning a very wet British Empire Trophy race in Ken Tyrrell's Eighteen. Further down the scale, club drivers were also finding that a Lotus was almost a *sine qua non* for success in their own field.

Only towards the end of the season did the Lotus supremacy seem even to be challenged, when other constructors had had time to revise their first thoughts on design for the Formula. But one could not help feeling that they were all a year out of date, when the new Lotus Junior, the Twenty, was unveiled for the first time at the opening of the Racing Car Show in January, 1961. Undoubtedly the star of the Show, the main point of discussion was its incredibly small size—this time, it was felt (though with some feeling of having heard this somewhere before), that Chapman really *had* achieved the ultimate in this direction in this his final design of 1960.

The Twenty was simply a logical development of the Eighteen. Frontal area was becoming a critical factor in Formula Junior racing, and this was lessened considerably by lowering the overall height in three main ways. The fuel tank, which had been over the driver's knees, was now behind his seat. To make room for it, and to lower the driver's head, the seat was inclined to an unprecedented extent. The front wheels were now of 13 in diameter, lowering both height and unsprung weight. The body shape was smoothed in line and improved in shape, being now pretty as well as functional; all minor external protuberances were now recessed into the glass-fibre bodywork, while the totally enclosed carburettors received air via scoops incorporated into the general shape. The exhaust pipe was also enclosed.

The chassis was in principle the same, but altered in detail to conform with the new line. The rear drum brakes were mounted inboard, and track was increased slightly to reduce weight transfer during cornering. The 13 in steering wheel soon became accepted by all who used it. The retail price of the Twenty (in kit form) was £1,450, or £1,525 fully assembled for export.

Demand was tremendous, and nearly 40 had been sold before the Racing Car Show closed! It appeared that the latest Lotus might again be virtually unbeatable—but for the good of Formula Junior racing, it was sincerely hoped that other constructors would produce cars that would give the Lotuses a really hard run for their money in the coming season.

21.

Rapid therapy for Moss

AFTER STIRLING MOSS had crashed his Formula 1 Lotus so horribly at Spa, he was moved to St. Thomas' Hospital in London for orthopaedic treatment. In accordance with the hospital's progressive policy, Stirling was almost immediately up and about, in contrast to the three months in plaster to which a Continental doctor had condemned him! While still officially residing at the hospital, Moss took a day off to travel to Silverstone to drive his first car since the crash, a brand-new design, the Lotus Nineteen sports-racing car.

This model superseded the Fifteen, which had had a good run, and was based on the successful rear-engined 1960 Formula chassis, the Eighteen. Conforming with the current International Appendix C regulations, the new machine was reminiscent of other rear-engined sports cars, in particular the Cooper Monaco, and it was immediately jokingly dubbed the Lotus "Monte Carlo"; a name which stuck firmly, forever afterwards.

The chassis was a space frame similar in principle to that of the Eighteen, but the side rails of the front foot wells and rear, engine bay diverged in order to make room for the two occupants of the cockpit. Suspension was also similar to the Formula car, but anti-roll bars of a different rate were fitted front and rear, and the rear radius arms were similar in dimensions to Rob Walker's own Formula 1 machine. Track and wheelbase measurements remained the same, but of course the width of the all-enveloping body was greater. Steering the brakes were as on the Formula car, the rear discs being mounted outboard in this case, in the interests of better brake and gearbox cooling. Separate hydraulic systems were used at front and rear.

The bodywork was in glass-fibre, both the quickly detachable nose section and engine cover being one-piece units. The spare wheel was carried in the front above the driver's knees, and the battery, and oil and water radiators were also accommodated in the front bay.

Petrol capacity was eighteen gallons, and this was all carried in pannier tanks on each side of the cockpit (no scuttle tank as on the Formula car), and more petrol could be carried if need be in long-distance races. Twin electric pumps conveyed the fuel to the power unit.

Instrumentation was identical with the Formula model, with the addition of an ammeter and an ignition/starter switch. Lights, horn and wiper switches were on the door sill by the driver's right hand. The windscreen was typically Lotus, and a tonneau could be fitted over the passenger seat.

Slightly different engine mountings were used in the Nineteen. The oil filter and gearbox oil tank were mounted in the engine bay, and only the engine oil was pumped to the oil radiator in the nose, the gearbox oil being circulated in a separate system at the rear.

The engine was the latest FPF 2½ litre Coventry Climax unit in full Formula 1 tune with the addition of a starter motor, transmitting the drive through a Lotus five-speed gearbox, which incorporated a reverse gear. The clutch was the twin-plate 8½ in assembly. A large cooling vent at the rear, as on the Formula cars, helped to keep the transmission cool.

Early trials of the prototype were more than encouraging, and soon Moss was lapping nearly 1.5 seconds inside the current Silverstone sports car lap record. So pleased was he with his latest acquisition that Stirling drove his first race since the accident in it, taking the Nineteen to Karlskoga and winning the 75 kilometre sports car race there on August 7th.

Following the successful debut, Lotus announced that it had been decided to produce a strictly limited number of replicas, fitted with the 2½ litre Climax engine and Lotus five-speed box. Only six cars would be available for sale in Great Britain, and a similar number for overseas customers; the potential shortage of 2½ litre FPF engines had much to do with this decision.

While the car was still in Sweden after the Karlskoga race, Jo Bonnier borrowed the Nineteen for attempts on the Swedish record for the flying kilometre, being successful at a speed of 252.3 kph (157.5 mph).

In readiness for the 1961 season three new Nineteens were bought by the U.D.T. Laystall racing team, to be driven by Stirling Moss, Henry Taylor and Cliff Allison, the remainder of the twelve built going to prominent sports car drivers in the United States, where interest in big sports car racing was not on the decline, as it appeared to be in Europe. There the Lotuses remained, to enhance the firm's considerable Transatlantic reputation for sports/racing cars.

Below: Stirling Moss at the wheel of the UDT-Laystall Racing Team's Lotus 19 at Aintree, complete with regulation tall screen. Bottom: Moss took time off from St. Thomas' Hospital, following his serious accident at Spa, to give the Lotus 19 an initial try-out at Silverstone in 1960.

22.

One man's Mille Miglia
By Gregor Grant

WHEN I FIRST mentioned the idea of driving a Lotus Eleven in the 1957 Mille Miglia, many people thought that I was plain crackers. They said that such a lightweight machine would fall to bits, and that a thousand miles was a long, long way. It was also pointed out that the smaller-capacity classes were practically 100 per cent Italian, filled with such formidable machinery as Osca, Fiat specials, Abarth, Cisitalia, Moretti, Stanguellini and Nardi.

However, Colin Chapman listened carefully, and thought that it would be a good idea to see how a Lotus would go in this classic road race. He agreed to prepare an Eleven at Hornsey, but I would have to take care of everything else, including the entry, insurance, re-fuelling, transport, service and so on. As it was my intention also to do a story on the race, I sure was in for a busy time.

In due course the entry was accepted, re-fuelling and oil arrangements made with Dennis Druitt of BP, and a trailer borrowed from Cliff Davis. It was arranged that photographer George Phillips would accompany me, and that we would tow the Lotus behind my MG Magnette, actually the same car with which I had made 4th place in the 2000cc GT category, the previous year. We planned to cross over to the Continent on a Monday; the Eleven was supposed to be ready for collection by the previous Wednesday. Therefore I arrived at Hornsey, complete with trailer, only to discover that the car wasn't even built!

"Not to worry", remarked Chapman: "Everything's here, we're just waiting on the petrol tank. It'll be absolutely ready early Friday".

Actually, I didn't receive the car until the Sunday morning, and only managed to drive it for about 30 miles before it was loaded on to the trailer, and sheeted-up ready for the trip. It certainly felt like a nice little machine, and it was extremely well turned out, but I had a slight panic when I saw the alleged hood. This seemed to consist of some thin fabric, and what looked like the framework of an umbrella. The Mille Miglia regulations stated quite clearly that all entries in the sports car class had to have an efficient form of weather protection in the case of open cars. It also stated that the scrutineers may demand that the hood be erected, and the vehicle driven to prove that the weather protection was efficient.

Clearly if I had to erect this Heath Robinson affair, the scrutineers would boot me out *pronto*! I telephoned Chapman, and his only comment was to the effect that it had always passed the scrutineers in the past—and who the hell wanted a hood on an Eleven anyway?

We took the Simplon route into Italy, but before that, near Chaumont, we ran into a fierce blizzard, not entirely expected in early May. The outfit was nearly wrecked when a tyre on the trailer blew out, and the whole bang-show began to swing about. Trying to hold the Magnette on an icy, snowy road with a trailer doing its damnedest to haul us off the road, is not one of my better memories. However I managed to stop before we jack-knifed, and ruefully surveyed a tyre completely in ribbons.

Obtaining a replacement took ages, for none of the garages in Chaumont had the size. We did think of fitting French wheels and tyres, but the hub fixing presented a problem. By a stroke of luck the Dunlop service truck stopped outside a bistro, and even luckier, they had a tyre of the proper size. I thought it rather sporting of George Phillips to volunteer to go back 10 kilometres or so to the hotel where we had left the trailer, re-fit the wheel, and leave me to have a snort along with the Dunlop boys!

Naturally, in Brescia, all sorts of things required attention. The battery had developed a leak, and a new one had to be fitted, but the replacement would not fit the Lotus cradle. So a local blacksmith produced a new one, which for rather less than a quid, was a jolly sound job. Wheels were badly out of balance, and once again Dunlop came to the rescue. Then, after a short practice run, it was discovered that the wrong grade of sparking plugs had been fitted, which coked up almost immediately. Thanks to Laurie Hands of Champion, the exact grade was found, and thereafter the engine ran like a sewing machine. The tachometer drive broke, requiring a new cable which was a devil to fit. I also had trouble with sticking throttles, which were cured by Wilkie Wilkinson of Ecurie Ecosse. Incidentally, I had come to an arrangement with EE boss David Murray to share their service facilities *en route*, provided I did not interfere with any work required on their 'D' Type Jaguar.

At Rome, my pit was to be manned by Malcolm Bateman, of the Yorkshire Sports Car Club, a tremendous enthusiast, and at Bologna, John Eason Gibson and the BARC's Bob Lawry would be helping, along with the second crew of Ecurie Ecosse.

I did manage one decent practice session, and was absolutely charmed with the speed and roadholding of the little green and silver Lotus. I made more arrangements for possible assistance. George Phillips would be taking the Magnette to cover the event photographically, and Harry Mundy in his car was doing a story for "Autocar". Both promised to look out for me, and gave me the location of possible places where they might be.

The scrutineers passed the hood without even looking at it being erected, but the senior man said that I did not have sufficient Italian insurance, so I had to produce a further 20,000 lire, bringing the total up to 80,000 lire, otherwise I would not be permitted to start. Then, suddenly, another official arrived who said that my insurance had been cancelled, as an objection had been lodged by another competitor that the seats were too small. John Patara, of BP Italy, produced a tape-measure, and proved conclusively that the dimensions were well within the permitted sizes. Then came another request, to erect the hood. This was done, and although I could not have travelled more than a few yards without the whole thing disintegrating, the official appeared to be satisfied.

Then followed apologies, a present of a couple of bottles of Asti Spumante (which I detest), and the formal return of 20,000 lire, as they now admitted that the charge should rightly have been 40,000 lire. Thank heavens for Johnny Patara, and also for Count "Johnny" Lurani, who did all the necessary interpretation for me.

There was another Lotus Eleven in the race, entered by Bruno Ferrari, which was a doubtful starter owing to gearbox troubles. However, Colin had supplied me with sufficient spares for the MG box to put it right, and we passed the scrutineers with something like an hour to spare.

Later, that evening, Patara came along to see me at the Gallo Moderne, and gleefully told me that the competitor who protested about the seats had had his car pinched from a car park and would be unable to start. He rather suggested that I knew something about this, and I had the devil of a job convincing him, and others, that I knew absolutely nothing about the affair.

The twin SU carburettors had no choke arrangement fitted, and as the weather was unusually cold for May, the engine was difficult to keep running. So Phillips "invented" his own version of a choke, comprising of piece of cardboard which could be held over the air-intakes. This worked admirably, and became standard equipment on the car—the idea also being passed on to Bruno Ferrari.

I had just one more practice run, and this time I was able to let the little car have its head. It seemed to be perfectly happy at 7,300 rpm, which was roughly equivalent to 130 mph. The seat, however, was terribly uncomfortable, but beyond

Gregor Grant asks how he is placed during one of his brief pauses in his lonely but gallant drive in the 1957 Mille Miglia with Lotus 11. His number, 337, indicates his starting time that morning at Brescia.

adding a rubber air-cushion, there was little I could do about it.

My number was 337, which meant that I started at the unearthly hour of 3.37 a.m. There were enormous crowds to watch the cars taking off down the starting ramp, and I gently eased the Lotus down to avoid bottoming. Then, it was a case of accelerating through the packed lanes of spectators, the powerful Lucas Le Mans headlamps providing a splendid spread ahead of me. I soon arrived at a level crossing, marked with a huge sign "Pericolo". Stirling Moss had mentioned this bumpy crossing to me, and said that it was at a place called Pericolo, which I had already learned meant simply "Danger".

It was a bumpy run on the twists and turns to Verona, and the crowds seemed to become thicker and thicker in the villages. At any rate, whenever one saw the largest congregation, one automatically realized that this was a main danger spot. I soon came on to some red tail lights ahead, and instinctively knew that these belonged to my rivals in the 1100cc class. To my delight, there were no signs of approaching headlamps in my rear mirror.

The car was going like a dream, with 7,000 rpm on the clock on the straights, and the Coventry-Climax engine running perfectly with a healthy burble from the exhaust, almost drowned by the thrilling scream of the racing Dunlops. Yet, my backside was already beginning to ache, and there were many hundreds of miles still to go!

At dawn, an annoying ground mist slowed me down considerably, and for about an hour this persisted in patches. But finally the sun broke through to a cloudless blue sky, and apart from my posterior, I began to enjoy myself thoroughly. I overtook and passed a couple of red Oscas, which for maximum speed could not look at the Lotus.

Down the Adriatic coast the weather was perfect, with a shimmering blue sea alongside. Chief hazards were the crowds, and it was more than a trifle disconcerting travelling at around 120 mph, to approach a solid mass of humanity, and watch them wait until the last possible moment before parting to let one through. In one or two places, with sharp bends, over-enthusiastic Italians even risked giving the car a pat as it went through.

By this time, I had passed quite a number of cars, but being alone I had no way of knowing my position, or how I was doing as regards average speed. In 1956 I had been able to use a Halda Speed Pilot on the Magnette, but the Lotus was not provided with such a luxury. I do, however, recall seeing a group of people waving an enormous Union Jack, and giving me a "thumbs up" sign. Whether or not they were merely pleased to see a British car, or were indicating that I was doing well, I hadn't the slightest clue.

It was at Ravenna, the first passage control, that I experienced the first signs of trouble. I had started with a vizor, but discarded this in favour of goggles when it began to mist up. The goggles were even worse, and there was a strong smell of petrol everywhere. I put on the vizor again, for trying to drive without anything in the way of protection for my eyes caused petrol to be sprayed straight on to my face.

The petrol spraying suddenly disappeared, but my neck was stiff having had to peer upwards from beneath the vizor, and with that damnnable seat I had to keep shifting my position. One of the Oscas shot past, and it was several kilometres before I could again overtake it.

Through Forli, Cesena and Rimini, the crowds were beyond belief. I have a hazy recollection of talking to Wilkie Wilkinson of Ecurie Ecosse when I refuelled at Pesaro. I was feeling rather groggy from the petrol fumes, and Wilkie told me later that I never even got out of the car.

Apart from the spectators and parked cars, I had a lonely race for many kilometres. Near Ancona, Maglioli's Porsche hurtled past, travelling very rapidly. I then overtook an Alfa Romeo, which suddenly began to weave all over the road. I had to brake hard as it broadsided in front of me. A rear wheel had come off, and the car was cutting deep ruts in the road on its brake drum. It came to rest without further incident, and I squeezed past. Not much further along the route, I saw a Fiat on its side, the crew sitting miserably on a wall, still wearing their crash hats.

Coming into Pescara, crowds were trying to right a Lancia which had obviously been on its roof. A couple of Fiat "Millicentos" had been abandoned, apparently one having shunted the other. Close to a level crossing I glimpsed a somewhat battered Triumph TR2, which I recognized as belonging to Nancy Mitchell/Pat Faichney. To my relief, I saw that both girls were OK, but the TR2 was definitely *hors de combat*.

Again, the crowds were so dense that the approaches to the city were most hazardous. My backside was so stiff that the pain had gone long ago, and although I still felt groggy the engine was running sweetly and my spirits were high. I took several slugs from my bottle of glucose, and looked forward to Rome, where I would have some respite, and a cigarette.

However, in the mountains from Aquila, the grogginess persisted, and so did the all-pervading stink of petrol. I began getting slower and slower, and was overtaken first by a V8 BMW, and then by Robin Carnegie in his works MG. I then had a grandstand view of a particularly fierce duel, with the BMW driver nearly putting the MG into a ditch, as Carnegie managed to squeeze past.

The groggy feeling then passed again, and off I set to try to catch the BMW and the MG. The German did everything possible to prevent me getting through. I tried the inside, then the outside, of every bend, but the gate was always shut. I felt like ramming him, but thoughts of the lightweight Lotus and the massive German car soon put these out of my mind. Then, coming down towards a double bend, the driver completely lost it, and for one sickening moment I anticipated his going end-over-end, but the car slewed sideways in a cloud of dust and a shower of stones, and in it went into a deep ditch. I just couldn't resist giving him the "Churchill" sign as the Lotus shot ahead!

Coming into Rome, I overtook the MG, and we both stopped at our pits together. Malcolm Bateman and his friend Jim Furze took charge of everything, checking tyres, petrol, oil, battery and so on. I swallowed a quick sandwich washed down with coffee, and was told afterwards that I smoked two cigarettes at once. Malcolm told me that I was fourth in the 1100cc sports class, not far behind a couple of 1100cc Oscas, but that Cabianca and his tremendously rapid "950" Osca were well out in front.

That halt put new life into me, as I set off for Firenze (Florence) over the tough mountain sections. At Viterbo I passed one of the 1100cc Oscas, and left it far behind as I moved towards Radiocofani. The crowds on the hillside slopes were enormous, the gay colours of the girls' dresses, the men's shirts and the bright sunshades creating a real holiday atmosphere. What a contrast from 1956, when this section was covered, during torrential rain, with thousands of umbrellas looking like a multitude of toadstools!

Just outside Siena, another Osca appeared in front, which I passed without any difficulty. I suddenly realized that the Lotus was second in its class, and that I might not be badly placed in the Index of Performance. Then the petrol vapour started again, and by the time I reached Florence, I was dizzy and my eyes were smarting dreadfully. I vaguely recall signing the control card, and racing off towards the Futa. On the famous pass, I performed a spectacular gilhooley, right in front of about ten thousand people. Practically blinded by petrol vapour, I was on a corner before I realized it, slammed on the anchors, and spun completely round, clouting a wall with a resounding crunch with the offside rear wheel.

I re-started gingerly, but thereafter the steering began to feel peculiar. The Lotus also had a tendency to shudder, as if it was resenting coming into contact with a hard, stone wall. On the descent of the Futa, I suddenly saw George Phillips and Harry Mundy. I asked them to have a quick look—see at the car, which they did, but they could find nothing wrong. So off I went once more, and it wasn't till afterwards that I learned that both had shouted after me, having spotted that the offside rear wheel was wobbling violently.

At Bologna, the Ecurie Ecosse boys said that the wheel was so badly buckled that it would have to be changed, so they swopped it for the one and only spare. Then John Eason Gibson and Bob Lawry demanded what capacity my petrol tank was supposed to be. They had pumped in something like 100 litres, and it was still far from full. Then one of the EE boys spotted that most of the petrol was running down the drain. He found that the tank had split wide open, along the bottom bend. With the tank immediately above my knees, this was not one of the best things that

Gregor Grant found on the Mille Miglia that the size of the crowd was a useful navigational aid — the larger the crowd the trickier the corner! Gregor was well-placed at this point, before a leaking fuel tank slowed him.

could have happened. Anyway, the mechanics did the best they could by closing the split with a copper clout and packing it up with "goo".

Eason Gibson took a quick look, and said that with luck the jury-rig would hold. He pointed out that I was still third in the class, and that the second place Osca had just pulled out and was only about a minute ahead.

That stop at Bologna now seems more like a dream. I remember seeing Enzo Ferrari with a glum face, and someone telling me that Peter Collins' Ferrari was out of the race, the rear axle having broken up when he was in the lead. I also recall informing the EE people that Ron Flockhart's D-type Jaguar was also out, which Wilkie had told me at Pesaro, and which I had completely forgotten.

So, off I went again, and in what seemed to be a very short time I had caught and passed the second-place Osca, and really started motoring towards Modena. All was not well, however, for the engine was spluttering badly, and the stench of petrol was overwhelming. Not far out of the town, the engine finally stopped altogether. I clambered stiffly out, and raised the bonnet, whilst a great crowd appeared literally from nowhere. I gave the SU petrol pump a clonk, it raced, and it then began to slow as fuel came through. I looked at the patched tank, but only a few drips were apparent, so on the way I went again, and with no sign of the Osca I had overtaken.

About 10 kilometres further on the engine again stopped. This time I managed to spot the trouble. When the tank was patched up, the polythene pipe to the SU pump had been shifted, and was being jammed by the bonnet. This was soon rectified, and the pump began to work normally.

The Osca had not appeared, so I felt that it must have met trouble, for I had lost many minutes sorting out the pump bothers. But the steering was, to say the least of it, very dodgy. On left-hand bends it seemed fairly accurate, but on right-hand turns, the over-steer was simply unbelievable. I then realized that what had happened was that the spare wheel must have been a front one, and that it was a smaller-section than the rear. There was nothing I could do about it, for the spare was too badly twisted to be of any

The Lotus 11, complete with regulation hood and side screens, was trailed across Europe and back again behind an MG Magnette which photographer George Phillips used to cover the event.

further use, so I pressed on, watching out carefully for all right-handers, for the Lotus appeared to be quite stable in a straight line.

Then, on the very fast straight between Cremona and Mantova, I found myself almost waist-high in petrol. The tank had finally burst, and I realized that there was a real danger of an explosion and fire—the worst thing that could occur to anyone!

It takes danger to bring on speedy reactions. I slammed on the brakes, and before the Lotus had stopped rolling, I was out, and going head-over-heels on the grass verge. I watched the car zig-zagging its way down the road, and finally coming to rest neatly parked on the roadside. By a miracle it hadn't caught alight. I struggled to my feet, and then to my horror, I saw crowds of people running towards me across the road. All seemed to be smoking cigarettes! I was soaked to the skin in high-octane petrol, and I stammered "pericolo—benzina"!

This didn't seem to have any effect whatsoever, for they began swarming towards me, so I took to my heels and ran. By great fortune, a couple of policemen on motorcycles appeared, and quickly weighed up the situation, and angrily ordered the crowd back to the other side of the road, making certain that no cars were coming along.

One of them could speak French, and when I asked him where the nearest garage was, he told me "about five kilometres". He indicated the pillion seat on his Guzzi, and whilst his mate mounted guard over the Lotus, I was taken to the garage. Meanwhile cars roared past on the final leg to Brescia.

When the policeman told the garage proprietor of my plight, he wheeled out his Vespa, and was about to race down the road in the face of oncoming cars, before the copper managed to stop him. Thereupon he rode across the fields to examine the abandoned Lotus. He returned quickly enough, to inform me that he thought that it could be put right, and took me back to the car on his Vespa. The spilled petrol had by now completely evaporated, and there still remained a pint or so in the tank. The engine fired, and slowly I managed to coax the Lotus to his garage.

The tank was quickly removed, but found to be completely beyond repair. The whole affair had split wide open at the seams, and it was only the Ecurie Ecosse repair at the base that had held the last few remaining drops.

Time was running out, and it was pretty obvious that, with 70 miles to go, I would never reach the finish inside the time limits. The cheerful *padrone* offered to tow me to Brescia, after the roads had been opened, but this would not be for many hours, as the slower touring small cars had a much more generous time allowance. He then hit on the idea of a temporary tank, and rigged up a jerrican which he lashed to the bonnet, after having drilled the base and inserted a tap from a derelict motorcycle. From this, he led a rubber tube to the pump supply pipe. He found a large section of Dunlopillo (or was it Pirellipillo?) and formed it in the shape of a wedge, so that the jerrican was at an angle of about 45 degrees, with the filler-cap facing forward. I could see that this man knew what he was about, for he carefully drilled a small hole in the jerrican filler cap lid, and angled the "tank" forward, so that any vapour would be blown forward. I sat in the car, and found that I could see quite well over the top of the contraption. Moreover, it worked perfectly, and had it occurred to him earlier, I could well have finished within the time limit—or would I?

I cannot describe fully that nightmare 70 miles. I was in agony from petrol burns, and to add to the general discomfort, it started to rain push-rods. How I reached the Gallo Moderne I shall never know. I was black from head-to-feet, and stank of petrol. I vaguely remember having some food, and several glasses of wine. The strongest recollection, however, was of George Phillips painting my blistered parts with Germolene, and my nearly hitting the ceiling as a result!

Despite the painful blisters, the Phillips first-aid worked the trick, and I had several hours of sleep, before awaking to write the report for 'Autosport'. Many incidents came back to me, once my head had finally been cleared of the muzziness induced by the petrol fumes. I recall seeing the dreadful results of the tragic de Portago crash, which sounded the death-knell of the Mille Miglia. I also remember the eventual winner, Piero Taruffi, screaming past me in his Ferrari, possibly doing about 170 mph.

Naturally I was disappointed with the results of my run, but felt that in the main, the Eleven had proved that it could stand up to 1000 miles of racing speeds. My retirement had been entirely due to the faulty petrol tank, and when I returned to England, I was able to find out what had happened.

It was constructed of magnesium alloy, and when it was being produced by the suppliers, in order to mark the exact sections to be bent over, someone had carelessly used a scriber, thus producing a highly vulnerable edge when the shape was formed. It seems likely that my experience taught somebody a lesson, for magnesium tanks were also used on the highly-successful 1957 Le Mans Lotuses, and these gave no trouble whatsoever.

I might also add a footnote that a rather shame-faced George Phillips produced a considerably battered MG Magnette for our trip home. He had run into the back of Harry Mundy's Standard Vanguard, and had modified the frontal appearance very considerably. One way and another it had been quite a trip!

LOTUS MARK 9

Colin Chapman designed this, his second aerodynamically-bodied sports car, primarily to accept the Coventry Climax 1,100cc engine, and in this form it was used for the first Team Lotus entry at Le Mans, in 1955

LOTUS 12 (FORMULA 2)

Simplicity, minimum drag and maximum power-to-weight ratio were the guiding principles of the design of the first single-seater Lotus, which was also the first car to feature the Chapman strut-type rear suspension.

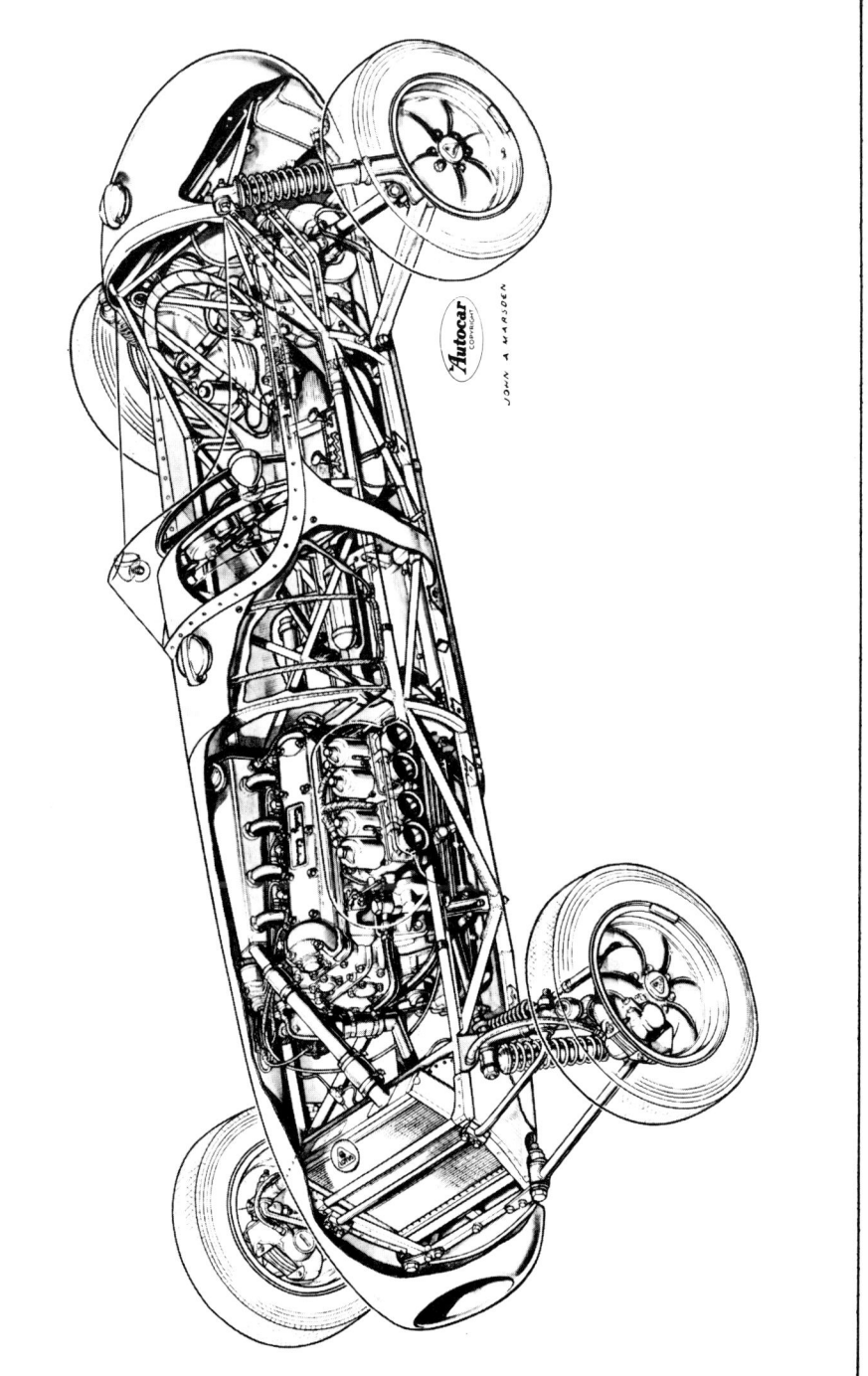

LOTUS 14 (ELITE)

Revolutionary in concept and unique in style, the Elite was the Lotus company's passport to acceptance as a serious manufacturer of high-quality Grand Touring passenger cars, although the glass-fibre coupe was also a prolific race-winner.

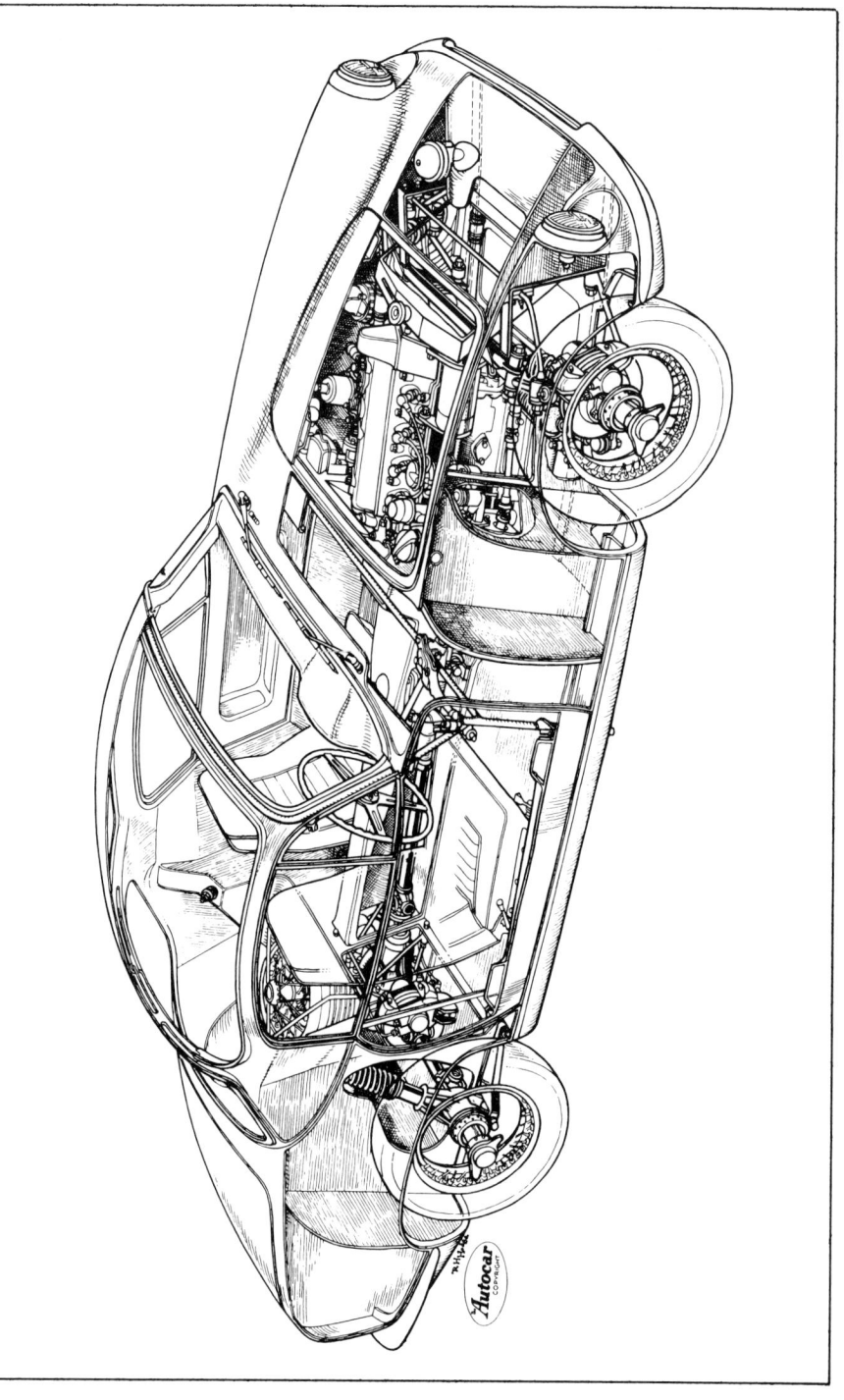

LOTUS 15

Designed primarily as a Le Mans challenger in 1958, the 15 was to be the last of Colin Chapman's large-displacement front-engined sports cars, ultimately to be replaced by the rear-engined 19 after an active competition life of three years.

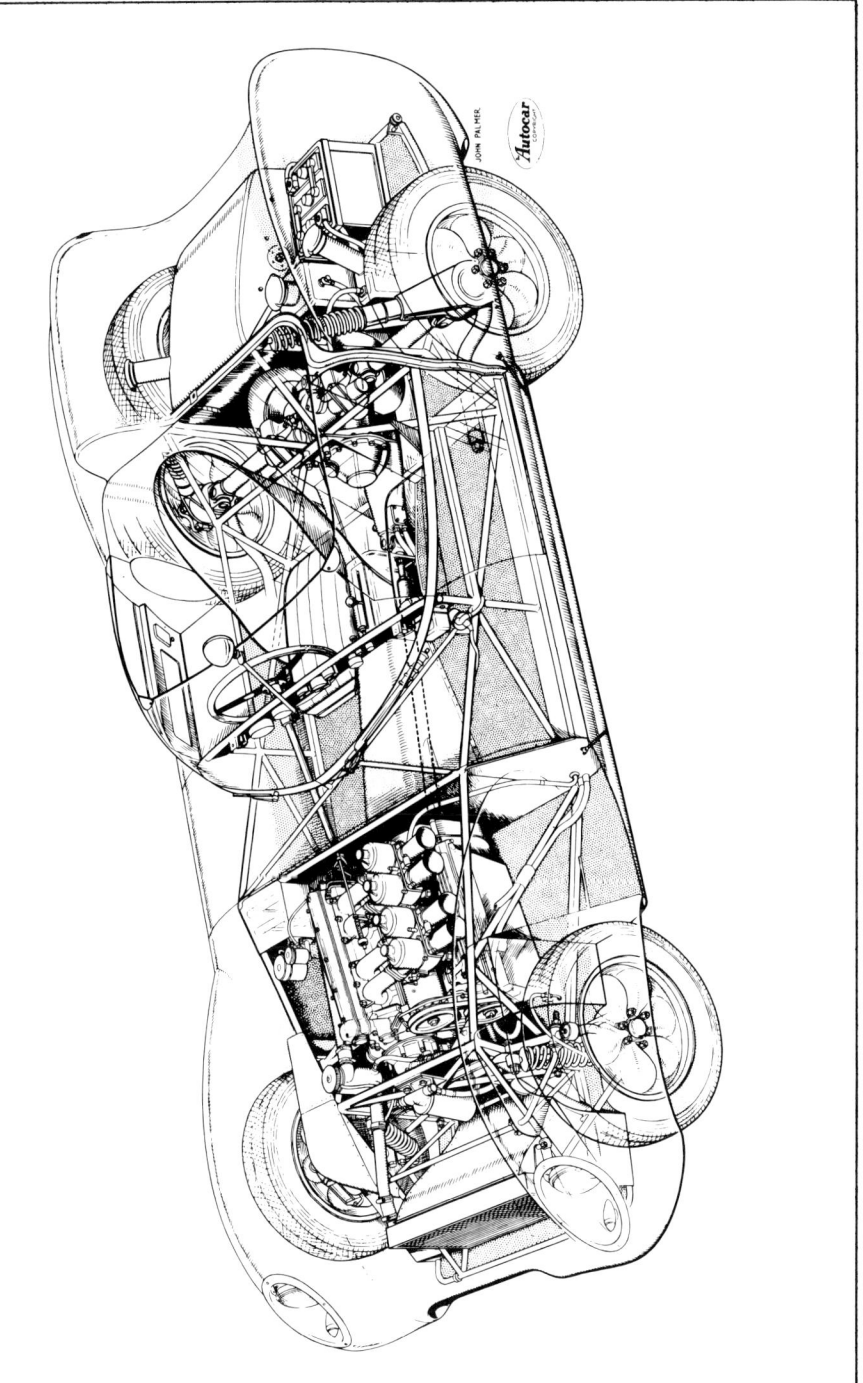

LOTUS 18

A multi-purpose single-seater, the 18 was to prove virtually invincible in Formula Junior form (as drawn), and as a Formula 1 car driven by Stirling Moss was to give Lotus their first victory in a world championship grand prix, at Monaco in 1960.

LOTUS LINE-UP 1947-1960

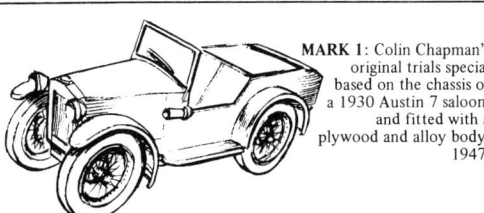

MARK 1: Colin Chapman's original trials special based on the chassis of a 1930 Austin 7 saloon, and fitted with a plywood and alloy body. 1947.

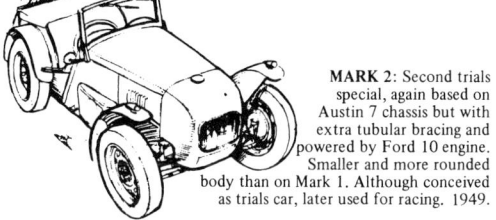

MARK 2: Second trials special, again based on Austin 7 chassis but with extra tubular bracing and powered by Ford 10 engine. Smaller and more rounded body than on Mark 1. Although conceived as trials car, later used for racing. 1949.

MARK 3: Racing car built to 750 Formula with modified Austin 7 chassis and engine featuring unique divided inlet manifolding and ports. Aluminium body. 1951.

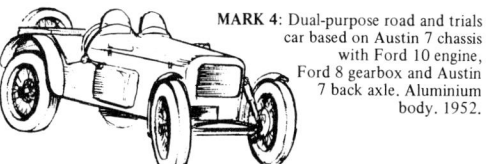

MARK 4: Dual-purpose road and trials car based on Austin 7 chassis with Ford 10 engine, Ford 8 gearbox and Austin 7 back axle. Aluminium body. 1952.

MARK 5 Never produced. Was to have been 100 mph Austin 7-engined sports-racing car based on the Mark 3. 1952.

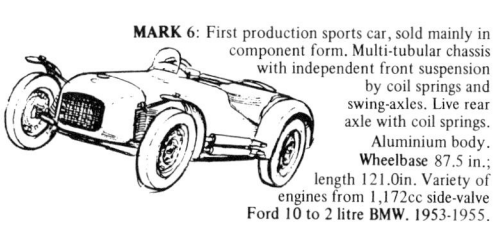

MARK 6: First production sports car, sold mainly in component form. Multi-tubular chassis with independent front suspension by coil springs and swing-axles. Live rear axle with coil springs. Aluminium body. Wheelbase 87.5 in.; length 121.0in. Variety of engines from 1,172cc side-valve Ford 10 to 2 litre BMW. 1953-1955.

7: Replacement for Mark 6. Multi-tubular chassis with independent front suspension by coil springs and wishbones. Live rear axle with coil springs. Aluminium body, later with glass-fibre nose cowl and wings. Wheelbase 88.0 in.; length 123.0 in. Variety of engines from 948cc BMC to 1,500cc Coventry-Climax. 1957-1960. (Seven still in production in improved forms).

MARK 8: First sports-racing car with aerodynamic bodywork. Spaceframe chassis with independent front suspension by coil springs and swing axles. De Dion rear axle with transverse coil spring. Aluminium body. Wheelbase 87.5 in; length 164.0 in. Variety of engines from 1,100cc Coventry Climax to 1,500cc Connaught. 1954.

MARK 9: Smaller-engined successor to the Mark 8. Spaceframe chassis with independent front suspension by coil springs and swing-axles. Live or De Dion rear axle with coil springs. Aluminium body. Wheelbase 87.5 in.; length 140 in. Variety of engines from 1,100cc Coventry-Climax to 1,500cc MG. 1955.

MARK 10: Larger-engined version of the Mark 8. Spaceframe chassis with independent front suspension by coil springs and swing-axles. De Dion rear axle with coil springs. Aluminium body. Wheelbase 87.5 in.; length 164.0 in. Engine 2 litre Bristol or 2 litre Connaught. 1955.

LINE-UP CONTINUED

11: Replacement for Mark 9. Spaceframe chassis with independent front suspension by coil springs and swing-axles. De Dion rear axle with coil springs. Aluminium body. Wheelbase 85.0 in.; length 134 in. Variety of engines from 1,100cc Coventry-Climax to 1,500cc Maserati. 1956-1958.

12: First Formula 2 single-seater. Spaceframe chassis with independent front suspension by coil springs and wishbones. Early cars De Dion rear axle with coil springs, later cars independent rear suspension by Chapman struts incorporating coil springs. Aluminium body. Wheelbase 88.0 in.; length 131.0 in. Engine, 1,500cc Coventry-Climax. 1957.

13. Model number not used for superstitious reasons, but successor to original 11 designated instead 11 Series 2. Main changes: independent front suspension by coil springs and wishbones, and stronger De Dion rear axle. Variety of engines from 1,172 cc Ford to 2 litre Maserati. 1957.

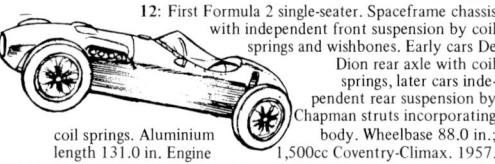

14: First closed passenger car, the Elite. Glass-fibre monocoque structure comprising eight box sections and reinforced with steel tubing and plates. Independent front suspension by coil springs and wishbones. Independent rear suspension by Chapman struts incorporating coil springs. Wheelbase 88.0 in.; length 144 in. Engine, 1,216cc Coventry-Climax. 1957-1961.

15: Successor to Mark 10, for larger-capacity sports-racing classes. Spaceframe chassis with independent front suspension by coil springs and wishbones. Independent rear suspension by Chapman struts incorporating coil springs. Aluminium body. Wheelbase 88.0 in.; length 137.0 in. Variety of engines from 1,500 to 2,500cc Coventry-Climax. 1958-1960.

16: Formula 1/Formula 2 car, successor to 12, with 'Mini-Vanwall' body. Spaceframe chassis with independent front suspension by coil springs and wishbones. Independent rear suspension by Chapman struts incorporating coil springs. Aluminium and glass-fibre body. Wheelbase 88.0 in.; length 140 in. Variety of engines from 1,500 to 2,500cc Coventry-Climax. 1958.

17: Successor to 11 for small-capacity engines. Spaceframe chassis with independent front suspension by Chapman struts incorporating coil springs and lower wishbones. Independent rear suspension Aluminium and glass-fibre body. Wheelbase 88.2 in.; length 131 in. Engine, 750 or 1,100cc Coventry-Climax. 1959.

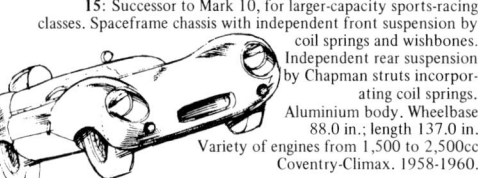

18: Multi-purpose rear-engined single-seater design for formula racing from Formula Junior to Formula 1. Spaceframe chassis with independent front suspension by coil springs and wishbones. Independent rear suspension by coil springs, double transverse links and radius arms. Aluminium and glass-fibre body. Wheelbase 92 in. length 133 in. Variety of engines from 1,000cc Ford to 2,500cc Coventry-Climax. 1959-1960.

19: Rear-engined sports-racing car developed from 18. Spaceframe chassis with independent front suspension by coil springs and wishbones. Independent rear suspension by coil springs, double transverse links and radius arms. Aluminium and glass-fibre body. Wheelbase 92 in.; length 141 in. Engine, 2,500cc Coventry-Climax. 1960.

Index

Abecassis, George 64
Adams, Jill 18
Adamson, Dennis 25
Allard, Sydney 30
Allen, Michael 19, 21, 25-26, 28-29, 33-34, 36
Allen, Nigel 19, 21, 23, 25-26, 34, 36, 38-39, 51-52
Allison, Cliff 65-66, 77-78, 79-80, 81, 83-84, 87, 90-91, 95, 101-103, 106, 109-114, 116-118, 136-138, 141-142, 145-146, 154, 159, 175
Ansdale, Richard 98
Anstice-Brown, John 67
Anthony, Mike 36 40-41, 47-48, 51-54, 56-57, 63, 65, 73, 104
Arundell, Peter 170, 172-173
Ashdown, Peter 67-78, 83-84, 106, 109-115, 117-119, 136

Badcock, Roy 113
Baillie, Sir Gawaine 83
Baird, Gil 84
Barber, Chris 67, 133
Barnard, Tom 88
Barth, Edgar 119-120
Basson, Mr 146
Bastrup, Len 59, 67, 82-83
Bateman, Malcolm 177, 180
Bauer, Erwin 48, 51
de Beaufort, Count Godin 112
Beauman, Don 72
Behra, Jean 90, 142, 151
Bell, Peter 62
Bennett, Colin 47, 104, 113
Bentley, — 91
Berchem, Pierre 136
Beresford, George 17, 23
Bianchi, Lucien 160, 164
Bicknell, Reg 76-77, 79-80, 81, 84, 90-91
Biggs, Harold 25
Bik, Tony 83
Birkett, Holland 25
Birrell, Alistair 81
Black, Duncan 67
Blanchard, Bob 118
Bloxam, Jean 52
Bloxham, Roy 52
Bonnier, Jo 142, 151, 157, 159, 161, 163, 165-168, 175
Boulting Brothers 18
Bowman, B. 57
Brabham, Jack 78, 83, 102-103, 152-154, 157-158, 160-161, 163-168
Bramley, L.I. 67, 84
Bristow, Chris 108, 153, 165
Brooke, — 103
Brooks; Tony 66, 84, 103, 137-138, 145-146, 154, 161
Brown, Alan 45, 52
Brown, John 72
Bryden-Brown, Louise 166
Buchanan, G.D. 67
Bueb, Ivor 59, 62, 64, 66, 76, 80, 109, 111-112, 142
Bulmer, Mr & Mrs Charles 79
Burgess, Ian 168
Butler, Phil 117
Buxton, David 153

Cabianca, Giulio 84, 180
Campbell-Jones, John 104, 111, 113
Carmichael, Ian 27
Carnegie, Robin 180
Castellotti, Eugenio 72, 87
Castro, Fidel 157
Chalk, Tony 50
Chamberlain, Jay 88, 105, 110, 114, 117-119, 138, 141
Chapman, Colin 6-12, 14-16, 17-21, 23, 25-26, 28-30, 33-34, 36-40, 42-43, 45-48, 50-54, 57, 59-73, 76-80, 81-84, 86-88, 90-92, 94, 97-98, 100-102, 104-106, 108-111, 113-117, 119-122, 127-128, 132, 146, 151-152, 154-157, 165-166, 168-169, 172-173, 176-177
Chapman, Hazel 52-53, 64, 67, 69, 76, 98, 115, 127-128
Chapman, S.F. 29, 39-40, 113, 168
Chivas, Doug 41
Clairmonte Brothers 29
Clark, Jim 134, 151, 160-161, 163-168, 172-173
Clarke, 'Nobby' 40, 42-43, 53, 80, 85, 113
Clover, Ron 104, 113
Collins, Peter 137, 145, 182
Coombs, John 38, 44, 46, 48, 52, 65, 67, 81, 83-84, 106, 108, 110, 112-113, 131, 142, 166
Cooper, John 92, 155
Cornet, — 90
Costin, Frank 18, 42-44, 47-48, 50, 58, 80, 101, 116, 128, 136, 138, 142
Costin, Mike 18, 38-42, 46-48, 50-51, 53, 57, 62-63, 66-67, 69-71, 73, 79, 81, 105-106, 113, 115-118, 122, 136, 172
Crawford, — 120
Crombac, 'Jabby' 41, 113, 117
Cunane, 'Tip' 52
Cunningham, Briggs 70, 72
Cunningham, Charles 83
Currie, Adam 22, 25-26, 39, 42

Dalton, John 80, 114-115, 120

Dare, Colin 7-8
Davidson, J.B. 22, 34
Davis, Cliff 57, 63, 81, 176
Davy, John 173
Dean, James 57
Derisley, John 41
Deschamps, H. 87
Desoutter, P.A. 37, 39
Dickens, M.G. 112
Dickson, Tom 81, 111-112, 138, 141, 150, 153, 160
Downing, Ken 25
Drew, — 23
Druitt, Dennis 176
Duckworth, Keith 113, 169
Duke, Geoff 167
Dungan, Dick 105
Duntov, — 72

Eason Gibson, John 69, 72, 91, 92, 105, 177, 180
Ellis, Tony 83
Emery, Paul 65
Endruweit, Jim 146
Escott, Colin 33

Faichney, Pat 180
Fangio, Juan-Manuel 72
Ferguson, Andrew 168
Ferrari, Bruno 177
Ferrari, Enzo 146, 182
Fifield, 'Fifi' 50
Fisher, John 148, 151
Fletcher, Paul 125
Flockhart, Ron 65, 68-70, 72, 84, 87, 102, 108-110, 112, 165, 182
Francis, Alf 167
von Frankenberg, Richard 91, 119-120
Fraser, Mackay 80, 84, 87, 90, 102, 106, 108-110, 114, 117-119, 121
Fraser, Marga 110
Frayling, John 127-128
Frère, Paul 160
Frost, Bill 78, 81, 106, 108-113, 138
Fuller, — 23
Furze, Jim 180

Gahagan, Dudley 17
Gammon, Peter 33, 36-38, 40, 42, 48, 50-51, 66, 81, 104
Gaze, Tony 65
Gendebien, Olivier 160, 164-165
Gibbs, Len 25
Gibson-Jarvie, Bob 69
Gilmour, Tom 41, 62
Goethal, — 110
Goddard, Geoffrey 6
Gonzales, Froilan 48
Graham, Malcolm 111-112
Grant, Gregor 6, 109-110, 176-183
Green, John 114
Greenall, Edward 81, 83-84
Greene, Keith 130, 146, 151, 154
Gregory, Masten 151
Griffiths, Bill 113, 116, 118
Gurney, Dan 166-167

Halford, Bruce 80, 148
Hall, Eugene 109
Hall, Jim 168
Hall, John 15
Hall, Keith 78-80, 81, 83, 85-87, 90, 103, 106, 109-114, 116-118, 136
Hands, Laurie 177
von Hanstein, Huschke 65
Harris, John 41, 79
Havard, Dr Vaughan 57
Hawes, Ken 23
Hawthorn, Mike 23, 72, 76-79, 81, 83-84, 86, 112, 137-138, 145-146
Hay, Arthur 29
Hechard, Andre 114-115, 141
Hennessy, Sir Patrick 30
Herrmann, Hans 51, 91, 119-120, 166
Hewitt, Bryan 67, 83
Hicks, Bob 81, 84, 109, 138, 141
Hill, Fred 37
Hill, Graham 77-78, 80, 81-85, 88, 95, 98, 103-104, 106, 111, 113-114, 116, 118-119, 126, 136-138, 141-143, 145-148, 150-154, 161, 164-165, 167
Hill, Phil 153, 163, 165-166
Hogg, Tony 43
Holder, Tony 43
Hugus, Ed 91

Ireland, Innes 78, 84, 87, 110, 113, 135, 138, 141, 146, 148, 151-154, 157-161, 163-168

Jackson, Peter 62
Jenkinson, Denis 132
Jepson, Peter 83
Jolly, Derek 25, 151

Index (continued)

Jones, Gordon 112
Jones, Ian 104
Jopp, Peter 60, 63-66, 68-70, 90

Kasterine, Dimitri 54
Kelsey, Dave 42-43, 52
Kirwan-Taylor, Peter 12. 131
Klinck, Bill 41
Knowles, Bill 79

Larreta, Rodriguez 157, 159
Laurent, Claude 92, 135
Laverock, Len 154
Laverton, Ken 40
Lawry, Bob 177, 180
Lawry, John 40, 88, 90, 117
Lawry, Ted 69
Lawson, Mike 18, 25-28
Layden, Godfrey MP 154
Leston, Les 62-63, 78, 134
Levegh, Pierre 72
Lewis, Edward 35, 66, 79, 109, 111, 122
Lewis, Graham 154
Lewis-Evans, Stuart 137-138
Lister, Brian 23
Lovely, Pete 138, 142, 148
Lozano, Ignacio 79
Lucas, Jean 110
Lumsden, Peter 62, 67 130, 134, 151, 153
Lund, Ted 33, 48
Lurani, Count 'Johnny' 177

McAlpine, Ken 63
MacDowel, Michael 67
McKee, Mike 173
Mackintosh, 'Mac' 38, 40, 42, 104
McKusker, Tony 43, 47, 51
McLaren, Bruce 159, 163-165, 167-168
Madan, Mike 29, 36
Maglioli, Umberto 91, 119-120, 179
Malle, — 151
Manton, Dr 111
Margulies, Dan 51, 106, 109
Marriott, Fred 41
Marsh, Tony 80, 110, 135, 154, 168
Martin, Tim 88
Masson, Roger 114, 119-120, 135, 141
Mayer, Harvey 79
Mayes, Peter 43, 51, 63, 69-70
Metcalfe, Chris 21, 23
Mica, M. & Mme 69-70, 72, 90, 92, 116-117, 120
Miller, Frank 59-60
Mitchell, Nancy 180
Monise, Frank 79
Moss, Bill 113
Moss, Stirling 48, 65, 76-77, 83-84, 90, 95, 103, 121, 137, 142, 151, 157-165, 167-168, 174-175, 179
Mundy, Harry 94, 98, 177, 180, 183
Murray, David 177
Musso, Luigi 87
Musy, Benoit 77

Naylor, Brian 44, 49, 52, 79, 81, 83, 87, 106, 108-109, 112-113, 168
Nicholl, S.D. 80
Nixon, George 57
Nuckey, Rodney 10, 17
Nurse, Austin 37, 52

Oddous, Jean 79
Onslow-Bartlett, — 16

Page, R.A. 65
Parker, Dennis 83
Parkes, Mike 88
Parnell, Reg 63, 76, 167-168
Parsons, Nicholas 27
Patara, John 177
Perkins, Bill 41
Phillips, George 176-177, 180, 183
Phipps, David 166
Piper, David 37, 64, 78, 83-84, 87, 142, 148, 154, 165-166
Playford, John 83
Polensky, — 91
Polivka, Jerry 67
Prior, Dick 78, 88

Rabe, George 60
Richards, Jack 31, 78, 81, 83, 118, 123, 125
Riley, Peter 134, 151, 153
Ross, Peter 38, 40, 42, 104, 109
Rouselle, — 92
Rudd, Ken 88
Russell, Jim 64, 76, 173

Salvadori, Roy 57, 64, 76-79, 81, 84, 103, 109-110, 113, 136, 138, 142, 145, 152, 161
Samuelson, — 59
Sanville, Steve 113
Scannell, Desmond 69
Schell, Harry 80, 81
Scott, Norman 59
Scott-Brown, Archie 48, 51-52, 78-79, 81, 111
Scott-Russell, Peter 53, 57, 63, 65
Scott-Watson, Ian 134
Sears, Jack 166
Shale, David 80
Shelby, Carroll 151
Sheppard, Joe 105
Short, Bill 55, 57
Sieff, Jonathan 135, 151
Singleton, Peter 43
Siracusa, — 84
Slade, Pamela 25
Smith, Alan 83, 118
Smith, Ian H. 6, 34, 62-63, 76-77, 88
Smith, Ken 64-65
Smyth, Mike 83
Somervail, Jack 78
Sopwith, Tommy 78, 80, 83-84
Sparrowe, Jim 25
Stacey, Alan 78, 83, 106, 109-115, 118-119, 135-136, 138, 142, 146, 148, 150-154, 157, 159-165, 168, 172.
Standen, John 43, 51, 63-64, 69-70, 113
Stanguellini, — 84
Steed, Dick 49, 52, 67
Steel, Anthony 57
Stephens, Pat 33-34
Storez, — 91, 120
Studdard, Fred 116, 118
Summers, Chris 160
Surtees, John 160-163, 165-168, 172
Swaters, Jacques 66
Sweeney, Sinclair 29

Tadgell, — 103
Tanner, Reg 120
Taruffi, Piero 183
Taylor, Dennis 103
Taylor, Freddie 33-34
Taylor, Henry 103, 112, 171, 173, 175
Taylor, Michael 138, 141, 146, 151, 161, 164
Taylor, Peter 78
Taylor, Simon 6
Taylor, Trevor 166, 168, 170, 173
Templeton, Malcolm 81
Terry, Len 147
Teychenne, John 29, 36, 42
Threlfall, Chris 173
Timanus, John 79
Titterington, Desmond 79
de Tomaso, Allesandro 110, 112
Trintignant, Maurice 137, 160
von Trips, Wolfgang 91, 160, 165-166
Tyrrell, Ken 173

Vandervell, Tony 167
Vidilles, — 151
Voegler, — 103

Wagstaff, John 135
Walker, Andy 111
Walker, Ian 88, 133
Walker, Rob 84, 160-161, 167, 174
Walshaw, Bob 114-115, 119-120
Warner, Graham 134-135, 172
Warwick, Dave 118
West, L. 23
Whatmough, — 33
Wharton, Ken 48
White, Bruce 50
Whitehead, Peter 80
Whitfield, June 57
Whitmore, John 135, 151
Wilkinson, 'Wilkie' 177, 179
Williams, Hazel 7-12, 16, 17-18, 23, 25, 34, 36-40, 47, 52
Williams, J.P. 130
Williams, Mr 8
Williams, Mrs 8, 10, 39-40
Williamson, Geoff 88
Woolf, Alfred 87, 106, 115
Wootton, Derek 11, 23, 80

Yates, Bob 25
Yorke, David 80
Young, John 65
Young, Mike 57

Zervudachi, Marke 83